179.3

All heaven in a rage

ALL HEAVEN IN A RAGE

E. S. Turner

ST MARTIN'S PRESS
NEW YORK

ACKNOWLEDGEMENTS

One source which has been of great help to the author in this not very well charted territory is a little-known work by Dix Harwood, *Love For Animals And How It Developed In Great Britain,* published in America in 1928. Two histories of the RSPCA provided useful background information: *Valiant Crusade* (1961) by A. W. Moss and *A Century of Work for Animals* (1924) by E. G. Fairholme and Wellesley Pain; so did the files of the *Animal World,* published by the RSPCA. Thanks are due to the Society for permission to reproduce illustrations from their journal and one of their advertisements, also for the print of the portrait of Richard Martin; and to Mr Kenneth Bird ('Fougasse') and the Universities Federation for Animal Welfare for permission to reproduce one of their posters.

CONTENTS

ILLUSTRATIONS

INTRODUCTION

THIS book sets out to describe how the British nation was persuaded, shamed, shocked and coerced into showing mercy to the 'brute creation'. It deals with the social, philosophical and legislative aspects of that struggle. For reasons chiefly of space it is concerned with the cruelties of peace, not of war. Much in these pages is capable of rousing passion and controversy, but the writer would like to think he has achieved a certain restraint in the telling.

The germ which led to this book was picked up long ago in a Chicago slaughter-house. A sign over a corridor read:

THIS WAY
TO SEE
THE KILLING

As the corridor changed direction the sign was repeated. Then a new notice appeared:

THOSE WHO DO NOT
WISH TO SEE THE
KILLING, STOP HERE

Nobody stopped there. Who could endure the shame of halting under a notice like that? Next moment all were spectators of semi-mechanised hog-spearing: a brutal sight, a brutal noise and a brutal smell. Then came the primitive pole-axeing of steers. Afterwards, in a canteen, all the sight-seers ate strips of cooked bacon and filled in a questionnaire saying which they preferred.

It was not like going to a bull-fight, one of the party argued, defensively. Slaughter for food was necessary, slaughter for art was not; people ought to know what was done to animals on their behalf. He may have been right. But the spirit in which most of the party went through the slaughter-house was that in which so many tourists go to the bull-fight: to see whether they would be sick or not.

The British would quickly find moral objections if slaughter-houses in their own land were thrown open to tourists, just as they would object to the introduction of bull-fighting. Their opposition would be based on fear of how such spectacles might degrade their fellow human beings. How such apprehensions have influenced the campaign against cruelty these pages will show.

In our attitudes to animals we are hopelessly, perversely inconsistent. There have been fox-hunters who revolted at the idea of performing animals. Game shots who litter the ground with cripples denounce deer-hunters as barbarians. Old ladies assault men who try to kill pigeons, but keep cats which destroy birds. Women wearing 'cruel furs' used to criticise women who wore 'cruel feathers'. People send cheques to the RSPCA and next day eat *pâté de foie gras*, which the Society begs them not to do. All of us applaud the trouble taken to tranquillise and lift hippos from the sites of dams, but none of us care whether rats are killed humanely or cruelly. Nobody has ever started a Society for the Prevention of Cruelty to Fish. The law is riddled with illogicality. A dogs' home is awarded damages against an author who said that its dogs were sent for scientific experiments; yet experimentation is not only legal but, in some contexts, compulsory. In a sentimental moment the law exempted stray dogs from being sent to the laboratory, while leaving householders free to sell their unwanted pets for this purpose. A clergyman has to pay damages for saying that a fox was dug out and thrown live to the hounds, but if the hounds catch a live fox and kill it, well, that is the purpose of hunting.

If there is much about hunting and shooting in these pages, it is because this is the ground on which people are always spoiling for a fight. The rules of sportsmanship ought to be taken out and re-examined by every generation. In 1951 the

Committee on Cruelty to Wild Animals, which found in favour of almost all field sports, said that future generations might well regard the cult of sportsmanship, with its basic lack of logic, as 'an outmoded virtue, tainted by its origin'. A hundred years earlier the *Quarterly Review*, after brooding over the ethics of playing a salmon, summed up thus: 'In no sport is the mere extinction of the animal's life the principal object – the very word implies the reverse; it implies time for pursuit, that is, time for mortal fear, time for anguish. In the exact proportion that you abridge your pastime you bring yourself nearer to your butcher; and abridge the process as you may, you never can be so humane, in your actual character of executioner, as the tradesman in the blue apron may be – and as the law should compel him to be in all cases whatever.'* Sport has been described as the observing of rules to make difficult what would otherwise be too easy – or should it read 'what would otherwise be too humane'? Up to a point the law upholds the sporting principle. If coursed hares have inadequate facilities for escape, the promoters of the event may be prosecuted. But the law does not mind how many foxes' earths are stopped up. The sporting Englishman refuses to worry over-much about these things. 'This amiable man,' wrote Miss Victoria Sackville-West, 'to whom organised cruelty would be abhorrent should he once recognise it as such is enabled by his peculiar national and racial capacity for the avoidance of lucid thinking to esteem himself rather a fine fellow under cover of that good totem name of sportsman.'†

In shooting, which causes far more suffering than hunting but attracts less indignation, the code of sportsmanship involves the man with the gun in idiotic dilemmas like that posed by the writer in *Shooting Times* (December 27, 1963). Faced with a very high-flying pheasant he said to himself: 'If this were a duck, it would be bad manners to fire at a bird so palpably out of shot . . . as it is a pheasant I suppose it would be bad form not to fire' (he fired and missed). The general standard of marksmanship in a land where anyone can buy and use a shotgun can never be high. Thousands of

---

* Vol. CLXV (1848).
† 'Outdoor Life', in *The Character of England* (ed. Ernest Barker).

'sportsmen' observe no rules whatever; in 1962 more than half the deer killed in the Forestry Commission's woodlands had gunshot wounds in them. Shooting is encouraged by a powerful industry and every effort is made to bring up new generations in the tradition. Another writer in *Shooting Times* (November 30, 1962), describing Christmas shoots for boys, said: 'Now and again a boy would "connect", to his own and everybody else's surprise, and you would see on his face the bliss that passes all understanding . . .' In the same issue a pundit said: 'Respect your quarry and do not think of it, or treat it, as some lowly form of animal life.' The hallmark of a sportsman is that he can do this and yet feel, if he does not always show, the bliss that passes all understanding when he 'connects'.

The basic question, in hunting and shooting, is: 'Should killing for amusement be left to the individual conscience?' Or is it one of those forms of self-expression, like rape and the seduction of minors, which call for legislative restraint? Long ago the law decided that baiting should not be left to the individual conscience. Under one Socialist Government an attempt to suppress hunting failed, the time being regarded as unpropitious. Next time a similar Bill might squeeze through. But it is difficult to imagine Parliament passing an Act to limit shooting.

Nowadays the animal 'crank' – the person who used to ask, when shopping, 'Was it humanely killed?' or 'Was it humanely trapped?' – finds it harder to make a personal stand against practices he detests. Before the last war it was possible to order coal from non-pony pits, thus causing a certain disorder in the coal trade; but zoning of supplies ended all that. The electricity we switch on may owe its existence to pit ponies. The anti-vivisectionist knows by now, or ought to, that hundreds of medicines are tested on animals – are they all to be rejected? Fats and cosmetics may come from whales killed by explosive harpoons (blow a hole in a man, anchor a rope in his wound and make him pull a loaded barrow for an hour or two – that is a rough comparison). Not many of us care about whales; they are majestic and mysterious, but readily overlooked. It is easier to boycott a circus than to boycott soap. It is easier still to live and ask no questions.

People have wondered whether the RSPCA came into being because Britain was exceptionally kind to animals or because some such body was exceptionally necessary. The answer, surely, is that it was formed when the British conscience was more sensitive than those of other nations. 'The greatness of a nation consists not so much in the number of its people or the extent of its territory as in the extent and justice of its compassion,' says the inscription on the memorial at Port Elizabeth to the horses lost in the South African War. A statement of this kind would have been a blazing irony if a similar monument had been erected in Britain overlooking one of those ports from which cavalcades of broken-down horses were shipped by 'sausage boat' to the Belgian abattoirs – in times of peace. But when all the ironies and anomalies and hypocrisies have been discounted, Britain can still claim a wider range for her compassion than most countries. In two lands which claim to be the founts of Liberty things are done to laboratory animals which are not tolerated here. And Britain at least has abolished the gin trap, while most of the world retains it (she still imports the products of other nations' gin traps).

Her next step, perhaps, is to temper the harshness of the industrial revolutions on her farms.

1

DOMINION OVER THE BEASTS

'DO not kick him,' said Pythagoras to a man abusing a puppy. 'In his body is the soul of a friend of mine. I recognised the voice when he cried out.'

Was it fear for his own soul that first led man to show compunction, if not compassion, towards animals? An occasional cynic has said so. The doctrine of transmigration of souls was abroad long before Pythagoras' day, notably in ancient Egypt. Yet whether or not he was moved by a moral idea, man has usually been able to show a rough solicitude for those animals which were willing to come over to his side. He might be brutal in his ways of capturing and breaking them; he never doubted that they were his to beat, to hobble, to hamstring, to castrate, to ride to death; but he was prepared within reasonable limits to treat them as members of the family. In the words of an eighteenth-century pamphleteer, 'infants to the teats of the tenants of the fields were not unseldom submitted.'* Nothing was to be gained by abusing the wet nurse; though there was no reason why she should not be eaten when her duties were over.

The notion of the migrating soul was given new currency in the sixth century B.C., by Pythagoras in Greece and Buddha in India. In many lands it still survives. Nobody would deny that it has had a softening effect on man's attitude to animals; equally, nobody would deny that those professing this belief indulge in gross inconsistencies. Even Pythagoras is credited with having ordered a hecatomb of animals in honour of a famous geometrical proposition.

* John Oswald: *The Cry of Nature* (1791).

It is more rewarding to start with Plutarch (*c.* A.D. 46–120), in whose pagan writings Alexander Pope found 'more strokes of good nature . . . than I remember in any author';* and whom the historian Lecky describes as 'probably the first writer who advocated very strongly humanity to animals on the broad grounds of universal benevolence.'† A tutor to the Emperor Hadrian, Plutarch lived in Rome at a time when conquerors were herding wild animals from a score of lands to butcher in the Colosseum, when epicures resorted to singularly hellish practices for their bellies' sake. 'Law and justice,' he said, 'we cannot in the nature of things employ on others than men; but we may extend our goodness and charity even to irrational creatures; and such acts flow from a gentle nature as water from an abundant spring.' Plutarch argued that man had a duty towards domestic animals, not only when they were foals and whelps, but when they were old. It was wrong to treat animals 'like old shoes or dishes and throw them away when worn out or broken with service.' If only for the sake of study and practice in humanity a man ought to accustom himself in such matters to be kind and gentle. Very plainly, Plutarch disapproved of the action of Cato, who left behind in Spain the horse which carried him through all the wars when he was consul, 'because he would not put the public to the charge of his freight.' Whether this was due to greatness or pettiness of spirit, 'let everyone argue as he pleases.' More to be praised, Plutarch thought, were the people of Athens who, after they had built the Parthenon, turned loose those horses and mules which had worked hardest; one horse which had rallied and incited the others was allowed to graze out its life at the public expense.‡

In his tract on flesh-eating, Plutarch argued that much of the world's cruelty flowed from man's ill-controlled rage for meat. An animal was entitled to cry, 'Kill me for thy feeding but do not take me for thy better feeding.' Yet man was deaf to such appeals. 'For the sake of some little mouthful of flesh, we deprive a soul of the sun and light and of that proportion

* *Guardian*, May 21, 1713.
† *History of European Morals* (1869).
‡ *Marcus Cato The Elder.*

of life and time it had been born into the world to enjoy.' Let us eat flesh, he said, but only for hunger, not for wantonness. 'Let us kill an animal; but let us do it with sorrow and pity and not abusing or tormenting it, as many nowadays are wont to do.' These torments included running red-hot spits through the bodies of swine, 'that by the tincture of the quenched iron the blood may be to that degree mortified that it may sweeten and soften the flesh in its circulation'; trampling and inflaming the udders of sows about to litter; and sewing up the eyes of cranes and swans, the better to fatten them in darkness. Of the fiends who indulged these tastes, Plutarch said: 'It is not for nourishing they want, or any necessity, but for mere gluttony, wantonness and expensiveness, that they make a pleasure of villainy . . .'

Further glimpses of the epicures' villainy are to be found in the pages of Martial. The poet gloats over goose livers swollen to a size larger than the goose itself (this trick was performed with the aid of fat and figs). 'You, perhaps,' writes Martial, 'will prefer the chitterlings of a virgin pig; I prefer them from a pregnant sow.' And again: 'We give you, from the first milk of the mothers, sucklings of which the shepherd has deprived the dams while yet unable to stand.' For emperors, dishes were made from the tongues of hundreds of singing birds, from peacock brains or from infinities of dormice.

In the long tale of man's inhumanity to beast the mass killings in the Roman amphitheatres form a baffling chapter. The butcheries began as a subsidiary attraction to the gladiatorial games; a mob accustomed to seeing human blood spilled for amusement was not likely to baulk at the blood of beasts. In the second century B.C. lions and panthers died for the glory of Rome. Aspirants to power earned themselves credit with the mob by bringing home rare creatures from the Republic's farthest confines. Pompey in 55 B.C. pitted elephants against criminals in the arena, a spectacle which seems to have stirred mixed feelings. 'He, a leader of the state and one who, according to report, was conspicuous among the leaders of old for the kindness of his heart, thought it a notable kind of spectacle to kill human beings after a new fashion,' writes Seneca.* Yet

* *On the Shortness of Life.*

The Roman *venatio*: man versus beast

by no means all the sympathy on that occasion was reserved
for the criminals. Julius Caesar produced the first giraffe,
Augustus the first tiger. Under the emperors, as the legions
brought back not only lions by the thousand but rhinos,
hippos, bears, bulls, stags, crocodiles and snakes, the mob
yawned at the tedious variety of Nature and could hardly wait
to see the hard-won menageries destroyed. Sometimes, the
animals were hunted through groves of greenery by men
armed with spears, javelins and torches, men of undisputed
daring who were prepared to stun bears with their fists and
throw cloaks over the heads of lions; at other times, the
victims would be cut to pieces by the imperial cavalry, as a
military exercise; or they might be engaged by unarmed, or
under-armed, criminals; or encouraged to destroy Christians
tied to stakes or wrapped in wild beast skins. For further
variation animals were matched against animals in every likely
and unlikely combination – rhinoceros *versus* bear, bull *versus*
elephant, bear *versus* bull, endlessly. Bulls were roused by giving
them red-wrapped balls to toss or by goading them with red-
hot irons and darts dipped in burning pitch. As art and luxury
advanced, more artistic and luxurious forms of killing were
devised. Martial has amused epigrams inspired by incidents in
the arena during Domitian's reign – a bear ludicrously caught
in bird-lime, a pregnant sow speared in such a way that her
litter was able to escape (it was Domitian who pitted dwarfs
against women and allowed criminals to be put to death to
give verisimilitude to plays). Emperors with a reputation for
humanity and enlightenment followed the bloody tradition;
Titus, who opened the Colosseum, caused 5,000 wild beasts
to be slaughtered on the first day, and 9,000 in the succeeding
hundred days. Trajan, who made the gentle Plutarch a consul,
butchered 11,000 animals to celebrate a Dacian triumph.
Commodus, the infinitely corrupt, himself descended into the
arena and led the slaughter. Even those who most loathed him
conceded that he was a brilliant marksman; for with crescent-
tipped arrows he could shoot off the heads of racing ostriches.
Writes Gibbon: 'A panther was let loose; and the archer
waited until he had leaped upon a trembling malefactor. In
the same instant the shaft flew, the beast dropped dead and the

man remained unhurt. The dens of the amphitheatre disgorged at once a hundred lions; a hundred darts from the unerring hand of Commodus laid them dead as they ran raging round the arena. Neither the huge bulk of the elephant nor the scaly hide of the rhinoceros could defend them from his stroke. Ethiopia and India yielded their most extraordinary productions; and several animals were slain in the amphitheatre which had been seen only in the representations of art or perhaps of fancy. In all these exhibitions the surest precautions were used to protect the person of the Roman Hercules from the desperate spring of any savage who might possibly disregard the dignity of the Emperor and the sanctity of the god.'*

Yet slaughter could pall. Under one emperor or another the spectacles were varied by making the more tractable beasts perform tricks. Elephants bowed before the royal box, tracing Latin or Greek flatteries in the dust with their trunks. Tigers licked the hands of those who lashed them, Domitian's lions carried live hares in their mouths and the most improbable animals were harnessed to chariots. Sometimes trained beasts were given as prizes during festivals. But for the vast mass of these creatures born under alien skies the entertainment demanded of them was that they should kill or be killed.

For the savageries of the amphitheatre there were many justifications. They were part of the accepted system of 'blood and circuses', of 'giving the public what it wants'; they were a safety-valve for a vast indolent mob on whose goodwill the emperor's safety depended; they enabled him to share the pleasures of the people and to receive their adulation. Philosophers said that scenes of blood and bravery helped to harden the spirit of a martial race, an argument which was used to defend bull-baiting in nineteenth-century Britain; but the amphitheatre, instead of teaching contempt for death, taught only contempt for life. Efforts to introduce games on the Greek pattern failed. As Lecky says, 'to men who were accustomed to witness the fierce vicissitudes of deadly combat any spectacle that did not elicit the strongest excitement was insipid.' Delicately, he points out that vices interact and that the blood frenzy of the spectacles led naturally to orgies (the opponents

* *Decline and Fall of the Roman Empire.*

of English bull-baiting were concerned about the wild sexual behaviour that followed).

Few philosophical voices were raised in protest against the slaughter of the amphitheatre and a good many poetical ones were raised in praise. What, after all, were animals? Yet the Rome which staged these abominations contained men and women who were kind to their domestic animals, who treated pets with an often exaggerated affection. On Seneca's evidence, there were skilled horse-breakers who scorned to ply the lash, knowing only too well that the creatures would grow afraid and obstinate unless caressed; and the trainer of game dogs was aware that abuse would only break their spirit and their native qualities.* Even Nero was fond of animals, in his fashion; and Commodus ordered that a favourite horse should be buried in holy ground. Indeed the list of tyrants who were pet lovers is embarrassingly long.

Even after the Christian emperors suppressed the gladiatorial games the wild beast shows continued, though on a reduced scale. One difficulty was that, after five or six centuries, the supply of wild animals was drying up. The Romans could claim that, thanks to the *venatio*, they had rid their lands of savage game; but as a technique of disinfestation this must rank as the costliest, most laborious and most degrading that history can offer. Many neighbouring nations were corrupted by the Roman blood lust, but not the Greeks. As an enduring legacy of the amphitheatre we have the bull-fight, the broad pattern of which was laid down in the time of Julius Caesar.

The most passionate defenders of Christianity do not pretend that it was a potent, positive force in teaching compassion towards the 'brute creation'. Today the Church of England Prayer Book still lacks a prayer for animals. The best that can be said is that Christianity, in its unsophisticated form, fostered a mental attitude in which respect for animals could subsist naturally with man's love for his neighbours. Bible text-hunters do not find a great deal for their comfort. In *Genesis* is a declaration that man has dominion over fish, fowl, cattle and all creeping things. After the Deluge, God blesses Noah and

* *On Mercy.*

says: 'And the fear of you and the dread of you shall be upon every beast of the earth, and upon every fowl of the air, upon all that moveth upon the earth, and upon all the fishes of the sea; into your hand are they delivered. Every moving thing that liveth shall be meat for you; even as the green herb have I given you all things.' Vegetarians have denied that this is a butchers' charter. The authorisation, they say, was an emergency one, because the Flood had destroyed all green herbs (yet was not Abel, in pre-Flood times, a keeper of sheep?), and the blame is laid on impious priests for sanctioning the practice of meat-eating after the calamity had passed.

Scattered through the Old Testament are various injunctions urging solicitude for animals, designed as much as anything to ensure efficient husbandry. 'A righteous man regardeth the life of his beast' (*Proverbs* xii, 10) is perhaps the most disinterested. Animals are to be rested on the Sabbath day. There are cautions against muzzling the ox which treads the corn, ploughing with an ox and ass together, seething the kid in its mother's milk and taking the mother bird with its young. But there are limits to the toleration which may be extended to domestic cattle: 'If an ox gore a man or a woman, that they die: then the ox shall be surely stoned, and his flesh shall not be eaten.' (*Exodus* xxi, 28).

Christ was no vegetarian, nor did he expect others to be. Critics of angling are careful to point out that the disciples were net-fishermen, who killed for food, not for sport. Christ's statement that not one sparrow is forgotten before God is followed by the assurance: 'Ye are of more value than many sparrows.' From the Gadarene episode, it is evident that man is of more value than many swine. This passage has embarrassed many generations of animal-lovers and has been hurled by medical students at the heads of anti-vivisectionists.*
God had hesitated to destroy Nineveh, the wicked city, because it contained, as well as six thousand people, 'much cattle'; yet his Son was willing to save one man's reason at

* In a polemical clash with Gladstone, Thomas Huxley described the Gadarene affair as 'wanton destruction of other people's property' and 'a misdemeanour of evil example.' Gladstone said the story was a moral allegory. – Gertrude Himmelfarb: *Darwin and the Darwinian Revolution.*

the expense of two thousand swine. 'Doth God care for oxen?' asks St Paul, contemptuously, overlooking the evidence. Christ cared enough for oxen to say: 'If your ox fall into the pit on the Sabbath day will ye not straightway pull him out?' St John in a vision saw animals in positions of honour at the throne of God; but the Church did not accept this as evidence that animals were immortal.

The attempts to corrupt Christianity, to confuse its simplicities with Greek metaphysics, were many and insidious. Gradually, medieval Churchmen fell under the revived spell of Aristotle, whose rational interpretation of the universe laid more stress on the immensity of the gulf which separated man from the beasts than on his kinship with them. By the time that St Thomas Aquinas defined and concentrated Christian thought in the thirteenth century, the status of animals, in scholastic circles at least, was low indeed. Man alone was rational, cogitative, contemplative; animals were instinctive. St Thomas could write of them: 'Beings that may be treated simply as means to the perfection of persons can have no rights and to this category the brute creation belongs. In the Divine plan of the universe the lower creatures are subordinated to the welfare of man . . . (but) the very essence of the moral law is that we respect and obey the order established by the Creator.'* Animals, being part of this order, were not to be needlessly harried, if only because men who were brutal to animals were likely to be brutal to each other. Primarily, the Church was obsessed with preparing man for the life to come; animals, with no expectation of this privilege, forfeited not only rights but, all too often, sympathy too. Only the eccentrics argued that animals, *because* they had no souls, merited special consideration; among these was Cardinal Bellarmine, who allowed vermin to pasture on him freely, saying, 'We shall have Heaven to reward us for our suffering, but these poor creatures have nothing but the enjoyment of their present life.'

But if theologians could turn their eyes from animals, the Church's saints, martyrs and hermits inspired innumerable legends which demonstrated kinship between man and beast. Ascetics who cut themselves off from the world's wickedness

* *Summa Theologica.*

to live in holes in the ground perforce had to come to terms with Nature. Sometimes, no doubt, they achieved improbable feats of domestication. The pages of hagiology teem with tales of strange alliances. Ravens brought bread to Paul the Hermit and when he died two lions came quietly up and dug his grave. Cuthbert of Lindisfarne was tended by swans and otters. Gerasimus drew a thorn from a lion's paw, in return for which the creature carried his water bottles and guarded his donkey. Froilanus had his baggage borne by a wolf. An eagle fanned Servetus with its wings when he slept in fierce heat on pilgrimage. Ida wrote by the light shed from the tips of a stag's antlers. Colman, a well-organised Hibernian, had a cock to announce his devotional hour, a mouse to nibble his ear if he slept on and a fly to mark his place on the page. Many stories sprang from the amphitheatre: Mamas was thrown to the beasts, but they fawned on him; Marcellus had to be beheaded, because the bears refused to touch him; Thekla was defended by a lioness against a bear, afterwards baptising the beast which saved her.

Such incidents as hinds offering their milk, stags drawing the plough, wolves atoning for depredations by guarding the flock or helping with the baggage crop up continually. Francis of Assisi was only one of many who preached to wild creatures (his 'brothers and sisters'); Anthony of Padua addressed the fishes; and Regulus and Herveus, if they did not preach to the frogs, requested their co-operation by keeping quiet. There were also legends in which an animal served as a divine instrument. Hubert, an ardent hunter, pursued a stag in the Ardennes on Good Friday; when it turned in a clearing the crucifix shone between its antlers and the voice of Christ said: 'Unless you turn to the Lord, Hubert, you shall fall into Hell.' The stag, it appears, did not object to being hunted, only to being hunted on Good Friday. Mysteriously, Hubert became the patron saint of hunting.

However extravagant these legends were, it is hard to doubt that, down the centuries, their effect on the minds of simple people was to spread sympathy and indulgence towards animals. If beasts could spare or succour man, had not man a duty to spare and succour animals? If they could display human virtues, did they not merit human compassion? We do not know whether, in fact, men's minds worked like this, but it seems probable that, where tomes of theology could not promote kindness, word-of-mouth superstition did. Sometimes superstition got out of hand. In the diocese of Lyons, the report that a dog had been mistakenly put to death on suspicion of killing a child led to pilgrimages by countryfolk to the canine martyr's grave; whereupon the affronted Church wiped out the reputation of St Greyhound with bell, book and candle.*

Although they were deemed to have no souls, animals could be possessed by evil spirits. St Thomas said that it was legitimate to curse such animals 'as satellites of Satan instigated by the powers of Hell.' That ruling, in conjunction with the harsh law laid down in Exodus, was enough to authorise the custom of putting animals on trial for grievous 'crimes' and executing them with all the ignominy and high-flown sentiment reserved for human offenders. In 1386 at Falaise a pig was condemned to be mutilated and hanged on a gibbet for having killed a child; it was dressed in man's clothes and executed in the public square. In 1408 the Russians sent a refractory he-goat to Siberia. At Basle in 1474 a cock was convicted of laying an egg (a dire offence, since cocks' eggs hatched cockatrices for sorcerers) and was publicly burned, along with its monstrous egg. Pigs seem to have been the usual victims, but cows, bulls, horses and cats were also strung up. In the fifteenth and sixteenth centuries men accused of 'un crime que nous ne pouvons désigner' were burned along with the violated beast, which might or might not be strangled first.† Winged nuisances could not be brought before a religious tribunal, but they could be cursed collectively. After the sixteenth century the custom of putting animals on trial petered out and the law took action instead against the owner of the offending beast.

The Renaissance brought a quickening of men's minds but no immediate quickening of their compassion. Old superstitions were replaced by new. The humanists, who saw man as the

---

* G. G. Coulton: *A Medieval Garner.*
† Emile Agnel: *Curiosités Judiciaires et Historiques du Moyen Age* (1858).

measure of all things, had as little charity for the animal kingdom as had the theologians. Reviving science picked on animals as something to be carved and taken apart, in search of the secret of life. Only the feeblest flame of humanitarianism stirred in the cold wind of humanism.

2

RUDE PLEASURES

ENGLAND'S national obsession was hunting. In Saxon times it was not only an obsession but a very necessary activity; wolves were so numerous in Yorkshire that forts were built where travellers could take refuge from bloodthirsty packs. Under the Normans, who rewrote the rules of the chase and seized the forests, wolves were almost wiped out and wild boars reduced; but there were still deer innumerable to pursue. In the twelfth century John of Salisbury mocked the passion for hunting which bred a fierce arrogance in its devotees: 'In our time hunting and hawking are esteemed the most honourable employments and most excellent virtues by our nobility; and they think it the height of worldly felicity to spend the whole of their life in these diversions; accordingly they prepare for them with more solicitude, expense and parade than they do for war; and pursue the wild beasts with greater frenzy than they do the enemies of their own country. By constantly following this way of life they lose much of their humanity and become as savage, nearly, as the very brutes they hunt.'* Even churchmen became infected with the passion for the chase, and had to be reminded that time so spent was time stolen from devotions. Eventually angling became the accepted field sport of monks and nuns; it was supposed to allow ample time for divine meditation.

By Tudor times no animal, save the occasional boar, offered any mortal challenge to man. Hunting was primarily a sport, one which in the process provided meat and helped to limit

* *Policratus*, quoted in Joseph Strutt's *Sports and Pastimes of the People of England* (1801).

those animals which were too numerous. In one fashion or another all England hunted. Monarchs pursued deer; ladies flew merlins against larks; farmers loosed greyhounds against hares or splashed after otters; labourers dug up foxes or badgers; artisans shot stones at birds; boys set dogs after rabbits. These were the natural recreations in a land where heaths, wastes, marshes, lakes, woodlands and fens were alive with wild life. Animals possessing strong fighting instincts, when taken alive, were kept for baiting; in this way the excitements of bloodshed and death were brought within reach of the townsman.

Pursuit of the larger game bred a certain hardihood and contempt for comfort, and for this reason hunting was sometimes represented as a preparatory school for the battlefield; it was also regarded as a corrective for the effeminacy which went with courts. But, in the main, men hunted because it was a traditional pursuit, a source of exercise and an excuse for conviviality afterwards. Outwitting and killing inferior creatures was an appeasement of an ancient instinct; and skill was flattered at the same time as this instinct was assuaged.

Criticism of hunting on humanitarian grounds – as distinct from those on which John of Salisbury assailed it – was almost unknown. The young Henry VIII wore out eight horses a day in the chase; who was to accuse him of cruelty? Yet in 1516 appeared Sir Thomas More's *Utopia*, with this passage:

'What delight can there be, and not rather displeasure, in hearing the barking and howling of dogs? Or what greater pleasure is there to be felt when a dog followeth a hare than when a dog followeth a dog? For one thing is done in both, that is to say, running, if thou hast pleasure therein. But if the hope of slaughter and the expectation of tearing in pieces the beast doth please thee, thou shouldest rather be moved with pity to see a silly innocent hare murdered of a dog: the weak of the stronger, the fearful of the fierce, the innocent of the cruel and unmerciful. Therefore all this exercise of hunting, as a thing unworthy to be used of free men, the Utopians have rejected to their butchers, to the which craft . . . they appoint their bondmen. For they count hunting the lowest, the vilest and most abject part of butchery, and the other parts of it more profitable and more honest, as bringing much more commodity, in that they kill beasts only for necessity, whereas the hunter seeketh nothing but pleasure of the silly and woeful beast's slaughter and murder. The which pleasure in beholding death they think doth rise in the very beasts, either of a cruel affection of mind or else to be changed in continuance of time into cruelty by long use of so cruel a pleasure.'

In essence, Sir Thomas More's criticism contains all the objections advanced by the opponents of blood sports today.

Deer-hunting was the most fashionable sport. In its least strenuous form, as staged for royalty, ambassadors, ladies and the higher clergy, it involved no more than driving the animals into an enclosure and executing them at leisure. As guest of

Ladies hunting: fourteenth century
From Strutt's 'Pastimes'

Lord Montacute at Cowdray, Sussex, in 1591 Queen Elizabeth entered a bower where a nymph presented her with a cross-bow. Thirty deer had been rounded up for her pleasure; and, while musicians played, she took aim and killed three or four of them. One of her ladies, the Countess of Kildare, accounted for another. In the evening, looking down from a turret, Elizabeth saw sixteen bucks pulled down by 'greyhounds' (according to George Turberville, a red deer would sometimes bear four or five brace of hounds before collapsing). The Queen also hunted deer in the traditional manner in the forest, dismounting to cut the animal's throat with her own hand. Sometimes it pleased her to show clemency, as when on a

visit to Kenilworth, she allowed a captured hart to return to
the forest, though not before depriving it of its ears 'for a
ransom'. It was at Kenilworth that the Queen's Buck Hounds
were housed by the Earl of Leicester.

George Turberville, who published his *Noble Art of Venerie*
in 1575, described the method of dispatching the hart at bay.
A huntsman with a sword crept up behind and, if the hart
rounded on him, retreated behind a tree (the Queen presumably was offered a more exhausted quarry). The death of
a deer was an occasion for savage or mock-savage rejoicing,
on the pattern described centuries earlier by John of Salisbury:
'One would think that the capture of the King of the Cappa-
docians was being celebrated, to judge by the blare of the
trumpet and squeal of pipe proclaiming the victory.' The body
was cut up on the spot, the head being raised to bay the
hounds and the heart flourished in triumph; the nobler
portions were claimed as perquisites, the less noble portions
thrown to the hounds. Blood was freely splashed over guests
and onlookers. The first of the Stuarts, in the belief that the
sinews of his legs would be thereby strengthened, used to
paddle in the quarry's gore.

In Scotland deer were rounded up in great drives and
massacred indiscriminately. James V and Queen Mary, in
1563, watched a three-day operation by two thousand High-
landers who concentrated the deer of the Atholl area, and
then fell upon them with dogs, daggers, arrows and firearms.
Many of the attackers were trampled to death under the
gigantic herd. Elsewhere, deer were sometimes driven into
special dykes for slaughter.

The hare, described by Edward II's huntsman, William
Twici, as the most marvellous beast on earth, was the next
most popular quarry. It was hunted by scent, both on horseback and on foot, and coursed on sight by greyhounds. Gervase
Markham, that prolific writer on rural sports, described hare-
hunting as 'every honest man, and good man's chase . . . the
freest, readiest and most enduring pastime.'* James I, who
used to hunt hares freed from baskets, assured his son Henry
in a letter that this was 'the most honourable and noblest

* *Rural Contentments* (1615).

sport', a far more distinguished recreation than mangling game with guns and bows, which was 'a thievish form of hunting'.

George Turberville thought the coursing of hares with greyhounds was a nobler pastime than coursing a deer. Chaucer's monk was a devotee:

> Therfore he was a pricasour aright;
> Grehoundes he hadde, as swifte as fowel in flight;
> Of priking and of hunting for the hare
> Was al his lust, for no cost wolde he spare . . .

The hare was not regarded as a timid, defenceless animal; its speed and cunning were its armoury. But to ensure that competitive coursing should not become a succession of quick kills, the Duke of Norfolk in Elizabeth's reign laid down rules which limited the number of pursuing greyhounds to two and stipulated that the hare should receive 'fair law'.

As yet, the fox did not rank as a sporting adversary. Like the badger it gave off a hot scent and for that reason, says Gervase Markham, little cunning was needed to pursue it. But, sporting adversary or not, the fox had to be destroyed, with other vermin. A common practice was to hunt it on foot, dig it from its earth and then – if the captors were in the mood for sport – allow terriers to worry it in a confined space. Badgers were caught in sacks placed over their earths and afterwards baited to death in inn yards. Otters were hunted by hounds and impaled on long spears; occasionally, if taken alive, they too were baited. The poorest sport, perhaps, was offered by rabbits, which were caught by dogs or ferrets or taken in snares. Sometimes they were reserved for the amusement of townsmen. Paul Hentzner, a German traveller in Elizabeth's reign, describes a wrestling match before the Lord Mayor of London and says: 'After this is over a parcel of live rabbits are turned loose among the crowd, which are pursued by a number of boys who endeavour to catch them with all the noise they can make.'* The cat, whether wild or domesticated, had need of all its nine lives. Britain had few cat lovers and a great many cat haters, much of the animus against it

* *Travels in England* (1598).

stemming from the fact that it was the witch's favourite animal. Boys set terriers on cats and huntsmen used them for blooding young hounds. Wildcats, once deemed worthy of pursuit by Norman kings, were wiped out by any crude and convenient method.

The bastard sport of baiting – which looms large in these pages – afforded pleasure to princes and ruffians alike. For no discernible reason, the English were more addicted to this pastime than other nations; and their favourite victim in Tudor days was the bear, which needed little incitement to

A horse baited with dogs: fourteenth century
From Strutt's 'Pastimes'

ferocity. The animal was tethered by a chain and relays of mastiffs – up to six at a time – were loosed at it. Some it would mutilate or kill; others would withdraw when mauled; the fiercest, or the most adept, would 'pin' the bear by sinking their teeth into its nose or other convenient toothhold, and holding on. The bait continued until the bear had routed its rivals or had been mauled sufficiently for the bearward to stop the fight. It was a valuable animal, and the mere fact that herds of them were maintained in England (as Erasmus testifies) did not mean that their lives could be cheaply sacrificed. Bearwards took pride in the performance of their beasts, showed them a rough affection and plied them, when necessary, with strong liquors. The public eagerly followed the careers of famous fighting bears like Sackerson (mentioned by Shake-speare), Tom of Lincoln, Ned of Canterbury and Blind Robin. Blind bears were baited by men as well as by dogs. Hentzner saw one scourged 'by five or six men standing circularly with whips, which they exercise upon him without any mercy as he cannot escape because of his chain; he defends himself with all his force and skill, throwing down all that come within his reach and are not active enough to get out of it, and tearing the whips out of their hands and breaking them.'

The most famous bear-garden was built in Henry VIII's reign on Bankside at Southwark. It held one thousand specta-tors who paid one penny admission and was the scene of great din and disorder. Mary and Elizabeth both enjoyed baiting and staged displays for visiting ambassadors. There is a description of the bait at Kenilworth Castle in 1575, which resulted in 'such expense of blood and leather . . . as a month's licking . . . will not recover'. The narrator says: 'It was a sport very pleasant of these beasts, to see the bear with his pink eyes leering after his enemies' approach, the nimbleness and wait of the dogs to take his advantage and the force and experience of the bear again to avoid the assaults; if he were beaten in one place, how he would pinch in another to get free; if he were taken once, then what shift, with biting, with clawing, with roaring, tossing and tumbling, he would work to wind himself from them, and then he was loose, to shake his ears twice or thrice, with the blood and the slaver about his phisnomy, was a matter of goodly relief.'*

Unlike bear-baiting, bull-baiting had ancient legal authority behind it. The flesh of the bull was thought to be indigestible and unwholesome if the animal was killed without being baited and butchers were liable to prosecution if the brutal pre-liminaries were omitted. Numerous butchers were still being fined for this offence in Stuart times; in 1612 Michael Alford of Wells, Somerset and five other butchers were convicted of selling bull meat to the lieges when 'the bull aforesaid was not first *pulsatus*, in English, bayten . . .'† Court rolls and sessions books of other English towns yield similar instances.

* Robert Laneham's *Letter* (1575).
† *Notes and Queries* CLV.

By those in authority, baiting was regarded as a lusty, manly, traditional sport which gave the people an outlet. If they drew from it lessons of courage, so much the better. In the view of Elizabeth and her ministers it was a more fit national pastime than the theatre, which put new and irreverent ideas into men's heads. Late in her reign, the Queen was sufficiently disturbed by the growing vogue for play-going to call for an order restraining the production of plays on a Thursday, which was baiting day. The Lord Mayor of London thought it wrong that 'in divers places, the players do use to recite their plays, to the great hurt and destruction of the game of bull-baiting and such-like pastimes which are maintained for Her Majesty's pleasure.' The Queen's taste for this pastime did not diminish with age. Her Chief Master of the Bears had power to seize bears, bulls and dogs from any part of England.

The early Puritans were not afraid to condemn baiting. They did so mostly on the grounds that it was a profanation of the Sabbath and a focus for gamblers, rogues and bawds. Thomas Cartwright, mainspring of the Puritan movement, in his *Admonition to Parliament* in 1572 said: 'If there be a bear or a bull to be baited in the afternoon or a jackanapes to ride on horseback, the minister hurries the service over in a shameful manner in order to be present at the show.' But Philip Stubbes in 1583 struck a clear humanitarian note: 'What Christian heart can take pleasure to see one poor beast to rent, tear and kill another, and all for his foolish pleasure? And though they be bloody beasts to mankind and seek his destruction, yet we are not to abuse them for his sake who made them and whose creatures they are. For notwithstanding that they be evil to us and thirst for our blood, yet are they good creatures in their own nature and kind, and made to set forth the glory, power and magnificence of our God and for our use, and therefore for his sake we ought not to abuse them. It is a common saying among men, borrowed from the French, *qui aime Jean aime son chien* . . . so, love God, love his creatures . . .'*

James I opposed cruelty in principle, but curiosity led him

* *Anatomy of Abuses.*

to conduct wild beast baits at the Tower. Stow in his *Annals*
tells of a lion bait which cost the lives of two dogs; a third
held on to the lion's lip, and was with difficulty dislodged,
after which the lion withdrew from the engagement. Prince
Henry took charge of the wounded dog, saying, 'He has fought
with the king of beasts and shall never fight an inferior
creature.' In 1610 two lions and a bear were put in a pit
together, but refused to fight; nor did they show any interest
in a high-spirited horse which joined them. Six mastiffs were
then introduced and would have torn the horse to pieces, but
were dragged off by the bearwards. The lions and bear ignored
the whole affair.

Unearthing a fox: fourteenth century
From Strutt's 'Pastimes'

Cock-fighting, or cocking, also received the patronage of
monarchy. During Henry II's reign it had been the custom
of London schoolboys to bring cocks to school on Shrove
Tuesday and match them under the supervision of a master.
In many parts, cock-fights were held in churchyards, with the
full approval of the incumbent. Henry VIII built a cockpit
as part of his Palace of Whitehall and many more were erected
in Elizabeth's reign. 'There is no pleasure more noble, delight-
some, or void of cozenage and deceit than this pleasure of
cocking,' said Gervase Markham. A Norfolk vicar, the Rev.
George Wilson, argued in his *Commendation of Cockes and Cock-
fighting* (1607) that by watching cocks the citizens learned
courage. He recalled that Themistocles, before besieging

Dalmatia, staged a preliminary cock-fight before his troops. It was fiercely contended and both birds died. Then, addressing his troops, the commander expressed the hope that they would show as much courage as 'these silly fowls of the air'. Thus fortified, the army went on and massacred its enemies. Puritans vigorously denied that cock-fighting taught courage. It was the school, said Stubbes, of swearing, forswearing, deceit, fraud, collusion, cozenage, scolding, railing, covetous talking, fighting, brawling, quarrelling, drinking and whoring.

Cock-fighters could always plead that cocks would have fought each other in nature. It was more difficult to find a justification for the ancient Shrove Tuesday pastime of 'throwing at cocks'. Sometimes the creature was tied to a stake and became the prize of the first marksman who killed it with sticks or stones; if its leg was broken, rough splints were applied so that it could still stand up to receive punishment. Sometimes it was buried in earth, with only its head visible; or it might be thrust in an earthen vessel, with head and tail protruding, and become the prize of the first person to break the vessel. Why the cock should have been selected for this treatment on Shrove Tuesday was a question no divine could answer; nor could any patriot give a good reason why the English alone should be addicted to this barbarity. The only half-plausible explanation ever advanced was that the cock was the national emblem of France and abusing it was a suitable and necessary expression of contempt. If so, it is surprising that any frog was left alive in Britain. Children were encouraged to throw at cocks; even the kindly Sir Thomas More, as a boy, was said to have shown promise at this pastime.

Hawking had reached the zenith of its popularity in Tudor and early Stuart times. It was the sport of the nobility and subject to elaborate rules. Nobody thought it cruel to set two merlins after a lark, one to strike it down, the other to catch it – least of all the ladies, whose special exercise this was (and who returned home to lavish affection on caged larks). The wild lark would have died anyway, so the argument ran; man was merely imposing a certain discipline on the random strife of Nature. Lesser citizens caught birds by every stratagem, sporting or otherwise, that ingenuity could devise: by liming

branches; by bat-fowling, that is, by rousing sleeping birds in
their roosts, confusing them with torches or hot coals, and
striking them down as they fluttered in fright; by low-belling,
or ringing a bell and causing them to huddle together in
alarm, then netting them; by shooting them with arrows from
behind stalking-horses (life-like models of horses); by setting
out decoys or flashing mirrors and then collapsing nets on the
inquisitive; by setting springes (nooses on the end of pliant
rods) or loops of horsehair; and by every variety of gin and
pitfall. Here and there the musket was beginning to be pressed
into service; but the sport of 'shooting flying' had not yet arrived.

Monks, those patient, meditative anglers, had a curious
capacity for ignoring the sufferings of the live bait they
fastened to their lines. The perch had the reputation of being
able to live longest on the hook; its fins were stripped off and
it was threaded with wire through the length of its body, in
which condition it remained wriggling until a pike seized it.
Those who have read their unexpurgated Izaak Walton will
be familiar with that old humbug's instructions for sewing up
a live frog as bait. The idea was 'to use him as if we loved
him, that is, harm him as little as possible, that he may live
the longer.'* One way of heightening the sport was to tie the
line to the leg of a duck and chase it about the water, in the
hope of stimulating a tug-of-war between pike and bird.†

Even the insect world contributed to human amusement.
Each new generation of children was taught the art of threading
a cockchafer on a string, in such a way that the creature buzzed
fiercely in its efforts to escape.

The people who followed these pursuits were great pet lovers.
They kept ponies, spaniels, lap-dogs, monkeys, squirrels, hedgehogs, badgers, rabbits, dormice and every kind of bird; and
in the main treated them with every kindness. An Englishman,
as John Bunyan complained, would rather go for a walk with
a dog than with a Christian. When the inescapable seventh
day came he took his dog into church with him.

On balance, Puritan agitation against savage sports probably

* *The Compleat Angler* (1653).
† An idea attributed, perhaps unjustly, to Dame Julyana Berners, prioress of
a nunnery at Sopwell, near St Albans, in the *Book of St Albans* (1496).

did more harm than good. It was difficult to convince the common man that Nature's internecine strife and the beasts' dread of man stemmed from the Fall. 'I never read of any in the volume of the sacred Scriptures that was a good man and a hunter,' wrote Stubbes, arguing that no animal should be slain for food except in the fear of God. That was not the mood in which Englishmen hunted.

Macaulay's jibe is well-known: 'The Puritan hated bear-baiting not because it gave pain to the bear but because it gave pleasure to the spectators. Indeed, he generally contrived to enjoy the double pleasure of tormenting both spectators and bear.'* Lecky appears to agree with this verdict; Samuel Gardiner, historian of the Commonwealth, insists that the Puritans were chiefly concerned to end 'the immorality which these exhibitions fostered.'

That the Puritans were by no means devoid of humanitarian feelings is evident from their writings. But on coming to power they seem to have decided that the best way to abolish baiting was to kill off the bears. When Charles's Queen arrived, defiantly, from Holland in 1643 she brought with her a company of savage bears, which were distributed among various county towns. Cromwell's men entering Uppingham found a Sabbath bait in progress, tied the bears to a tree and shot them. Baiting went on, despite efforts to legislate it out of existence. In 1653 Colonel Pride, as Sheriff of Surrey, decided to put an end to defiance from the Keeper of the Bears at Southwark. He 'caused all the bears to be fast tied up by the noses and then valiantly brought some files of musketeers, drew up, and gave fire: and killed six or more bears in the place (only leaving one innocent white cub) and also cocks of the game. It is said all the mastiffs are to be shipped for Jamaica.' On his death-bed Pride is reputed to have said: 'The first thing that is upon my spirits is the killing of the bears, for which the people hate me and call me all the names in the Rainbow. But did not David kill a bear? Did not the Lord Deputy Ireton kill a bear? Did not another lord of ours kill five bears?'†

* *History of England.*
† Macaulay: *History of England.*

With the Restoration, baiting lost prestige. The theatre, and, increasingly, horse-racing were now the fashionable pursuits. Evelyn, from curiosity, went to the Bear Garden and found the proceedings 'butcherly'; he left 'heartily weary of the rude and dirty pastime which I had not seen I think in twenty years before.' Pepys was similarly disgusted. But the rougher elements still derived much pleasure from baiting and were resolute to protect their sport from any new breed of Puritans.

In the sixteenth century an urge to 'witch the world with noble horsemanship' spread to England from Renaissance Italy. The princes of the South, losing interest in jousting, bred a lighter, more spirited, more supple steed, capable of sophisticated and graceful feats which enhanced the reputation of its rider. These animals were not broken by brutal methods, as brutality was then understood; the idea was to train a lower intelligence by the exercise of a higher one. Hence came the arts of *manège* and equine ballet. All the courts of Europe displayed an eager interest in the new science, including that of Henry VIII. An Italian riding master travelled to England to instruct the boy King Edward VI, who had need of princely accomplishments.

It would be absurd to pretend that the influence of the Italian school spread a new lenity towards horses throughout Britain; but it did show, to those who cared to learn, that subtler methods of training could produce gratifying results. Gervase Markham, a champion of the new approach, wrote copiously and repetitiously on the theme of horsemanship. A one-time soldier in the Low Countries, he is said to have imported the first Arab horse to Britain. Books like his *Cavelarice, or the English Horseman* (1607) and *Country Contentments* (1615) reveal the barbarities from which the horse had still to be delivered:

'It hath been the practice of some horsemen, when they could not make their horse go forward, to tie a shrewd cat to a pole, with her head and feet at liberty, and so thrust it under the horse's belly, or between his legs, to make her scratch, bite and claw him by the cods and other tender parts of the body; the strange torment

and violence whereof will make any horse start to run away. Others
have taken a hedgehog and tied it straight by the feet under the
horse's tail, the hideousness of the cry of that little beast will make
a horse not only go forward but run away violently . . . Others
have used to put a cord with a running knot about the horse's
stones, and to take the other end of the cord into their hand and
so at their pleasures to pull it straight, which torment being most
insufferable hath made a horse to go forward violently.'

The huntsman moves up to stab the hart
From Turberville's 'Noble Art of Venerie' (1575)

The latter device was also used, Markham says, not to urge
a horse forward but to serve as a brake, or to discourage the
animal from settling down in water. Often it caused such
injuries that the horse had to be gelded. Markham makes the
point that cruel methods breed other faults; for example, to
stop running horses with the aid of wisps of fire on poles only

brings out cowardliness and fear. His recommended way of
urging a stubborn horse forward is to 'thrust forth your feet
hard and stiff upon your stirrups,' and at the same time offer
'cherishings', that is, words of affection and encouragement
like 'there, boy, there', or 'so, boy'. With a vicious horse the
rider should use his spurs, the terror of his voice ('Ha, traitor!'
or 'Ha, villain!') and, in great extremities, 'the stroke of your
rod between his ears'. He disagrees strongly with French
writers who are for ever beating a horse about the head; 'by
rubbing the withers of the horse with the butt end of the rod
you shall more cherish and delight your horse than with anything else whatsoever.' If a horse will not amble, Markham's
advice is to take him into a ploughed field for a quarter of an
hour, and then ride him on the road again. He is suitably
scornful of those masters who cut the horse's mouth to fit the
bit, instead of adapting the bit to the horse. He rejects bits
with sharp wheels, roughened portions and fittings like the
rowels of a spur, 'which hath made me admire how men for
pity could be so tyrannous, when the greatest fault in the
horse is the soonest reclaimed with gentleness.' Always he
enjoins patience and gentleness, through which the horse will
understand the rider's nature and intention.

Not all ballet movements, it is clear, were taught by superior
intelligence alone; if a horse was not ready to turn at the
appropriate moment, in a cornet or a capriole, a bystander
prodded it with a spike. Markham does not object to teaching
a horse tricks, 'because these unprofitable toys show in a horse
an extraordinary capacity, an observant fear and an obedient
love, all of which are to be esteemed worthy qualities.' The
tricks include picking up gloves, counting out numbers by
pawing the ground and 'making a horse to piss when you
would have him'.

Markham is reluctant to give instructions on how to prepare
hunting horses to win wagers (which became a considerable
scandal in the eighteenth century), on the grounds that wagers
cause too many quarrels.

It is evident that the methods of gelding horses, to make
them less 'rammish and unruly', were often crude and cruel;
strangulation by horse hairs is a method condemned by

Markham. He informs his readers that cutting off a horse's mane and tail will not abate its lust; unlike Samson, the horse does not have its strength in its hair. His advice for 'stirring up lust' in horse or mare is to rub the vital regions with nettles, 'a thing ordinarily used'.

Other writers pleaded eloquently for the horse, among them Michael Baret in his *Hipponomie, or the Vineyard of Horsemanship* (1618). He condemned the training of horses with weights, sandbags, trammels, oversize shoes, lead pasterns and deep earths. 'Of all the creatures that God made at the Creation there is none (except man) more excellent or so much to be respected as a horse,' he says.

Yet Britain remained the proverbial hell of horses. 'The English, especially Northern men, ride from daybreak to the evening without drawing bit, neither sparing their horses nor themselves,' says Fynes Moryson in his *Itinerary* (1617). And James Howell, in his *Instructions for Foreign Travel* (1642) writes: 'The English generally are observed by all other nations, to ride commonly with that speed, as if they ride for a midwife or a physician, or to get a pardon to save one's life as he goeth to execution . . .'

3

NO SOULS, NO FEELINGS

A REPELLENT, and largely forgotten, feature of the seventeenth century was the rage for vivisection which, all over Europe, seized speculative philosophers and their adherents. The Church which had been so reluctant to allow the dissection of human corpses, or experiments on living criminals, showed little or no concern over the cutting up of living animals.

It has been said that 'the anatomists began by denying souls to animals and concluded by denying them feeling also.'* Descartes was their beacon of darkness in the surrounding light. The great geometrician found some difficulty in fitting animals into his mechanistic theories, but he was able to show that they were mere automatic devices with 'animal spirits' flowing through their nerves. They functioned like watches, without mind, soul or destiny. Descartes' followers contended that a dog felt no pleasure when it wagged its tail and a cat suffered no pain when its tail was trodden. The shriek when a limb was torn off was no different from the shriek when a branch was torn from a tree. Animals had reflex actions only. The human body was also a machine, but it had been united by God with a rational soul; even a slavering idiot stood immeasurably higher than the most intelligent ape. To argue otherwise was to court trouble with the Church, which discouraged any attempt to raise beasts to the status of men. The views of Descartes, for all their ingenuity, caused no distress in the bastions of orthodoxy.

Before Descartes, Montaigne had dared to express the view

* Dix Harwood: *Love for Animals* (1928).

that man showed unseemly arrogance in assuming superiority over the animal kingdom. Men and animals alike were guests in the Creator's household and for that reason alone we ought to show them respect, affection, grace and benignity.* In these views, Montaigne echoed his favourite Plutarch. A handful of others had voiced similar opinions, but had not cared, or dared, to propagate them.

Of the *dilettanti* who cut living animals like turnips, probably few bothered what the Church thought. It was useful to have a religious or philosophical warrant for cruelty, but the spirit of inquiry was not to be shackled. Nothing could be discovered save by experiments. If experiments were too painful to be carried out on human beings then the obvious course was to try them out on the expendable creatures so lavishly furnished for man's utility. There were, of course, no anaesthetics; and if there had been, it would have been regarded as farcical to anaesthetise machines. How many investigators fully deluded themselves into thinking that cats and dogs were non-sentient we cannot tell; more probably, the experimenter schooled himself to watch dispassionately for reactions and reflexes and to ignore what might or might not be cries of pain.

Vivisection was a pastime open to all. Physicians and professors, princes and courtiers, divines and medical students – all were scientists. In France fashionable ladies who used to attend the disembowellings of dead criminals for the *frisson* now watched living dogs turned inside out. There was no attempt to co-ordinate research, if research it could be called; anyone who could think of an audacious or amusing experiment proceeded to carry it out. Nor was it always pretended that the overriding object was to save human suffering, or to improve the human lot. For every experiment conducted to elicit new information, a score were performed to demonstrate what was already well known, or to show off the manipulator's skill. Yet, out of cruelty, great discoveries were made. William Harvey, with the aid of stags put at his disposal by the King, established his theory of the circulation of the blood; whereupon a hundred little Harveys followed in his wake, demonstrating the same principle in opened-up dogs, cats and pigs.

* *On Cruelty.*

In England the game gained a grip after the Civil War. The new intellectual pursuits were dismembering, poisoning, drowning, suffocating, gutting, burning, impaling, draining, starving and injecting. In 1664 Samuel Pepys called on 'Mr Pierce, the surgeon' to see a dog killed by 'letting opium into his hind leg'. The operators' knowledge of anatomy seemed deficient. 'He and Dr Clerke did fail mightily in hitting the vein and in effect did not do the business after many trials; but, with the little they got in, the dog did presently fall asleep, and so lay till we cut him up.' Another dog was made to swallow opium, staggered and fell asleep – 'it is a strange and sudden effect'. Whether this was primarily an experiment in anaesthesia is not clear.

Could the characteristics of an animal be changed by changing its blood? Pepys in 1665 describes a 'pretty experiment' in transfusion at Gresham College. It involved 'the blood of one dog let out, till he died, into the body of another on one side, while all his own ran out on the other side.' The dog into which the substitute blood was siphoned was reported as 'likely to do well'. What would happen, the onlookers speculated, if the blood of a Quaker was run into the veins of an Archbishop?

John Evelyn, like Pepys, a member of the Royal Society, in 1667 watched blood transfused from a sheep into a dog, 'till the sheep died, the dog well, and was ordered to be carefully looked to'. In 1668 his *Diary* says, 'I saw the experiment repeated, of transfusing blood out of a sheep into a man, celebrated at Arundel House.' One night the Society would poison birds with *nux vomica*, another night it would allow vipers to bite dogs and cats. At Gresham College Evelyn was privileged to demonstrate killings in a vacuum to the Danish Ambassador; it was not easy to preserve laboratory discipline because of the press of bishops, statesmen and poets. Robert Boyle was not without pity and admiration for the 'admirable engines' in the shape of kittens, snakes and frogs which he methodically suffocated. Sometimes lady spectators would beg him to break off the experiments, which he did, only to resume them at night when the unscientific sex had gone home. He weighed creatures immediately before and after death, in an effort to discover if anything tangible departed from them; and he compared how long various animals took to drown.

From these and a thousand other physiological experiments the lesson learned was a somewhat humiliating one: namely, that the mechanism of animals much more closely resembled that of human beings than had been dreamed of in Descartes' philosophy. It became more and more difficult to maintain that God had given animals the means of feeling so that they should *not* feel (as Voltaire later put it). Perhaps the Preacher in *Ecclesiastes* had not been so far wrong:

'For that which befalleth the sons of men befalleth beasts; even one thing befalleth them: as the one dieth, so dieth the other; yea, they all have one breath; so that a man hath no pre-eminence above a beast: for all is vanity.

'All go unto one place; all are of the dust, and all turn to dust again.

'Who knoweth the spirit of man that goeth upward, and the spirit of the beast that goeth downward to the earth?'

Man was reluctant to think that his soul was extinguished in the earth; but if he now conceded that animals had feelings, must he also concede that they had souls? The Church told him to dismiss such a notion from his mind. Nevertheless the suspicion grew – it was voiced by Locke and Addison, among others – that even with the exclusive possession of a soul man might stand at a greater remove from God than from the higher animals. This was a timely deflation of his self-importance. He now knew that he was very much a part of the family of Nature; hence it seemed reasonable to concede that animals, while they might have no *rights*, perhaps deserved a fairer deal from him than hitherto. Men and beasts alike were fellow pensioners of a benevolent Providence; therefore it was for privileged man to show the lesser tenants some of that same benevolence. This theme was taken up by Locke's pupil, the Earl of Shaftesbury, whose *Characteristics* (1711) moulded much of the moral philosophy of the eighteenth century. Essentially, the new doctrine of benevolence was only what Plutarch had advocated seventeen centuries before; and Pope, for one, was very willing to acknowledge Plutarch's lead. The changed attitude was not one of sentimentality, nor as yet was it coloured by Romantic sensibility. There was no question of elevating animals to human rank. Man still enjoyed master status, but with superiority went responsibility. In the words of Pope: 'The more entirely the inferior creation is submitted to our power, the more answerable we should seem for our mismanagement of it.'* Man was a reasoning animal, but

> . . . short of reason he must fall
> Who thinks all made for one, not one for all.†

The essayists of the Augustan age, spokesmen of a politer world in which not only manners but morals were being refined, expressed doubt whether man had any more right to carve up the brute creation than he had to bait or otherwise abuse it. Their objections had no effect on the vivisectors, other than to induce them to conduct their experiments in private, but they did much to mould the public mind into a more compassionate attitude towards animals. Pope disputed with Dr Stephen Hales his right to cut up dogs: 'How do we know that we have a right to kill creatures that we are so little above as dogs, for our curiosity, or even for some use to us?' Addison, in the *Spectator*, rebuked the 'innumerable retainers of physic' who slashed and stifled animals, for want of other amusement. He describes a 'barbarous' test of animal love: 'A person who was well skilled in dissection opened a bitch, and as she lay in most exquisite tortures offered her one of her young puppies, which she immediately fell a-licking; and for the time seemed insensible to her own pain; on the removal she kept her eye fixed on it and began a wailing sort of cry which seemed to proceed rather from the loss of her young one than the sense of her own torment.'‡

The essayists were intolerant of many popular cruelties, among them cock-throwing and baiting (Pepys and Evelyn had disliked baiting, but chiefly because it was noisy and vulgar). 'It will be said that these are the entertainments of the common people,' wrote Steele. 'It is true; but they are the entertainments of no other common people. Besides, I am afraid there is a tincture of the same savage spirit in the

---

* *Guardian*, May 21, 1713.
† *Essay on Man.*
‡ *Spectator* No. 120 (1711).

diversions of those of higher rank and more refined relish . . .'*
Hunting was not included among savage diversions. Sir Roger
de Coverley in the *Spectator* figures as an obsessive hunter, ready
to kill a brace of geldings and half his hounds to catch one
fox; but he is also shown as displaying unusual chivalry to the
hare. Eustace Budgell, author of the hare episode, quotes
Pascal with approval: 'What, unless it be to drown thought,
can make men throw away so much time and pains on a silly
animal which they may buy cheaper in the market?' Budgell,
however, thinks hunting ideal for mending a bad constitution
and preserving a good one; and suggests that if Pascal had
taken more exercise he would not have died at forty.†

Neither Addison nor Budgell was ready to argue that
exercise could be obtained on horseback without killing anything. Pope was somewhat more critical of hunting. In the
Guardian in 1713 he wrote: 'I dare not attack a diversion
which has such authority and custom to support it; but must
have leave to be of opinion that the agitation and the exercise,
with the example and number of the chasers, not a little
contribute to resist those checks, which compassion would
naturally suggest in behalf of the animals pursued.' Some
usages of hunting were too much for him, among them 'that
savage compliment our huntsmen pass upon ladies of quality'
by handing them a knife to cut the throat of a trembling stag.
This, thought Pope, was a custom barbarous enough to be
derived from the Goths or Scythians.

Echoing Locke, Pope urged that children should be taught
compassion; in practice, they were commonly taught the
opposite. 'One of the first pleasures we allow them is the
licence of inflicting pain upon poor animals; almost as soon as
we are sensible what life is ourselves we make it our sport to
take it from other creatures. I cannot but believe a very good
use might be made of the fancy which children have for birds
and insects.' He deplored the 'unaccountable animosity' against
the cat; 'scarce a boy in the streets but has in this point out-
done Hercules himself who was famous for killing a monster
that had but three lives.'

* *Tatler* No. 134 (1709).
† *Spectator* No. 116 (1711).

Swift, in his own fashion, befriended the horse. Gulliver found himself in a land where horses were civilised and men were brutes; the Houyhnhnms could not believe that in Gulliver's own land persons of quality allowed their ageing horses to be sold into drudgery and then killed for dog-meat. This satire failed to make Englishmen ashamed of themselves; they recommended *Gulliver's Travels* to their children as a comic book.

The Church lay stiff in spiritual paralysis. But 'about a quarter before nine' on May 24, 1738 occurred an event not without significance for the brute creation. That was the hour at which John Wesley, in Aldersgate Street, London, felt his 'heart strangely warmed'. The Methodist preachers who re-animated the heart of English Christianity reanimated its conscience too; they spread a spirit of humanitarianism which did not exclude the claims of the beasts. John Wesley condemned brutal sports. His followers were invited to consider such propositions as this: 'What if it should please the All-Wise and All-Gracious Creator to raise [animals] higher in the scale of beings? What if it should please Him when he makes us equal to angels to make them as we are now?'* Gradually Methodists earned a reputation for showing unaccountable tenderness to birds, beasts and butterflies. Though this brought mockery, the same tendency was later to be detected in the Evangelical Party within the parent Church.

* Quoted by Lewis Gompertz in *Fragments in Defence of Animals* (1852).

4

TOM NERO'S WORLD

WHEN William Hogarth devised his notorious *Four Stages of Cruelty* (1751) he made it clear that he wanted the message to be understood at the lowest levels of humanity. The message was that cruelty to animals begets cruelty to human beings and leads to the scaffold. It was a proposition easier to assert than to prove; drovers who maltreated cattle on the way to Smithfield were often degraded men, but it is unlikely that they were more often guilty of murder than, say, footmen. A critic has complained that these drawings by Hogarth 'savour too much of that inventive school of morality which in defiance of real facts inculcates the pious theory that "Don't-care comes to a bad end".'* But Hogarth's object was to secure the starkest possible impact on simple minds. He said that if his works served to check the progress of cruelty, he would be more proud of being their creator – with all their crudities of subject and technique – than if he had painted Raphael's Cartoons.

The *Four Stages* shows the decline and fall of Tom Nero, a charity boy. In the first picture Tom is engaged in a 'horrible business' which, says Dr John Trusler in a commentary, 'let us hope was never realised in this or any other country.'† He has fired, or thrust, an arrow in a dog's fundament; a deed which inspires a youth of superior rank to offer him a pastry in the hope of redeeming the dog from torture. Other children are tormenting birds and beasts. One throws a cat suspended on bladders from a window; another encourages a dog to

* H. S. Salt: *Humanitarianism* (1891).
† *The Works of William Hogarth.*

51

disembowel a cat; another ties a bone to a dog's tail; a 'group of embryonic Domitians' have suspended two cats from a lamp bracket; a boy holds a cock for another to kill; and two

The Second Stage of Cruelty: by William Hogarth

youths are blinding a bird. In the second picture Tom Nero, now a coachman, hammers the head of his fallen horse; a drover beats a fallen sheep; a donkey sags under two heavy men and a chest; and a bull beset by heroes tosses a boy. Posters on the wall advertise cock-fighting and John Broughton's boxing amphitheatre. In the third picture Tom, hopelessly brutalised, has cut the throat of his pregnant mistress, the servant girl whom he trained as a thief; and in the fourth his cut-down corpse is being dissected by surgeons, with a dog sniffing at one of his vital organs on the floor.

At all levels the prevailing sottishness, as shown in Hogarth's *Gin Lane*, led to brutality, but animals suffered no less grievously from the attentions of the sober. There were scores of other cruelties the artist could have depicted, from the wantonly malicious to the merely heedless. Game-preserving squires set dog-spears in their coverts. Deer poachers followed the pregnant hind and when she dropped her calf they pared its heels to the quick, thus preventing its escape; when it had grown fat enough, they killed it.* Bumpkins tortured hedgehogs, which they suspected of sucking cows, by putting them against a fire to make them unroll and then lacerating them with notched sticks.† Squirrels were kept in treadmill cages outside shops. Horses had their ears cropped with shears to make them look fierce; their tails were docked so that a coachman should not have his face swished, or excruciatingly nicked to make them stand up unnaturally. At the Tower menagerie visitors could save the admission money by bringing a live dog, cat or other pet and pushing it between the bars for lions or tigers to eat.

The cruelties visited on creatures destined for the table, perhaps for Hogarth's table, were sometimes demoniacal. For the epicure's benefit, pigs were scourged to death with knotted ropes to make their flesh more tender. Pope protested in the *Guardian* at the practice, adding: 'I know nothing more shocking or horrid than the prospect of . . . kitchens covered with blood and filled with the cries of creatures expiring in tortures. It gives one an image of a giant's den in a romance bestrewed with the scattered heads and mangled limbs of those who were slain by his cruelty.' This was written in 1713; more than a hundred years later the whipping of pigs was still not extinct. 'Let such of us as may read with horror of cutting steaks from

* Gilbert White: *Natural History of Selborne* (1789).
† *London Magazine*, February, 1762.

the living bullock in Abyssinia remember that pigs whipped
to death have been in frequent use and praised as a delicacy
in a Christian country and in this reign of George III,' says
a writer in 1822, noting gratefully that this 'abomination
scarcely to be named' seemed at last to be dying out.*

Kitchens like those described by Pope were to be found, not
only in the abodes of gluttons, but in the homes of otherwise
impeccable citizens. Servants bled turkeys to a prolonged
death by hanging them upside down with a small incision in
a vein of the mouth; other birds they butchered bloodily in
the hope of ensuring pale, tender flesh. Men and women of
refinement sat down to salmon which had been crimped (that,
is, hacked into collops while alive), eels which had been
skinned alive and chickens which had been sewn up at the
vents to fatten them.

The art of cramming was well understood. In Wiltshire
geese were nailed to the floor through the webs of their feet
after the French fashion, to prevent them taking exercise. The
French added the 'refinement' of putting out the creatures'
eyes, presumably so that they could concentrate their entire
attention on their stomachs. Some breeders mixed gin with
the bean meal, which made the victims sleepy and helped to
fatten them – and their much-prized livers – more quickly.
The goose was not left to gorge of its own accord; food was
manipulated down its throat in dexterous fashion, always far
more than enough but never enough to suffocate. Mechanical
crammers later appeared on the market but skilled manual
stuffing was thought to yield better results.

While some geese were nailed to the floor for life, others
were forced to waddle hundreds of miles to the London
market – from Somerset, from the Anglian fens, from Ireland
and parts of Europe. In 1783 a drove of 9,000 geese passed
through Chelmsford on their way to the capital. While being
reared, fenland geese shared the homes and even bedrooms of
their owners (the nursery rhyme about 'goosey-goosey gander'
wandering in 'my lady's chamber' was not wholly fanciful).
They were plucked five times a years; first at Lady Day, for
quills and feathers; then four more times, for feathers only,

* Henry Crowe: *Zoophilos*.

before Michaelmas. Many denuded geese died in cold spells. The process of stripping, a painful one, was loudly resisted by the young geese but the older ones eventually accepted it with something like resignation.

In the main, those animals privileged to share the household roof were well treated, but an exception was the turnspit tyke, a short-legged mongrel appointed to rotate the roast by operating a treadmill. The dog rapidly tired in the heat but could be stimulated, if necessary, by popping a hot coal into the wheel. John Gay, in one of his *Fables*, tells of a turnspit dog pursued by an angry cookmaid. The cur reflects that it might have been a lap-dog and laments:

> Am I for life by compact bound
> To tread the wheel's eternal round?
> Inglorious task! Of all our race
> No slave is half so mean and base.

However, the ox assures the dog that it could have been worse off:

> You by the duties of your post
> Shall turn the spit when I'm the roast.

Whereupon the dog resumes its task with a cheerful heart. And Gay's youthful readers were left with the idea that the turnspit dog was performing the duty to which Providence had called it; and as dogs continued to do until roasting jacks were introduced.

Another potential field for Hogarth was Eton College, where abuse of animals was almost part of the curriculum. The most notorious pastime, dating from about 1687, was the annual 'hunting' and clubbing to death of a ram provided by the college butcher. The young Duke of Cumberland (the future victor of Culloden) watched this sport in 1730 and was allowed to strike the first blow; he was also in at the death, his club being 'blooded according to custom'. On one occasion an unusually active ram crossed the Thames and ran through the market-place at Windsor with the boys in full cry. 'Such severe exercise in summer being deemed dangerous to the health of the boys, the unfortunate rams were thenceforth hamstrung and, after the regular speech, deliberately beaten to death in Weston's Yard,' says an Eton historian.* By 1747 the College had decided that this exercise was not essential to character-building and the ram hunt ended. For long afterwards, however, the boys baited badgers with dogs on the common and attended bull-baitings and dog-fights staged for them in Bachelor's Acre and elsewhere. Another public school diversion was duck-hunting, an ancient sport which involved tying an owl on a duck's back and sending a dog to swim after the squawking double prey. As the dog approached, the duck dived, causing the owl to claw it fiercely; the game was over when the owl was drowned and the duck captured. In general, any dog, cat or bird venturing near a public school could expect to be maimed or killed. The boys of Harrow bought or stole cats, carried them in bags to a field and worried them to death with dogs.

In 1759 Hogarth published his drawing *The Cockpit*. Its central figure is Lord Albemarle Bertie, a sportsman of the day, who is following the proceedings with a relish scarcely impaired by the fact that he is blind; he can feel the fierce excitement round him and that is enough. The rest of the audience is made up of aristocrats, swells, ruffians and thieves, one of whom is stealing from his blind lordship. Also present is the public executioner. A fastidious Frenchman walks from the scene in disgust at English barbarity, or perhaps at the excessively mixed company.

In that hard-gambling century the popularity of cock-fighting had increased, since it was an excellent medium for wagers. Often matches would be staged at race meetings and after prize fights, along with baitings. Breeding the birds was a considerable industry, especially in Norfolk. An article on gamecocks' diet in the *Gentleman's Magazine* in 1754 said that for four days before fighting a cock's drinking water should be scented with musk and have plenty of balm leaves soaked in it, and that immediately before facing its antagonist the bird should be given twenty or thirty millet seeds soaked in sherry and a few drops of vinegar. The antagonists were fitted with

* H. C. Maxwell Lyte: *A History of Eton College.*

sharp metal spurs designed to draw blood more freely (more cleanly, said the apologists) and were partially clipped so that feathers should not give the adversary an easy grip or confuse the thrust. At every stage of the combat, money changed hands. Odds were lengthened or shortened as the life-blood splashed; the creature that took 'an unconscionable time a-dying' would be the subject of wild jubilation or execration; and a severe pinch by the handler would remind a flagging bird of its duty to teach the human race courage. The most exceptionable forms of combat were the battle royal, in which a number of cocks fought indiscriminately until only one could stand, and the Welsh main, which started with sixteen pairs of cocks pitted against each other, the sixteen winners being opposed to each other in a second round, the next eight winners in a third, the four winners in a fourth and the two winners in a final round. In some areas church bells were rung in honour of the survivor.

The eulogists of cock-fighting continued to produce far-fetched vindications of their sport. William Machrie, a fencing-master who popularised the amusement in Scotland, saw it as a substitute for war: 'village may be encouraged against village, city against city, kingdom against kingdom; nay, the father against the son; until all the wars in Europe, wherein so much Christian blood is spilt, be turned into that of the innocent pastime of cocking.' Machrie thought that cocks could teach men lessons not only in courage, but in fidelity and virility: 'The noble passion of love is so conspicuous in the cock . . . for he most courteously entertains and indus-triously provideth for his females. Aristotle tells us how singular he is in the work of generation, that "sadness seizeth on every creature after coition except the cock".'* Another pamphleteer, 'R.H.', thought that cocking could do much 'to divert the English gentry from effeminate dancing, whoring and drinking, which are three evils grown now almost epidemical.' The sport, he says, is more manly than 'to run whooting after a poor timorous hare' or to ride madly over hedge and ditch after a thieving fox; in short, cocking 'fits a man either for peace or war, and creates both courage and constancy, with

* *An Essay upon the Royal Art and Recreation of Cocking* (1705).

good nature and ingenuity all glued together.' He concludes: 'How anyone can prove cocking to be unlawful or wicked I cannot imagine, seeing God Almighty has nowhere declared against it.'*

The rage for wagering which packed the cockpits also packed the race-courses. If a horse was not whipped and spurred all the way the jockey was suspected of 'pulling' it;

The Cock-pit: by Hogarth

occasionally a horse was spurred so savagely that its entrails were visible as it passed the winning post. Attempts were made to curb furious riding, but improvement was slow. On the open highway still more wagering went on. In that plethoric sporting world where aristocrats and squireens found common ground with butchers and grooms, nobody objected to destroying horses so long as the size of the stake rendered it worth

* *The Royal Pastime of Cock-Fighting* (1709).

while. Young horses, aged horses, newly foaled mares – all were liable to be called upon to perform feats of 'emulation and exertion' at their masters' whim. Sometimes these feats called for considerable human endurance as well, but in general the partner whose feet touched the ground performed the real work. In pre-Revolutionary France bored aristocrats conducted similar amusements, hacking and slashing not only at their mounts but at critical spectators.

Many wagers were described in the *Sporting Magazine*, under 'Extraordinary Equestrian, Pedestrian and Other Performances.' The most-told, but not the most reliable, tale of barbarity had for its 'hero' Tregonwell Frampton, of Moreton, Dorsetshire, the so-called 'Father of the Turf' who died in 1727. According to the version in the *Sporting Magazine* of January 1798, Frampton, keeper of the running horses to William III, Anne and the first two Georges, owned a celebrated stallion, Dragon, which had helped him to win £40,000. When it seemed that there was nothing left to win, Dragon was honourably retired to 'the seraglio'; but then came a £1,000 challenge from the owner of a mare. Dragon raced again and won. The challenger then wagered £2,000 that his mare would beat any gelding in the world next day. Frampton accepted, and to his 'eternal infamy and disgrace' decided to qualify Dragon for the contest. When the stallion was brought forward for the race 'the burst of indignation can be better conceived than described.' Nevertheless, 'Dragon was thrown, castrated, mounted and spurred on to the goal!' He beat the mare, says this account, but fell and died after passing the post. The writer of the above cites Dr John Hawkesworth's account of the supposed incident in the *Adventurer* of March 13, 1753: 'When I had heard this horrid narrative, which indeed I remembered to be true, I turned about in honest confusion and blushed that I was a man.' According to Hawkesworth, the bet was a £10,000 one. Another contributor to the *Sporting Magazine*, in July, 1794, said: 'Had I been an absolute prince and such a deed had been perpetrated in my dominions I would have fulfilled the *lex talionis*.'

In Patrick Chalmers' *History of Hunting* this atrocity is said to have occurred towards the end of Anne's reign. But Alsager

Vian, author of the life of Frampton in the *Dictionary of National Biography*, discredits the tale. Dr Hawkesworth, he says, could have had no personal knowledge of the affair which, if it happened at all, occurred in the time of Charles II. He quotes a letter from Lord Conway in 1682: 'His Majesty's horse Dragon, which carried seven stone, was beaten yesterday by a little horse called Post Boy carrying four stone and the masters of that art conclude this top horse of England is spoiled for ever.' This, says Vian, implies an operation but there is no mention of Dragon falling dead. Another letter, written eighteen months afterwards by the Duke of York to the Prince of Orange, mentions a match between the famous horses Dragon and Why Not. Vian says there is no reason to suppose that Frampton, active though he was on the Turf at that time, was connected with Charles II's racing establishment; and one may assume that the monarch would scarcely have approved an act of this kind. Vian also cites a testimonial from one of Frampton's contemporaries to the effect that 'cruelty was no part of the old gentleman's character.' He concedes, however, that Frampton was 'by no means always scrupulous' and was known as 'the oldest and cunningest jockey' in the land. 'Probably not guilty' is Vian's conclusion. Whatever the facts, the story was given the widest credence during the eighteenth and early nineteenth centuries. Humanitarians made it their favourite horror story and sportsmen told it as a classic example of unsportsmanlike behaviour.

The *Sporting Magazine* reported many wagers contested on the open road. One 'whimsical performance' was the non-stop drive by a London couple, weighing thirty-two stone between them, in a one-horse chaise to the gates of Windsor Castle and back; 'the horse was neither to stop nor the parties get out of the chaise.' Ten hours were allowed for the feat which was performed 'with ease' in less than nine. A peruke-maker of York rode his horse to London in 32 hours, 40 minutes, a distance of 192 miles. At Hyde Park Corner a crowd gathered to watch a pony set out with the Exeter Mail; the wager was that it would be in Exeter, with or without a rider, before the stage coach, no matter how many times the stage changed horses. The journey of 182 miles usually took twenty-eight

hours. Thomas Walker and Captain Mulcaster rode against
each other from London to Ousebridge, in Yorkshire, covering
the first ninety miles in six hours. Walker's hackney tired near
Tadcaster 'and it is supposed it will die.' The winning mare
drank twelve bottles of wine on the forty hours' journey and
afterwards 'was so well as to take exercise on Knavesmire.'
Said the *Gentleman's Magazine* in 1773: 'There is no name
disgraceful enough to characterise this sort of diversion.'

Sometimes the *Sporting Magazine* condemned wagers like
these, sometimes it offered no comment. In December, 1793,
it told how the fifth Duke of Bedford had offered, for £1,000,
to produce a jockey to ride 100 miles in three hours and forty
minutes, ten horses to be allowed. 'Such wagers,' said the
magazine, 'should always be brought before the public that
they may know whether there is any cruelty in them to
animals which by their services and nature are peculiarly
under the protection of man and that they may punish it when
found by contempt and abhorrence of the perpetrators. In
this instance it seems improbable, from the number of horses
. . . as well as from the character of His Grace, that any
cruelty can happen to them.'

At country fairs feats were performed which are as difficult
to credit as the act attributed to Tregonwell Frampton. In
1748 a London newspaper reported that, for £50, a man of
Kildare ate five live fox cubs; 'it is, however, to be observed
that the devourer was a natural fool, having been born deaf,
dumb and without a palate.' It is also to be observed that
those who encouraged him, and watched him, were in their
right minds. In 1777 a shepherd at Beverley, Yorkshire undertook to eat a live cat on fair day. He was given the biggest
black Tom in the neighbourhood, 'not fed for the purpose';
and how he ate it is described in the *Sporting Magazine* of
March, 1794. In less than a quarter of an hour he had
'devoured every part'. He was a raw-boned fellow of about
forty and seemed perfectly satisfied with his reward of two
guineas; for the rest of the afternoon he walked about the
fair and was 'neither sick nor sorry'. On March 1, 1788,
according to the same source, a wager was agreed between
the Duke of Bedford and Lord Barrymore: 'His Lordship

betted His Grace £500 to £400 that he produced a man who should eat a live cat, which was performed at the time appointed by a labouring man of Harpenden, near St Albans.'* This was the fifth Duke of Bedford, already mentioned. He and the rapscallion Barrymore were associates of the Prince of Wales. An encomium published in the *Sporting Magazine* in February, 1795, credited the Duke with 'all the nicer sensibilities of the heart . . . those amiable qualities that so highly honour human nature.'

Other fair-time indulgences included the game of 'mumbling a sparrow', as described in Captain Francis Grose's *Classical Dictionary of the Vulgar Tongue*. A clipped cock sparrow would be put in the crown of a hat and competitors with arms tied would attempt to bite off the bird's head. Very often the sparrow was able to defend itself sharply enough for its adversary to desist with a bleeding face. In goose-pulling, horsemen would compete for the privilege of pulling off the greased head of a live, and lively, goose suspended upside down from a gallows. This went on in Scotland but was not unknown as a fashionable *divertissement* in London. The game of 'cat in barrel', as practised at Kelso and elsewhere, involved suspending a cat in a barrel half-full of soot, riding at the barrel with hammers and clubs until the bottom was knocked out, then chasing and killing the blackened, blinded cat. There were many similar pastimes; but these give some idea of the level from which the less philosophical elements of society had still to be lifted.

It has been said, by Henry Alken and others, that the eighteenth century became noticeably less brutal after the death of the Duke of Cumberland. Certainly the 'Butcher' Duke (of whom we have already had a glimpse at Eton) was a keen patron of the assorted barbarities staged in the amphitheatre of his pugilist crony, John Broughton. He once tried to enliven an Ascot race week by loosing a tiger at a stag, in a forest enclosure. When the two Negro keepers unhooded the tiger it crept forward on its belly like a cat stalking a mouse.

* John Lawrence in his *British Field Sports* (1818) refers to 'the devouring of living cats by obscene and loathsome human beasts.' Henry Crowe in *Zoophilos* expresses the view that a cat-eater is capable of cannibalism and murder.

The stag, a veteran, lowered its antlers and frustrated any attempt to turn its flank. When this 'cautious warfare' became tedious the Duke suggested irritating the tiger; after some objections, on the score of danger, this was done. The tiger then cleared the fencing, spreading considerable panic, and darted into a wood which contained a herd of fallow deer, one of which it pulled down. Its keepers at length ventured to approach and slit the deer's throat. The tiger refused to give up the haunch, so they cut it off and led the beast away prize in mouth.*

To foreign visitors this might or might not have seemed a singular distraction for an English race meeting. For their part, English travellers came home with strange tales of wild beast entertainments in Central Europe. Dr Charles Burney, reading the advertisements in Vienna in 1772, thought the local attractions were 'hardly fit for a civilised and polished nation to allow.' He gave this as a literal translation of a handbill typical of those distributed in the streets every Sunday and festival day:

This day by Imperial Licence in the Great Amphitheatre at five o'clock will begin the following diversions:

1st A wild Hungarian ox in full fire (that is, with fire under his tail and crackers fastened to his ears and horns and to other parts of his body) will be set upon by dogs.

2nd A wild boar will in the same manner be baited by dogs.

3rd A great bear will immediately after be torn by dogs.

4th A wolf will be hunted by dogs of the fleetest kind.

5th A very furious and enraged wild bull from Hungary will be attacked by fierce and hungry dogs.

6th A fresh bear will be attacked by hounds.

7th Will appear a fierce wild boar, just caught, which will now be baited for the first time by dogs defended with iron armour . . .

11th and lastly, a furious and hungry bear, which has had no food for eight days, will attack a young wild bull and eat him alive upon the spot; and if he is unable to complete the business a wolf will be ready to help him.†

The Emperor Leopold put a stop to the Vienna wild beast shows about 1791.

* Rev. W. B. Daniel: *Rural Sports.*
† Dr Charles Burney: *Continental Travels.*

For Englishmen who could turn a blind eye to the bull baits in their own country there was rich scope for indignation in the Spanish bull-ring. Many of the bulls at this time were of indifferent fighting quality and were handed over, if they would not fight, to fierce dogs of prey bred for the purpose. Usually the dogs won, and the bull died disgracefully. By mid-century Pedro Romero, slayer of six thousand bulls, had arrived to make bull-fighting an art, thus eliminating some part of the animal's suffering. Horses were disembowelled freely, to the disgust of none but Englishmen. Padding was not made compulsory until 1928.

5

THE ASS FOR BROTHER

ONE of the major ironies of the eighteenth century was that, as the laws of England grew progressively more brutal, private compassion and benevolence expanded. By 1800 there were two hundred capital offences. Yet, while aristocrats turned over their thieving valets to the hangman, while squires caught their tenants in man-traps and had them shipped to Van Diemen's Land, while tradesmen imprisoned their pettiest debtors, there were voices ready to demand justice for cocks and cockchafers. The lone humanitarian was liable to be suspected of every aberration from old-fashioned Puritanism to new-fangled Rousseauism or Methodism. He was dismissed as one suffering from the scourge of 'sensibility', that often morbid obsession with the sufferings of others; and his seeming unmanly hysteria, his claim to kinship even with creatures that crawled, roused only derision in hardier breasts.

Humanitarianism was not a movement but a state of mind which animated small pockets of the literate world. Its propagandists had no common social, religious or intellectual background; they included essayists who carried on where Pope and Addison left off, philanthropists, Romantic poets, novelists of sensibility, clergymen, utilitarian philosophers, 'miscellaneous writers', the infrequent sportsman, the eccentric and crank, and the pious, conscience-torn citizen who could not believe that God had condemned his innocent creatures to misuse and oblivion.

These propagandists reached the broad road to compassion by devious routes. Some regarded indulgence to animals as a natural extension of that spirit of philanthropy which had provided hospitals and foundling homes. Others regarded 'rights for animals' as a natural extension of the 'rights of man' and the 'rights of women'; unfortunately, the championing of animals by those who appeared to have absorbed libertarian political notions from France was not always calculated to advance the cause. Many believed in Hogarth's proposition that cruelty to animals corrupted those who indulged in it, and were determined to fight it for that reason. Dr John Hawkesworth said, of killing for pleasure, that 'every practice which, if not criminal in itself, yet wears out the sympathising sensibility of a tender mind, must render human nature proportionately less fit for society.'* Yet many who believed themselves to be humane hunted and shot, reserving their censure for the cruelties of drovers and coachmen. A few took the vegetarian standpoint, denying that the possession of canine teeth entitled men to eat meat, and commending the ways of the 'tender-hearted Hindoo'.† But Dr Hawkesworth argued: 'If man had lived upon fruits and herbs the greater part of those animals which died to furnish his table would never have lived; instead of increasing the breed as a pledge of plenty he would have been compelled to destroy them to prevent a famine.' Dr Samuel Johnson said as much to Boswell: 'There is much talk of the misery which we cause to the brute creation; but they are recompensed by existence. If they were not useful to man and therefore protected by him they would not be nearly so numerous.' Boswell wondered whether the beasts which underwent so much for the service and entertainment of man would, if they had the chance, accept existence on those terms.‡ Of Johnson's humanity, there was little question. In the *Idler*, of August 5, 1758, he wrote scathingly of the 'race of wretches' who, in the name of physic, cut up dogs alive and, 'by familiar cruelty', prepared themselves for that profession which they proposed to exercise on the tender and the helpless; 'and if the knowledge of physiology has been somewhat increased, he surely buys

* *Adventurer*, March 13, 1753.
† *See* John Oswald's *The Cry of Nature* (1791), the author of which says: 'Vegetation allures our every sense and plays upon the sensorium with a sort of blandishment which at once flatters and satisfies the soul.'
‡ James Boswell: *Life of Samuel Johnson*.

AN
APOLOGY
FOR THE
BRUTE CREATION,
OR
Abuſe of ANIMALS cenſured;

In a SERMON on PROVERBS xii. 10.

Preached in the Pariſh Church of *Shiplake,*
in *Oxfordſhire, October* 18, 1772,

By JAMES GRANGER, Vicar.

Sævitia in Bruta eſt Tirocinium Crudelitatis in Homines.
Le Clerc in Prov. xii. 10.

*** This Diſcourſe is not only intended for
ſuch as have the Care of Horſes, and other
uſeful Beaſts; but alſo for Children, and
thoſe that are concerned in forming their
Hearts.

Dedicated to *T. B.* Drayman.

LONDON:

Printed for T. DAVIES, in *Ruſſel-ſtreet, Covent-Garden*; and
ſold by W. GOLDSMITH, in *Paternoſter-Row.*
MDCCLXXII.

This sermon 'gave almost universal disgust to two
considerable congregations'

knowledge dear who learns the use of the lacteals at the expense of his humanity.' The Doctor went out himself to buy oysters for Hodge, his cat, suspecting that if he sent a servant on such a humiliating errand the cat would be the sufferer. He rebuked his wife for chastising the cat in front of the maid, who would thus be able to cite her mistress's example for doing the same.

In the main, compassion for animals was spread by the printed word. Though societies were formed for the suppression of vice, the succouring of small debtors and numerous other purposes, upholders of animals' rights were still too sparse to band together. The literate individual who felt strongly enough about ill-treatment of horses or stoning of cocks could vent his indignation by writing to the *Gentleman's Magazine* or the *Sporting Magazine*, or to the daily newspapers, which were always open to correspondence on such topics. Inevitably, there was much preaching to the converted. 'The misfortune is, the writings of an Addison are seldom read by cooks and butchers,' lamented a writer in the *World* of August 19, 1756; and that was the measure of the problem. This writer said he had tried to intercede on behalf of ill-treated dogs, cats and sheep but had usually come off worse; moreover, the animals had suffered more grievously as a result of his intercession. 'I soon found it necessary to consult my own ease as well as security by turning down another street whenever I met with any adventure of this kind . . .' The usual reaction of an offender, when tackled by a 'busybody', was to point out, with oaths if not violence, that the animal was his own, or his master's, and that he was committing no offence in law. Gentlemen hesitated even to reproach their friends for cruelty. 'I once attempted to reason with a fellow (and he was of the rich vulgar) who was cruelly beating an innocent horse, till the blood spun from its nostrils,' wrote John Lawrence, the sportsman-farmer; 'the reply I obtained was, "G— d— my eyes, Jack, you are talking as though the horse was a Christian".'* Occasionally, in the annals of the times, one finds a reference to a vicar who would not allow boys to rob nests, a crank who bought captive birds from boys to set free,

---

* *A Philosophical and Practical Treatise on Horses* (1796).

a sentimentalist who allowed his old horse to live out its last days in comfort, a woman who succoured stray cats. But examples of this kind were rare and a subject for amused comment.

The spirit of humanitarianism was strengthened by the poets of Nature who took over from the poets of Art. Their contribution cannot be measured in precise terms. The cynic is entitled to point out that, despite a score of odes to the skylark, the world continued to guzzle these birds as never before; but the poets' influence on the collective mind of the nation, down the generations, may have been more potent than anyone supposes. One of the first of the new poets was James Thomson, whose *The Seasons* came out between 1726 and 1730. He notes the fowler engaged in his 'falsely cheerful barbarous game of death'; he is unable to admire the valour of men on horseback chasing hares, or even stags. But, in the absence of lions, wolves and boars, there is still one worthy foe – the fox:

> . . . give, ye Britons, then
> Your sportive fury pitiless to pour
> Loose on the nightly robber of the fold . . .

Reynard, whom even Pope describes as 'obscene', is to be pursued remorselessly through hedges, ditches and 'the shaking wilderness', until he dies hard –

> Without complaint, though by an hundred mouths
> Relentless torn . . .

But Thomson does not care for the sight of pesticide practised by women. He deprecates

> Uncomely courage, unbeseeming skill
> To spring the fence, to reign the prancing steed,
> The cap, the whip, the masculine attire . . .

More passionate in their defence of the brute creation were Burns, Cowper, Blake and Wordsworth. Burns' poem *On Seeing A Hunted Hare Which A Fellow Had Just Shot At* begins:

> Inhuman man! curse on thy barbarous art
> And blasted be thy murder-aiming eye;
> May never pity soothe thee with a sigh
> Nor ever pleasure glad thy cruel heart!

A flight of alarmed water fowl fills him with anger at the inhumanity of

> Man, to whom alone is given
> A ray direct from pitying Heaven . . .

and the mouse turned up by the plough finds in the poet a

> . . . poor earth-born companion
> An' fellow mortal.

Cowper, whose Evangelical compassion was nothing if not catholic, wrote poems to, or about, the hare, halibut, cat, spaniel, glow-worm, silkworm, grasshopper, parrot, sparrow, swallow, nightingale, bullfinch, goldfinch and robin. For ten years he kept a tame hare ('one at least is safe') and gave shelter to many other creatures. Field sports revolted him. The huntsman was a boor who took delight in defiling with blood scenes calculated to exalt the mind and compose the passions, a man incapable of feeling for

> The spaniel, dying for some venial fault,
> Under dissection of the knotted scourge.

In *The Task* (1785) Cowper sets out his philosophy in detail:

> I would not enter on my list of friends
> (though graced with polished manners and fine sense
> yet wanting sensibility) the man
> Who needlessly sets foot upon a worm . . .

The poet allows that intruders in man's domain, venomous creatures and 'the creeping vermin, loathsome to the sight' may be dispatched; 'a necessary act incurs no blame.' Man's rights 'are paramount and must extinguish theirs.' But, as a broad principle,

> . . . they are all – the meanest things that are –
> As free to live and to enjoy that life
> As God was free to form them at the first . . .

For all his advanced sensibility Cowper was no vegetarian:

> Feed then, and yield
> Thanks for thy food. Carnivorous thro' sin,
> Feed on the slain, but spare the living brute.

The poet yielded thanks for his food, not only to God, but to various good ladies who sent him presents of game, fish and oysters (the oyster was a 'living brute' but Cowper did not see fit to spare him). Some might feel that his lines to the halibut, a fish never before and perhaps never since apostrophised, lacked the humanitarian fire of some of the others:

> Thy lot thy brethren of the slimy fin
> Would envy could they know that thou wast doom'd
> To feed a bard and be addressed in verse.

Blake's compassion was confused with mysticism, but even the simplest minds could get the message of

> A robin redbreast in a cage
> Puts all heaven in a rage.
> A dove-house filled with doves and pigeons
> Shudders Hell through all its regions.
> A dog starved at his master's gate
> Predicts the ruin of the state.
> A horse misused upon the road
> Calls to Heaven for human blood.
> Each outcry of the hunted hare
> A fibre from the brain does tear.
> A skylark wounded in the wing,
> A cherubim does cease to sing.
> The game cock clipped and armed for fight
> Does the rising sun affright . . .

If Burns was ready to claim kinship with the mouse, Blake claimed it with the fly:

> Am not I
> A fly like thee?
> Or art not thou
> A man like me?
>
> For I dance
> And drink and sing
> Till some blind hand
> Shall brush my wing.

Those to whom such verses were the ravings of sick minds enjoyed a coarse laugh when Coleridge, in the *Morning Chronicle* in 1794, wrote a 'Poem to a Young Ass' containing the words 'I hail thee *Brother*'.

To catalogue all the appeals for humanity to animals in the works of the Romanticists is unnecessary. Coleridge's *Rime of the Ancient Mariner* (1798) puts a simple moral into simple words; but the poem was read for its imagery and notoriously failed to stop men shooting albatrosses. Of Wordsworth's many poems invoking sympathy for animals, the most-quoted was *Hart-Leap Well* (1800), based on the legend of a hunted hart which leaped to its death near Richmond, Yorkshire. It ends with the appeal

> Never to blend our pleasure or our pride
> With sorrow of the meanest thing that feels.

Correspondents of the *Gentleman's Magazine* were wont to comment on the apparent reluctance of the clergy to plead the cause of animals. It was not a complaint which could be upheld against the Rev. Laurence Sterne, that high priest of sensibility, who was such a potent influence on English literature; here was an eye as ready to weep over a dead donkey as a caged bird. In the Anglican Church a vicar who expressed undue solicitude for animals was liable to be suspected of Methodism, or premature senility. On October 18, 1772, the Rev. James Granger, who had no other object than to be 'an honest man and a good parish priest,' rose in his church at Shiplake, Oxfordshire to preach against cruelty to animals, taking as his text *Proverbs* xii, 10: 'A righteous man regardeth the life of his beast: but the tender mercies of the wicked are cruel.' The result seems to have been deeply discouraging. To a published version of his sermon, Granger added a postscript: 'The foregoing discourse gave almost universal disgust to two considerable congregations. The mention of dogs and horses was censured as a prostitution of the dignity of the pulpit, and considered as a proof of the Author's growing insanity. It was written in great haste, of which indeed it carries the marks; but it was dictated by his heart and he published it as it fell from his pen.'

In this despised sermon Granger appealed especially on behalf of the horse: 'How often is he whipped, spurred, battered and starved to death? What a piteous spectacle is his lean, hide-bound, scarred and maimed carcase, thus miserably disfigured by man, before he is dismembered and devoured by dogs. . . . It hath been observed that there is no country upon the face of the earth that is not totally sunk in barbarism where this beast is so ill-treated as it is in our own; hence England is proverbially "the Hell of Horses". Our humanity hath also with great appearance of reason been called in question by foreigners on account of our barbarous customs of baiting and worrying animals and especially that cruel and infamous sport still practised among us on Shrove Tuesday. But this character of cruelty, which is hardly to be equalled among savages, . . . is only applicable to the most stupid, ignorant and uncivilised of our countrymen. Those of higher rank and knowledge are far more humane and benevolent than those that endeavour to fix so ignominious a reproach upon the whole body of the people.'

However, foreigners continued to express surprise that a Christian people should expend such cruelty on so many creatures of the God they worshipped. In 1776 Dr Humphrey Primatt published *A Dissertation on the Duty of Mercy and Sin of Cruelty to Brute Animals*, telling how the Mussulman regarded it as a part of his religion to buy caged birds from Christians and free them. Christians, said Dr Primatt, seemed to take an especial pleasure in reserving for their worst abuses the Bird of Repentance and the Beast of Humility, namely the cock and the ass. They looked on all brutes as 'mere excrescences of Nature . . . infinitely unworthy of the care and cognisance of the Almighty.' Echoing this, Soame Jenyns in his *Disquisitions* (1782) wrote: 'The carman drives his horse and the carpenter his nail by repeated blows; and so long as these produce the desired effect and they both go, they neither reflect nor care whether either of them has any sense of feeling . . . The social and friendly dog is hanged without remorse if, by barking in defence of his master's person, and property, he happens unknowingly to disturb his rest.'

Yet, before the century's end, humanitarians were ready to

risk a multiplication of taunts by demanding legal rights for animals. Jeremy Bentham, the political philosopher, did so in his *Introduction to the Principles of Morals and Legislation* (printed 1780, published 1789). Utilitarianism, of which Bentham was the chief exponent, stood for the greatest happiness of the greatest number; and that greatest number, in Bentham's view, included animals. He complained of the long neglect beasts had suffered at the hands of jurists, who had degraded them into the class of things, and said: 'The day *may* come, when the rest of the animal creation may acquire those rights which never could have been withholden from them but by the hand of tyranny.' Men might yet recognise that 'the number of the legs, the villosity of the skin, or the termination of the *os sacrum*,' were reasons insufficient for abandoning a sensitive being to torture. 'What else is it that should trace the insuperable line? Is it the faculty of reason, or, perhaps, the faculty of discourse? But a full-grown horse or dog is beyond comparison a more rational, as well as a more conversable animal, than an infant of a day, or a week, or even a month, old. But suppose the case were otherwise, what would it avail? The question is not, Can they *reason*? nor, Can they *talk*? but, Can they *Suffer*?' In his *Principles of Penal Law* Bentham asked: 'Why should the law refuse its protection to any sensitive being? The time will come when humanity will extend its mantle over everything which breathes . . .'

From a robust quarter came support for Bentham. John Lawrence, farmer, hunter and humanitarian, wrote in 1796: 'No human government, I believe, has ever recognised the *jus animalium* which surely ought to form a part of the jurisprudence of every system founded on the principles of justice and humanity . . . I therefore propose that the Rights of Beasts be formally acknowledged by the State and that a law be framed upon that principle to guard and protect them from acts of flagrant and wanton cruelty, whether committed by their owners or others.'*

The expression of this opinion, John Lawrence thought, would no doubt gain him 'a snug corner in the holy temple of Methodism.' As a boy at grammar school he had risked

* *Philosophical and Practical Treatise on Horses.*

derision by writing an essay 'In Favour of Kindness to Animals', but he was no sentimentalist. He inveighed against that 'general unfeeling foolery, under the guise of sensibility, which induces an aversion to taking away the lives of deserted or aged and diseased dogs and cats in the same people who feast without reluctance or remorse upon the flesh of the finest, happiest and healthiest animals duly slaughtered for the purpose!' To turn moribund pets into the streets rather than kill them was an act inspired by 'stupidity, indolence and hypocrisy or a mixture of the three' and an offence against true sensibility.*

* 'John Scott' (pseud.) *The Sportsman's Repository* (1820).

6

MRS TRIMMER TAKES A HAND

HOW, in a brutal world, were children to be schooled in compassion towards animals? How was the new benevolence which filled the philosophers to be instilled in those who saw their elders lashing horses and stoning cocks? 'Pity is not natural to men,' said Dr Johnson. 'Children are always cruel. Savages are always cruel. Pity is acquired and improved by the cultivation of reason.'* Pope, as we have seen, thought 'a very good use' might be made of the fancy which children felt for birds and animals, but how was that fancy to be controlled and directed? Animal stories of the type on which children are nurtured today did not exist. Most of the 'Mother Goose' nursery rhymes taught to children were cheerfully heartless fancies in which the cow with the crumpled horn tossed the dog that worried the cat that killed the rat that ate the malt; the world of the little man who had a little gun, of cats down the well, of mice docked by carving knives, of blackbirds baked in pies. It is improbable that these rhymes, of themselves, fostered cruelty to animals, but few of them were calculated to rouse kindness. Even the better-intentioned rhymes probably misfired. 'Has any child ever felt any real sympathy towards Mother Hubbard's dog?' asked Miss Victoria Sackville-West. The average child, she thought, would be more likely to regard the dog's disappointment as an excellent practical joke.†

In the last quarter of the eighteenth century a handful of authors, rising to Pope's challenge, tackled the task of rousing

* James Boswell: *Life of Samuel Johnson.*
† *Nursery Rhymes.*

sympathy for animals in the breasts of older children. Their writings are, to our taste, sententious, mawkish, equivocal and often ridiculous, but they became 'required reading' in innumerable homes. Many of them were reprinted over and over again, sometimes down to our own times; and their influence on Victorian middle-class attitudes may well have been considerable. Among notable writers in this class were Dr Thomas Percival, Mrs Ann Letitia Barbauld, Mrs Sarah Trimmer, Thomas Day and Mary Wollstonecraft.

Dr Thomas Percival, the author of a standard book on medical ethics, published *A Father's Instructions* in 1775. It is something of a ragbag of fable and observation. One story tells how Euphronius, a disciple of Dr Priestley, is conducting experiments with mephitic water, in other words, water impregnated with 'fixed air'. Alexis enters with several small fishes which he is anxious to put in the mephitic water to see what happens. At first Euphronius demurs, then does as requested, and the fish at once die. Surprise and joy sparkle in the eyes of Alexis, but he is quickly silenced: 'Beware, my son! of observing spectacles of pain and misery with delight. Cruelty by insensible degrees will steal into your heart . . . The Philosopher who has in contemplation the establishment of some important Truth or the discovery of what will tend towards the advancement of real science and to the good and happiness of mankind may perhaps be justified if he sacrifices to his pursuit the life or enjoyment of an inferior animal. But the emotions of humanity should never be stifled in his breast; his trials should be made with tenderness, repeated with reluctance and carried no further than the object in view inevitably requires.' Euphronius adds that he killed the fishes only to save them from a worse fate at Alexis's hands.

Later Euphronius, accompanied by two children, visits Duke's Wharf, Manchester, where they see an ass being beaten by its owner. Close by a crowd is cheering. 'Each individual present was deciding by the throw of a halfpenny whether the mule or ass employed in his cart should have a feed of corn at noon or whether the value of the provender should be applied to the purchase of spirituous liquors for himself; and whenever chance proved favourable to injustice and debauchery

the whole crowd united in the cry of exultation.' Euphronius
curbs his inclination to remonstrate with the crowd, knowing
that he will be covered with abuse and worse, but he draws
the necessary moral for his children.

Mrs Barbauld wrote fables, hymns and verses for children,
her most-quoted lines being 'The Mouse's Petition'. These
were prompted by a visit to Dr Priestley's house, where she
saw a caged mouse awaiting an experiment with brewery gases.
Next morning Mrs Barbauld attached to the cage a petition
which contained these verses:

> The cheerful light, the vital air
>   Are blessings widely given:
> Let Nature's commoners enjoy
>   The common gifts of Heaven.
>
> The well-taught philosophic mind
>   To all compassion gives;
> Casts round the world an equal eye
>   And feels for all that lives.

Dr Priestley's well-taught philosophic mind caught the
message and the captive was released; though no doubt
another victim was quickly found.

Mrs Sarah Trimmer, of Ipswich, mother of six sons and six
daughters, was urged by her friends to write books in the
Barbauld vein. Of particular interest is her *Fabulous Histories
Designed for the Instruction of Children Respecting Their Treatment
of Animals* (1786). Eager though she was to foster compassion
towards the animal creation, Mrs Trimmer was also much
concerned that children should not fall into 'the contrary fault
of *immoderate tenderness.*' Her *Fabulous Histories* introduces Miss
Harriet and Master Frederick, the children of Mrs Benson.
When Master Frederick demands food for the birds his mother
reproaches him: 'Would you deprive a poor little hungry boy
of his breakfast to give it to the birds?' Master Frederick, very
properly, replies: 'No, I would sooner give my own breakfast
to a poor boy than he should go without.' He then has the
idea of asking the servants to keep scraps for the birds. 'A very
good scheme,' says his mother, 'and I advise you, my dear, to
put it into execution; for I make no doubt it will answer your

purpose if you can prevail on the servants to indulge you. I cannot bear to see the least fragment of food wasted which may conduce to the support of life in any creature.' One morning Master Frederick, having slept late, rushes out anxiously to feed the birds, but is rebuked sharply for doing so before he has paid his respects to his mother; another salutary reminder that people come before birds.

Harriet and Frederick are much shocked by the arrival, as a guest, of Master Jenkins, who is acquainted with 'the whole art of tormenting animals' and proposes to tie a dog and cat together with string. He boasts how he has made cats fly – 'we tie bladders to each side of their necks and then fling them from the top of the house' (as shown in Hogarth's *Four Stages of Cruelty*). Mrs Benson complains to Master Jenkins' father of the boy's bad influence, but Mr Jenkins applauds him as 'a lad of life and spirit, fit to go through the world.' Consoling her children, Mrs Benson warns them not to be too distressed at the cruelties which Master Jenkins metes out:

'It is wrong to grieve for the death of animals as we do for the loss of our own friends, because they certainly are not of so much consequence to our happiness; and we are taught to think their sufferings end with their lives as they are not religious beings; and therefore the killing them, even in the cruellest manner, is not like murdering a human creature, who is perhaps unprepared to give an account of himself at the tribunal of heaven.'

At this point a lady who happens to be present interposes: 'I have been for a long time accustomed to consider animals as mere machines, actuated by the unerring hand of Providence, to do those things which are necessary for the preservation of themselves and their offspring; but the sight of the Learned Pig, which has lately been shown in London, has deranged these ideas and I know not what to think.' A gentleman who also happens to be present says it is evident that animals do not possess 'reasonable souls like the human race,' but thinks they may possess some portion of intellect. As for the Learned Pig, 'mere instinct would never lead the creature to distinguish one letter from another.'*

* The creature picked out the letters of a word with his snout and told the time by indicating figures.

Mrs Benson feels the conversation is taking a dangerous trend. Pigs, however learned, are animals. 'As Providence has placed them so much beneath us in the scale of being, I should think it equally wrong to elevate them from their proper rank in life and suffer them to occupy that share of attention and love which is due to our own species only.' She thinks the Learned Pig acts on a secret sign from his keeper and that great cruelty must have been used to train him.

The children now visit a Mrs Addis, who has fallen into the fault of pampering her cats, dogs and monkey, while neglecting her child. Mrs Benson explains: 'Mrs Addis, you see, has absolutely transferred the affection she ought to feel for her child to creatures who would really be much happier without it . . . the lap-dog is, I am sure, a miserable object full of diseases the consequence of luxurious living.' The children are faced with a further example of misplaced kindness when they overfeed a bird; 'the little creature gave his eyes a ghastly roll and fell on one side, suffocated with abundance.'

On a visit to a farm Mrs Benson says: 'I often regret that so many lives should be sacrificed to preserve ours; but we must eat animals or they would at length eat us, at least all that would otherwise support us.' She also points out that when we take wool and milk we take no more than is our due and only what the animals can very well spare; this enables them 'to return their obligation to us.' Some creatures have nothing to give us but their own bodies. 'These have been expressly destined by the *Supreme Governor* as food for mankind and he has appointed an extraordinary increase of them for this very purpose; such an increase as would be very injurious to us if all would be suffered to live. These we have an undoubted right to kill; but we should make their short lives as comfortable as possible.' Other creatures are of no use to mankind except in so far as they serve 'to furnish our minds with contemplations on the wisdom, power and goodness of God and to exhilarate our spirits by their cheerfulness.' Savage and venomous beasts are to be killed only if they leave 'the secret abodes allotted them.' As Mrs Benson never tires of saying: 'We should prefer the happiness of mankind to that of any animal whatever.'

Wherever they go, Harriet and Frederick are confronted with a useful moral. On one walk they hear a Mock-bird. A footnote explains: 'The Mock-bird is properly a native of America but is introduced here for the sake of the moral.' After being warned never to boil lobsters up from cold but to put them straight into boiling water,* and to stun eels before skinning them, the children retire to bed 'in peace after a day spent with so much pleasure and improvement.'

Interspersed with the children's adventures is the story of a family of robins whose parents try hard to instil in them the precepts of self-sacrifice, unselfishness and obedience. A young robin who heedlessly wanders in the path of a gun exclaims, as it dies: 'Oh, my dear father! why did I not listen to your admonitions which I now find, too late, were the dictates of tenderness!' The story of the robins was issued separately and republished many times during the nineteenth century.

One difficulty confronting Mrs Trimmer was what to say about blood sports. In *An Easy Introduction to the Knowledge of Nature* the mother of Charlotte and Henry describes how hounds pull down a hunted stag 'and tear him till he dies.' She comments: 'I suppose there is pleasure in hunting, but I think the poor creature should be allowed to return to his park again in order to make him amends for the terror he must have suffered and for the diversion he has afforded to his pursuers.' The children's father is addicted to shooting and coursing, which makes criticism difficult; but when coursing comes up for discussion the mother says: 'I don't know how it is with the gentlemen, Henry, but I should feel so much for the poor little frightened creature as would destroy all enjoyment of the sport.'

One of the most enduring of these didactic works was *The History of Sandford and Merton*, by Thomas Day, of whom it was said that his many eccentricities were but symptoms of his nobility of character. Even as a boy at Charterhouse, he went out of his way to be compassionate to animals. When Sir William Jones said to him: 'Day, kill that spider,' the boy replied: 'No, I don't know that I have a right. Suppose that

* This is the method advocated by animal welfare bodies today.

a superior being said to a companion, "Kill that lawyer", how should you like it? And a lawyer is more noxious to most people than a spider.'*

Sandford and Merton appeared in three volumes between 1783 and 1789. Harry Sandford, son of a plain honest farmer, does not steal eggs or torment animals, and is careful to step out of the way of worms, a course of behaviour which makes him 'a great favourite with everybody.' Less fastidious is Tommy Merton, a rich man's son, but Harry's influence redeems him. Harry's first big test comes when he sees a hunted hare limping past and resolves not to tell the huntsmen which way it went. The leading rider is the squire who lashes Harry with his whip when the information is not forthcoming. 'Now! you little rascal, do you choose to tell me now?' demands the horseman, and Harry says: 'If I would not tell you before I won't now, though you should kill me.' Another rider comes up and remonstrates with the aggressor: 'It is an happy day for you, squire, that his age is not equal to his spirit. But you are always passionate . . .' Just then the hounds recover the scent and the hunt gallops off, leaving Harry to boast that his ordeal was nothing compared to what the young Spartans had to suffer. In due course Harry saves the life of the squire, who is being dragged by his horse, and is offered a guinea. 'Harry with a look of more contempt than he had ever been seen to assume before rejected the present.'

The boys then hear of an impending bull-baiting. Harry tries to persuade his companions that they should not go to watch this cruel and dangerous spectacle, 'particularly Master Merton, whose mother loves him so much and is so careful about him.' This advice is 'not received with approbation.' When the bull breaks loose, rushing 'like lightning over the plain,' it is Harry who, with a pitchfork, saves Tommy from being gored; his own life is then saved by a young Negro whom he earlier rescued from bullying.

It is not too much to say that the author of *Sandford and Merton* was killed by kindness. In 1789 he set off on an unbroken colt to visit his wife and mother at Bear Hill, convinced that any animal could be controlled by gentle means. Near War-

* *Dictionary of National Biography.*

grove the colt shied and threw him on his head, with fatal results.

Mary Wollstonecraft's *Original Stories* (1788) were modelled on those of Mrs Trimmer. Mary and Caroline, children of wealthy parents who have allowed servants to fill them with every kind of vulgar prejudice, are taken in hand by Mrs Mason. Seeing her walk in wet grass rather than tread on insects, they ask why she does not kill them, and receive the reply: 'You are often troublesome – I am stronger than you – yet I do not kill you.' When a boy shoots a lark and badly injures it, Mrs Mason bravely puts her foot on its head, 'turning her own another way.' Eagerly the children enquire how they should behave to prove that they are superior to animals, and Mrs Mason says: 'Be tender-hearted . . . it is only to animals that children *can* do good. Men are their superiors.'

7

HUNTING: BECKFORD'S RULES

DEER-HUNTING, a traditionally royal sport, declined steadily throughout the eighteenth century. The growth of cultivation and the enclosing of fields cut down the areas in which wild deer roamed and the fashionable world found it easier to chase half-tame animals, kept in paddocks for that purpose. Gilbert White, of Selborne, tells how the Duke of Cumberland sent a huntsman and six scarlet-jacketed yeomen-prickers to capture all the red stags in Wolmer Forest and cart them off to Windsor. Some of them, when hunted, 'showed extraordinary diversion.'*

Fox-hunters, now in the ascendant, scoffed at the pursuit of paddock deer and called it 'calf-hunting'. The less affluent squires could not, in any event, afford to take part in a sport which called for much pomp and parade. There was an additional objection: hunting the carted stag rarely yielded blood, since the object was merely to chase the animal, not to kill it (though when the animal *was* killed the scene was often sanguinary to a degree).

Lyrical descriptions of outings with the Royal Buck Hounds used to appear in the *Sporting Magazine* during George III's time. The turn-out of the deer was watched by carriage-loads of ladies amid 'a blaze of sporting brilliancy beyond the utmost mental fertility to describe.' Ten minutes were allowed for the deer to get away, this period being made magical by 'the sonorous strains of the horns, the musical, melodious echo of the hounds, the mutual gratulations of so distinguished an assembly, and the condescending kindness and affability of the

* *Natural History of Selborne.*

Sovereign to the loyal subjects who loved to surround him.'
When the quarry was at bay, and the King's arrival was
imminent, the scene was 'so truly rich and ecstatic that the
tear of excessive joy and grateful sensibility' shone in almost
every eye. 'The utmost fortitude' would be displayed in
an effort to save the deer, which 'so largely and laboriously
contributed to the general happiness of the day.' On one
outing the yeomen-prickers were cheered as they struggled
hand-to-throat with hounds in water to save the stag, their
efforts being made more dangerous because the quarry could
not comprehend that the men in scarlet, far from wishing it
ill, merely sought to reserve it 'for future diversion'. Rescue
sometimes arrived too late; a stag would be 'pulled down and
broken up' in sight of 'those who anxiously wished but had
not the power to preserve his life.' In 1793 a stag swam the
Thames and was taken near Marlow 'after an almost incredible
run of *four hours and a half*; and although he sustained no
bodily wound from the hounds, yet he was so exhausted by
the persevering rapidity of pursuit that he dropped and expired
in a few minutes after he was taken.' Occasionally, the King
would condemn an injured stag to be killed. The longer chases
took sharp toll of horses; after a four-hours run 'one horse
dropped dead, another died before he could reach a stable
and seven more within the week.'

Not all the references in the press to deer-hunting were
calculated to bring the tear of excessive joy to the eye. On
December 16, 1813, a correspondent of the *Morning Chronicle*
described how a deer with a dislocated leg was uncarted and
chased for nearly two hours in order to blood a pack of hounds
newly presented to the Prince Regent. In the *Sporting Magazine*
'Humanitas' (probably John Lawrence) demanded: 'Who give
the orders, or, if ashamed of such orders, who give the hints,
or does the act of infamy originate with the under-strappers?
Where is the unnatural, base, grovelling, grinning, pimping
scoundrel who can put his unfeeling claws to the act of grinding
dislocation? Of what kind or degree are those unclean beasts
in human shape or those demons who combine to hold down
the agonised victim, the deer that weeps?' Another correspondent expressed surprise that 'Humanitas' had never heard

Death of the fox

From the 'Sporting Magazine', May 1813

of 'the old, barbarous and all too common practice of pur-
posely dislocating the joints of a deer intended to be hunted
in order that the hounds may have a better chance with them
in point of blood?' If anyone complained of the practice,
those responsible would 'stare with a stupid face of wonder.'
The huntsman concerned in this episode denied vigorously
that he had lamed the deer; but no one could claim that the
practice was an unheard-of one. Giles Jacob's *The Compleat
Sportsman* (1718) says: 'You may likewise enter your hounds
by taking a hart in nets, and after you have cut off one of his
feet, let him go. A quarter of an hour afterwards assemble
your young hounds . . .' Having reached the deer, the young
hounds were not to be allowed to break it, but were to be
encouraged to leap at its cut throat.

The only form of deer-hunting acceptable to real sportsmen,
in the view of authorities like Henry Alken and the Rev.
W. B. Daniel, was the pursuit of an outlying deer, unhar-
boured. This was warranted to provide plenty of exercise and
labour, but also much frustration. Daniel wrote: 'Were the
King once to see a fox well found and killed handsomely he
would in all probability give a decided preference in favour of
fox-hounds.' The stag gave off too burning a scent and was
often sulky; its pursuit could offer 'none of the enthusiasm of
hunting which the sportsman feels when he is following an
animal upon whose own exertions of speed and craftiness his
life is staked.'

John Lawrence, though detesting many so-called sports of
the day, was ready to defend hunting and in particular the
new strenuous form of fox-hunting popularised by Hugo
Meynell and others. Says Lawrence: 'In Reynard we pursue
a beast of prey which lives by rapine and blood – and *blood
demands blood*. We hunt a hunter and put in practice all the
wiles and stratagems of the chase against the most wily of
animals; we pursue an animal the courage of which is equal
to his character for rapine and spoil and which dies bravely
without a groan and selling his life as dearly as he can.' The
fox indulged in no infant screams like the hare and shed no
tears like the deer. A further justification for fox-hunting was
that it served to attach the landed aristocracy to their land;

it was the next best thing to that ancient tie, 'the first cut at every matrimonial dish of their tenantry.'*

The practices and ethics of the chase were first codified, in detail, by Peter Beckford, in his *Thoughts on Hunting*, which began to appear in 1779 and was reprinted very many times (several passages were lightly paraphrased by the Rev. W. B. Daniel in *Rural Sports*). Of Beckford, a man of culture who had talked to Voltaire and Rousseau, a reviewer wrote: 'Never had fox or hare the honour of being chased to death by so accomplished a hunter . . . never was a huntsman's table graced by such urbanity and wit. He would bag a fox in Greek, find a hare in Latin, inspect his kennels in Italian and direct the economy of his stables in exquisite French.'† By his erudition, Beckford helped to rescue fox-hunting from the sneers of Lord Chesterfield, who condemned those 'rustic, illiberal sports of guns, dogs and horses, which characterise our English bumpkin country gentlemen.' Says Beckford: 'The intemperance, clownishness and ignorance of the old fox-hunters are quite worn out.' Hunting as a recreation is so old-established that it cannot be supposed either 'to dread criticism or to need support'; and its recommendation is that it promotes health, content, early rising and sociability. Much of Beckford can be read with pleasure, but his advice on the training and disciplining of hounds comes as a shock. He mentions a clergyman of his acquaintance who trains his young hounds at a cat 'which he drags along the ground for a mile or two,' later turning out a badger for them after taking the precaution of breaking its teeth. Beckford's own huntsman follows similar practices. John Lawrence found time to condemn the sacrifice of a domestic cat to hounds as 'a blasted and unmanly act of barbarity,' adding, 'I know from long observation the ill effect this cat-hunting has upon the morals of stable boys and servants in general.'‡

To flog hounds in kennel, says Beckford, is 'unreasonably unjust and cruel,' though a common practice; 'carried to excess, as we sometimes see, it is a disgrace to humanity.'

---

* 'W. H. Scott' (pseud.): *British Field Sports* (1818).
† *Dictionary of National Biography.*
‡ *A Philosophical and Practical Treatise on Horses.*

Hounds deserving punishment for running off at hares should be flogged only at the time of their offence, and only under supervision, since many huntsmen derive undue pleasure from using the whip. If hounds are obstinately riotous it is better to put a live hare among them, flogging those which approach it; 'they will then have some notion at least for what they are beaten, but let me entreat you, before this charivari begins, to draft off your steady hounds.' If any dog is exceptionally interested in the hare, says Beckford, 'you may tie a dead one round his neck, flogging him and rating him at the same time. This possibly may make him ashamed of it. I never bought a lot of hounds in my life that were not obliged to undergo this discipline.'

A hound guilty of pursuing sheep was sometimes coupled to a ram for punishment, but Beckford disapproved of the practice; 'that is breaking them with a vengeance – you had better hang them.' A noble acquaintance of his tackled the problem by putting his largest ram in the kennel, then invited a neighbour to watch the sport. 'Egad, he trims them!' exclaimed the owner, 'there is not a dog dare look him in the face!' Asked if he was not afraid for his dogs, he replied, 'No, damn them, they deserve it, and let them suffer.' Later an unwonted quiet fell over the kennels. It was found that the ram had been devoured and the hounds had retired full-bellied to rest.

Beckford says he makes no claim to be called a 'fair sportsman' if that means sparing the fox, the whole art of fox-hunting being to keep the hounds well in blood. 'Sport is but a secondary consideration with a true fox-hunter . . . I confess I esteem blood so necessary to a pack of fox-hounds that . . . I always return home better pleased with an indifferent chase with death at the end of it, than with the best chase possible, if it ends with the loss of the fox. Good chases, generally speaking, are long chases; and if not attended with success never fail to do more harm than good.' When hounds are tired after a hard day without blood Beckford recommends turning out a bag fox (a captured fox) to 'give them as it were new strength and vigour'; but in the ordinary way he is against hunting bag foxes because, from the conditions of their incarceration, they 'must needs stink extravagantly' and the hounds consequently have no problem. Moreover, the animal is weakened, hungry and dispirited, not knowing where to turn in strange territory, all of which militates against good sport. He mentions one chase in which a bag fox was made to stink even more extravagantly by drenching it with a whole bottle of aniseed. Despite the odds against them, bag foxes – according to reports in the *Sporting Magazine* – were sometimes recaptured and 'reserved for another day's sport.'

Beckford admits having heard a new doctrine that blood is not necessary to hunting, but 'one would almost be inclined to think blood as necessary to the men as to the hounds, since the best chase is flat unless you kill the fox.' Yet foxes should not be killed wantonly, as this affords no pleasure and spoils future sport. Nor does Beckford favour hunting a bitch fox big with young: 'A gentleman of my acquaintance, who killed most of his foxes at this season, was humorously called *midwife of the foxes*'.

The poet Cowper by accident saw the end of a fox. In a letter to Lady Hesketh in 1788 he describes how the huntsman carried 'dead Reynard' into a grove with all his hounds round him:

'I determined to stay and notice all that passed with the most minute attention. The huntsman having by the aid of a pitchfork lodged Reynard on the arm of an elm, at the height of almost nine feet from the ground, there left him for a considerable time. The gentlemen sat on their horses contemplating the fox, for which they had toiled so hard; and the hounds assembled at the foot of the tree, with faces not less expressive of rational delight, contemplated the same object. The huntsman remounted; he cut off a foot and threw it to the hounds – one of them swallowed it whole like a bolus. He then once more alighted and drawing down the fox by the hinder legs desired the people who were by this time rather numerous to open a lane for him to the right and left: he was instantly obeyed, when throwing the fox to the distance of some yards, and screaming like a fiend, "Tear him to pieces!" at least ten times repeatedly, he consigned him over absolutely to the pack which in a few minutes devoured him completely. Thus, my dear, as Virgil says, what none of the gods could have ventured to promise me, Time itself pursuing its accustomed course has, of

Stag at bay

From the 'Sporting Magazine', October 1793

its own accord, presented me with. I have been in at the Death of a Fox and you know as much of the matter as I, who am as well informed.'

John Lawrence had much to say about this description. To him Cowper was 'that melancholy proof of the triumph of debasing fanaticism over reason, genius and common-sense – a man who, had his mind possessed fortitude sufficient to excite a rational contempt for his *blind guides*, equal to that which he seemed to express for fox-hunting, might have joined hunting and other amusements with his poetical pursuits and passed a life of health and happiness instead of sinking into a state of pitiable wretchedness from merely imaginary and panic terrors and ridiculous anticipations.' The poet had painted a true picture of a most curious scene; but 'as at present managed by persons of a refined and right way of thinking,' the scene was a perfectly harmless one. Nevertheless, it could not fail to inspire serious reflections:

'The wild savage air and attitude, his fierce and goggle eyes, and the infernal screams which issue from the brazen throat and leather lungs of a fellow of right stomach, exhibit the truest possible representation of the ferocious and savage nature of the ancient chase and its thirst for vengeance and blood, the same passion which inspires the breasts of beasts of prey. This indiscriminate mixture of sport and cruelty and vengeance has in former times excited the most extravagant and profligate acts. By this unclean spirit was actuated the Lord Raymond Venous, who burned alive thirty of his finest horses by way of a frolic! and no doubt danced around the flaming pile with the most frantic gestures and cries. The same fury inspires our London Sunday and market-day bullock-hunters and the bull-hankers of certain provincial towns even in the year of our Lord 1817! This is said not with the most distant idea of disparaging or condemning the fair fox-hunt or even witnessing the tearing to pieces, amid frantic screams, an animal which Nature has taught to exist by similar acts. This is not dragging a fox to death by a lengthened and barbarous process of torture but dispatching him in the most expeditious manner the instant he is taken.

'The company should be silent whilst the hounds are killing the fox. It is not in every hunt that the custom prevails of treeing him or that they celebrate the orgies of screaming over his mangled carcase. It is, however, not only a stimulating ceremony but has its use in giving time for all the hounds to come in and enjoy their share and also to recover their wind. They must not be kept baying the suspended fox too long for fear of cooling that appetite and voracity with which it is expedient they should devour him.'*

Lawrence obviously had divided views on such obsequies; one half of him was revolted by the welling up of 'unclean', primitive passions, the other fascinated. Henry Alken, a fellow sportsman, had a more amused approach. After writing of the huntsman's 'hellish screams . . . issuing as it were from the mouth and countenance of one of Milton's devils,' he says: 'A tolerably infernal phiz, with lungs and voice calculated for the utterance of a real fiend-like scream are, indeed, no ordinary recommendation of a huntsman. These rites, however are not celebrated on every common occasion and our huntsmen are often too jolly and comely-visaged to possess the needful high qualifications.'†

If hunting dogs had a hard life, so did shooting dogs. Richard Badham Thornhill, compiler of the *Shooting Directory* (1804), had no qualms about coupling a sheep-worrying dog to a ram, flogging it and letting the angry ram complete the punishment. These are his instructions for teaching a dog not to run after fowls: 'Take a cleft stick, at one end of it tie a live fowl, and put the dog's tail in the cleft at the other; be sure to tie his tail in it very tight so as to cause him some pain and as you let him go give him three or four smacks of the whip that he will not fail to run off.' The dog will suppose the pain to be caused by the fowl; 'when he gets tired – beat him well about the head with the fowl once or twice; this you may be certain will be sufficient to prevent his ever touching a fowl again.' The Rev. W. B. Daniel's method of breaking a dog from running after poultry was to tie a live fowl to his tail and make him run the gauntlet of the whip; which prompted John Lawrence to protest 'What crime has the poor fowl committed?'

Thornhill's advice for preventing a bitch from copulating involves the application of a red-hot iron. He ends his book with an expression of hope that 'whatever we do or whatever

---

* *British Field Sports.*
† *British Sports* (1821).

amusements we are in pursuit of, they may tend to the glory of God . . . and more especially remind us of that great and solemn account we must one day give for all our actions.'

Hare-hunting was a sport which had little appeal for Beckford. He thought a man might just as well ride along the turnpike to the three-mile stone and back as turn out with harriers. But he was careful to add that he thought any kind of hunting a manly and wholesome exercise. William Cobbett missed few opportunities to pursue the hare. On one of his rural rides he joined a hunt and sat on his horse 'from daylight in the morning to dusk (about nine hours) without once setting foot on the ground'; which suggests that 'poor puss' was not the only sufferer of that November day.

Hares roused pity by the near-human cries they emitted in extremities (the French have the word *couinement* to describe this sound). Timorous they might be, but many were far from weaklings. Daniel says that in 1800 a brace of greyhounds in Lincolnshire, within a space of twelve minutes, chased a hare from its seat for a distance of four miles measured in a straight line, but actually very much longer; the creature ran itself dead before the hounds touched it. He also tells of a hare pursued, near Bottisham, Cambridgeshire, by a field of twenty-two horses, of which only one could still gallop at the end. Again the hare died before the hounds could reach it; and they had to be bled to enable them to recover.

The sport of coursing was beginning to run into criticism. Defending it, in the *Sporting Magazine*, a writer said: 'Cavillers aver that the courser's pleasure is short; but to counter-balance this apparent rapid joy I can aver it is neither so wearisome nor so replete with danger as hunting.' Nor was it so expensive. Beckford said that in fair coursing only one hare in three was killed: 'we should give scope to all her (the hare's) little tricks, nor kill her foully and over-matched.' This meant, said a critical reviewer, that 'the result of a true sportsmanlike compassion is not to put a speedy end to the suffering of this little timorous animal; but to prolong its terror until it has tried all the efforts agonised Nature can dictate and until the utmost exertions of its feeble strength are painfully exhausted. Here we not only find that even a sportsman confesses himself subject to compassion but we are instructed how to indulge it in the most curious manner ever yet discovered.'* This, of course, is a criticism which applies to most field sports. According to the code of sportsmanship, the quarry – whether hare, fox, stag or salmon – must be given a chance to fight for its life, even if that means lengthening the creature's apprehensions and sufferings while protracting the enjoyment or flattering the prowess of the sportsman.

Coursing lent itself to the operations of gamblers, who were unfastidious about observing such ethics as the pastime possessed. On March 29, 1803, the *Morning Herald* had a sardonic account of a meeting on the Surrey Downs. 'Nothing in the long-dog annals will be found to equal the adventures of *Major* and *My Lady*, who at this genial season so gallantly ran three brace of doe hares turned out of boxes for the amusement of a numerous field of high-mettled *Cockney* sportsmen. *Major*, to prove the *ne plus ultra* of his Northern blood, ran the prolific ladies of the skut so hard that they were obliged to cast their progeny in preservation of their own lives; while *My Lady*, more than equally successful, picked up and killed all the young that *Major* thus heroically left behind him! The Coursing Colonel, who brought his greyhounds in winding sheets decorated with armorial bearings, offered to bet Mr Durrant 10,000 guineas to 1,000 that he would run the next Surrey dog stone dead that dared to enter the lists with his Major, to run a doe hare on the same Downs next Midsummer day.'

The Coursing Colonel who, according to another report, kept the company in roars of laughter was Colonel Thomas Thornton, a celebrated sportsman with estates in Yorkshire, Wiltshire and Bedfordshire. After the Battle of Waterloo he hired the Château of Chambord and called himself Prince de Chambord.

There was another way of taking hares and that was by employing an Iceland hawk. 'It is a refined cruelty,' said the Rev. W. B. Daniel, 'for the hare feels the hawk's superiority so much that she would not stir were she not impelled, by a slow greyhound, to keep upon her legs; the poor animal is thus placed betwixt two enemies and is a long time tortured before the hawk gives the *coup de grâce*.'

* *Monthly Review*, September, 1781.

8

SHOOTING FLYING

DURING the eighteenth century the art of 'shooting flying' ousted the inferior art of 'shooting sitting'. In the *Spectator* a yeoman friend of Sir Roger de Coverley is said to knock down his dinner with his gun twice or thrice a week; 'he is a very sensible man; shoots flying; and has been several times foreman of the petty jury.'* Pope's *Windsor Forest* (1712–13) contains the following:

> See! from the brake the whirring pheasant springs,
> And mounts exultant on triumphant wings:
> Short is his joy; he feels the fiery wound,
> Flutters in blood, and panting beats the ground . . .

Nor did sportsmen disdain to point their blunderbusses at larks:

> Oft, as the mounting larks their note prepare,
> They fall, and leave their little lives in air.

Giles Jacob in *The Compleat Sportsman* (1718) does not rule out the easier method of execution. 'When you shoot at a flock of birds on the ground,' he writes, 'level your piece at the centre or middle of the flock and let the particular bird you aim at be hid with the muzzle of your piece.' If the ambitious sportsman wishes to try for birds on the wing the secret is to 'fire at a mark about six yards before and then the shot will take them as they are passing.' The long-barrelled, muzzle-loading guns of the day were slow, cumbrous, inaccurate, deafening and dangerous to the user; but bird life

* No. 122 (1711).

96

was almost unbelievably profuse and even the most inept marksman aiming at a mass of birds, whether feeding or flying, could scarcely fail to confer death and mutilation. Often sportsmen shot in pairs, one at the sitting birds, the other at the survivors as they flew away.

According to the author of *Pteryplegia: or the Art of Shooting Flying* (1727) the English were indifferent marksmen: 'I have often wondered why the French, of all mankind, should alone be so expert at the gun, I had almost said infallible. It's as rare for a professed marksman of that nation to miss a bird as for one of ours to kill . . . They owe this excellence to their education. They are trained up to it so very young that they are no more surprised or alarmed with a pheasant than a rattle-mouse.'

Pteryplegia was the work of 'Mr Markland, a former Fellow of St John's College, Oxford.' He cautions sportsmen against blowing their bird to pieces at twenty yards:

> Full forty yards permit the bird to go,
> The spreading gun will surer mischief sow:
> But, when too near the flying object is,
> You certainly will mangle it or miss;
> And if too far, you may so slightly wound,
> To kill the bird, and yet not bring to ground.

Markland notes that 'twenty shall tumble maimed for one shot dead.' He advises marksmen to concentrate their aim on one bird, which is more productive than relying on 'random fate.' Sooner or later a gentleman will wish to shoot at larks on frosty ground:

> Now let the sportsman so dispose his charge
> As may dispense the circling shot at large . . .
> Destruction thus shall a wide compass take
> And many little bleeding victims make.
>
> And now proceed, not by approach but storm;
> Run, briskly fire amid the rising swarm,
> And you will treble slaughter thus perform.

The sportsman, says Markland, should restrain the 'base, ungenerous desire' to fire at a passing hare, thus robbing the

huntsman of his pleasure. The hare is meant to be taken by
hounds:

> . . . he who dares by different means destroy
> Than Nature meant, offends 'gainst Nature's law.

Devotees of hawking may well have pointed out to Markland
that destroying winged life with the aid of gunpowder was also
an infraction of Nature's law.

By the 1740s parties of 'unreasonable sportsmen', to quote
Gilbert White of Selborne, were shooting down between
twenty and thirty brace of partridges a day in Wolmer Forest
and were in process of extinguishing 'a nobler species of game
. . . the heathcock, black game, or grouse.' In 1753 Dr John
Hawkesworth commented sadly in the *Adventurer* on the rage
for shooting: 'No man is thought to become vicious by sacri-
ficing the life of an animal to the pleasure of hitting a mark.
It is, however, certain that by this act more happiness is
destroyed than produced; except it be supposed that happiness
should be eliminated, not in proportion to its degree only but
to the rank of the being by whom it is enjoyed.'

By the century's end 'shooting flying' was 'almost universal'
and even lads of sixteen brought down their birds with all due
accuracy. This is on the evidence of the Rev. W. B. Daniel.
Shooting, in his opinion, was a welcome addition to those field
sports which neither polluted the manners nor corrupted the
mind, but served 'to temper the polished effeminacy of the
age.' Some shooting enthusiasts were so far from being effeminate that they used to pepper each other's arms and legs with
shot for a joke. The author of *The Shooting Directory*, Richard
Badham Thornhill, was satisfied that religion and shooting
could go hand in hand, recreation being as necessary for the
body as contemplation for the soul. 'On charging the fowling-
piece,' he writes, 'we may look on the shot as a lively representation of mankind, who are sluggish and unable of themselves
to do any thing, till enlivened and actuated by spiritual
fire they are enabled to press forward to the mark of the
high calling God; they have then power to pursue the
way of his commandments when he has set their hearts at
liberty.'

Pheasant shooting

From the 'Sporting Magazine', November 1793

Although he looked on shooting flying as a worthy sport, the Rev. W. B. Daniel was unhappy about a growing tendency to shoot to excess. The lists of game killed in certain areas of England revealed 'such wanton registry of slaughter as no sportsman can read without regret.' He notes that Thomas Coke, perhaps the best shot in Britain, on his Warham manor in 1797, within a mile's circumference, obtained forty brace of partridge in eight hours with ninety-three shots, every bird being killed singly; then adds: 'Mr Coke is so capital a marksman that as he inflicts death whenever he pulls the trigger he should in mercy forbear such terrible examples of his skill.' To illustrate the excesses to which a man might be driven by the desire to pose as an expert marksman, Daniel says: 'It is a fact well authenticated that one gentleman who used to boast that he never killed less than twenty-five brace of partridge in the first day of September has been known to take the late-hatched birds that could scarcely fly above the stubble from before the noses of his pointers, hang them up and so shoot them that he might not fall short of his favourite number.'

Daniel was contemptuous of the new competitive sport of shooting pigeons from traps, already popular in Buckinghamshire, Berkshire, Hampshire and Surrey. For gambling purposes, it might be the least objectionable mode of shooting, but it did not train a man to shoot game birds in their natural surroundings. It was 'wanton barbarity', in his view, to practise on what were, in effect, domestic creatures. He despised, also, those marksmen who shot at swallows, waiting until the birds were stationary on the turn.

If Daniel had little admiration for the feats of slaughter performed on Norfolk manors, he had none at all for the massacres conducted in the hunting grounds of Europe. He observes that the unlucky Louis XVI shot 572 head of game in eight hours on his last day in the field; and quotes from the game registers of Chantilly, that graveyard of poachers, to show that the Prince de Condé destroyed 65,524 pieces of game between 1748 and 1778. 'The Germans, too, have a happy knack at a massacre,' writes Daniel, noting that in 1753 the Emperor Francis bagged 978 head of game in a day and that Princess Charlotte during one foray fired 889 times. Bohemia was the scene of the greatest execution; here game clustered so thick at the roadside that it could be slashed with whips before it would disperse. Hunting parties loosed off at everything that flew, roosted, stood or ran, and often they enclosed the woods in high nets to cut off all escape. The statistics of these contests show that for every shot which killed three or four failed to do so; the number of stricken birds which escaped to die or which the overworked *ramasseurs* could not be bothered to pursue was monstrously high. But no one looked on them as birds, as living entities; they were 'pieces of game'.

Among royal sportsmen, King Ferdinand IV of Naples enjoyed high notoriety. 'If the object of the royal vengeance be pheasants, he has three or four hundred of these poor animals, which are as tame as barn-door fowls . . . confined within a small inclosed compass, himself being seated in an alcove above, by the front of which the *chasseurs* drive the birds one after another without a minute's delay while His Majesty fires at them as fast as he can discharge his pieces, and when he is tired of this excellent sport boasts that he has killed with his own hand two or three hundred pheasants in an hour's time.' The royal vengeance was also worked off on tame boars, which were herded by their keeper into the crater of an extinct volcano at Astroni near Naples. From behind a wall the King shot fifty or a hundred in a day, then entered the details in a book.* The sea was also his covert. Sailing from Naples to Palermo, followed by one hundred boats, he shot incessantly at gulls from an eight-oar barge. By the age of forty he had killed more than 50,000 'pieces of game'.†

Obviously, the art of shooting flying needed a code of behaviour, if the division between sportsman and poulterer was not to become hopelessly fogged; and in the early years of the nineteenth century conventions began to be established. The *Sporting Magazine* in 1805 quoted this tariff of penalties from a shooting lodge in Sussex:

* *Sporting Magazine*, October, 1794.
† Henry Crowe: *Zoophilos*.

Killing a hen pheasant	....	....	....	....	£1	1	0
Shooting at ditto	....	....	....	....	....	10	6
Shooting at a pheasant on the ground or in a tree	....	£1	1	0
Shooting at ditto at more than 40 yards unless wounded	5	0
Shooting two or more partridges at one shot	....	10	6
Shooting at ditto on the ground	....	....	....	£1	1	0
Shooting at ditto at more than 45 yards if not before wounded	5	0
Shooting a hare in her form	5	0

Of these fines, half was to be paid to the parish poor, the
other half to the gamekeepers. They were designed as a
deterrent to the 'pot-hunter' – an expression which is contu-
meliously used by Lt-Col Peter Hawker, in his *Instructions to
Young Sportsmen* (1816). Hawker, a plain-spoken Peninsular
veteran, despised the man who boasted of never having missed
a bird all day. Such a fellow ought to ask himself: how many
birds *should* he have tried to shoot? The good sportsman, he
said, took pride in showing mercy to what was in his power.
But Hawker also ruled that the good sportsman should prefer
a difficult shot to an easy one; the result of which, if his aim
was not equal to his sportsmanship, might be anything but
merciful. Behind this advice was the notion that a man
should scorn to shoot at a bird when he was absolutely sure
of killing it, but only when it had a sporting chance of escape;
which meant, in practice, that it had a strong prospect of
being injured and dying painfully, instead of being destroyed
instantly at an easier, but less sporting, range. Down the
generations this rule, applied to all kinds of wild creatures,
must have caused an incalculable amount of gratuitous
suffering.

Lt-Col Hawker argued that a real sportsman ought to derive
more pleasure from the performance of his dogs than from the
size of his bag (at this time game was walked up by dogs,
not – as yet – beaten to give the sportsman a fast, high target).
But pot-hunters were everywhere. Outside towns 'two or three
unfortunate coveys [of partridges] are . . . contended for by
half the lawyers, doctors, schoolmasters, sporting parsons and
tradesmen in the place.' Hawker warned the sportsman never
to display his guns or dogs, otherwise everyone with a gun

would follow him; if his object was known, he should ride out
of town in the opposite direction to that which he planned,
and then double back.

The sporting code which was extended to pheasants and
partridges did not embrace wildfowl, presumably because this
sport, according to both Thornhill and Hawker, was not a
gentlemanly one (it imposed serious discomforts). Wildfowlers,
crouching in their punts, measured their prowess by the
number of birds they destroyed in one broadside. Lt-Col
Hawker told his readers that, by discharging two heavy duck
guns in quick succession, they could 'possibly secure a hundred
wildfowl as fast as yourselves and a dog can collect them.' As
the nineteenth century progressed the sport had its gentlemanly
adherents, who often boasted in the sporting papers of the
execution they achieved with single shots.

Boasting was the besetting vice of the man with the gun, if
William Cobbett is to be believed. In his *Rural Rides* (1830) he
said that he found shooters a more disagreeable class than
hunters, 'and the reason of this is, their doings are almost
wholly their own; while, in the case of the others, the achieve-
ments are the property of the dogs.' Shooters, he said, talked
altogether too much about their exploits; one could tell from
an adjacent room which voices belonged to shooters and which
to hunters. In short; 'A professed shot is almost always a
disagreeable brother sportsman. He must have in the first
place a head rather of the emptiest to pride himself upon so
poor a talent.'

9

BAITING: FIRST ROUND

THE first pitched battle to secure legal protection for animals was fought on behalf of the bull, an animal which had already enjoyed the doubtful benefit of being 'protected' by the Puritans.

Although animals enjoyed no legal rights as such, men were occasionally sentenced to death for ill-treating them. Their offence lay not in the act of cruelty but in maliciously destroying or depreciating other men's property. Proceedings were taken under the 'Black Act' – 9 Geo 1 c 22 – so-called because, among other things, it prescribed fierce penalties for poachers with blackened faces. In 1749 at Gloucester Assizes two men were tried for killing a mare with a billhook to spite the owner, and one of them received the death sentence. The *Sporting Magazine* reported various prosecutions under this Act. At the Old Bailey in December, 1793, John Cornish was charged with maliciously maiming a horse by ripping its tongue out;* but the judge ruled that 'it must appear from the evidence that the maiming of the horse should arise from malice towards the owner of it,' and the jury pronounced a verdict of not guilty. Decisions like this, the *Sporting Magazine* thought, must discourage all who wanted to extirpate 'such innate villainy'.

Sometimes brutal drovers and coachmen were brought to court on the grounds that their conduct was likely to cause a breach of the peace; in other prosecutions it is not clear what statute was invoked. The Commissioners of Hackney Coaches

* A law of Henry VIII imposed a fine of £10 for this offence, according to Lord Erskine in the House of Lords, May 31, 1809.

had disciplinary powers. In 1803 one of their coachmen summoned at the Mansion House for ill-using a horse said the animal was his own and he could do what he liked with it; 'if he ran one of them through, what was that? no one but himself must be the loser.' He was made to apologise to three gentlemen whom he had abused and was reprimanded. In 1808 and 1809 several boatmen were jailed for ill-treating horses towing barges on the Grand Junction Canal.

Dogs enjoyed as much, or as little, protection as horses. At Sussex Assizes in 1806 a Quaker was said to have rubbed his neighbour's dog with oil of vitriol, with the result that on the following day its bowels fell out through its corroded flank. This act rendered the offender liable only to civil proceedings for the value of the dog. The jury were warned against giving way to anger and awarding vindictive damages; they were there to compensate, not to punish. They awarded £5.

Obviously, the sum total of suffering endured by horses was vastly greater than that suffered by the handful of fighting bulls, but it seemed an easier proposition to put down the limited abuse of baiting, which was premeditated cruelty exercised for pleasure, than the beating and over-driving of horses, which were caused by loss of temper, economic pressure, the orders of superiors and other factors making it a difficult subject for legislation. As it turned out, the struggle to stop bull-baiting rapidly developed into a political and class wrangle which was to go on for nearly forty years.

The rich, by the end of the eighteenth century, had lost interest in bull-baiting. No one seriously invoked the ancient laws which said that bulls must not be killed until they had been baited. But the sport was still an attraction at fairs and wakes, and very often a bait followed an encounter between pugilists. Almost all sporting writers condemned the pastime in very strong terms. John Lawrence admitted that 'in the days of our youth we were excessively, madly attached to bull-baiting – shame to our teachers from whom we never heard one syllable of caution or reproof!'* In some parts magistrates suppressed the practice because of the disorders for which it was a cloak. At Dublin in 1790 the Sheriff decided to disperse

* *The Sportsman's Repository.*

a bull-baiting mob in the field below the Custom House and called in the military, who shot three persons dead. Some magistrates would have liked to end baitings because they drew peasants, labourers and servants from their employment; others, because the sport sometimes resulted in fatal accidents. At Stamford in 1801 Benjamin Overton, a horse-keeper, plunged after the bull into the icy Witham 'while violently perspiring' and died, thus affording 'a momentary check to the pleasures of the chase.'

Not all bulls were baited to death. The hanker who led his scarred beast from town to town had no wish to see it destroyed. He negotiated suitable fees and rules with anyone who wished to set his dogs at it. The animal would be chained to a stake to prevent it running amok and was generally provided with a hole in the ground 'in which to shelter his most vulnerable part.' Bulldogs were specially bred for the attack. They fastened, for preference, on the bull's lip or tongue and, once they had pinned the animal, were difficult to dislodge. Often a game bull would rip open the dogs or toss them high in the air, when it was the duty of their owners to try to catch them on their backs, to break the fall. Under-bred dogs would retire after a bad toss.

But there were also baitings in which the bull had no more chance of survival than the beast in a Spanish ring, and faced worse indignities. If it was slow to 'show sport' or 'evince bottom' fires were lit under it. It might be houghed, to prevent it running away; its tail might be twisted or dislocated; it might have acid applied to its wounds or gunpowder exploded under its nose. 'We have heard of a hot iron being thrust up the animal's fundament,' writes Henry Alken* (this was the fate meted out to Edward II).

Some of the most cruel baitings were held in towns where, to quote John Lawrence, 'the jolter-heads or moonstruck humbugs of the olden time left part of their property to the injury of their families or the neglect of holy charity for the base purpose of perpetuating abomination and nuisance.'† At least two of these 'jolter-heads' laid down that the bull, before

* *British Sports.*
† *The Sportsman's Repository.*

being baited, should first be run; that is, harried and pursued through streets and fields to the point of exhaustion.

At Tutbury, in Staffordshire, the privilege of baiting a bull was supposedly conferred by a fourteenth century prior on his minstrels. After morning church on the designated day the bull was turned loose with its horns cut off, its ears cropped, its tail half or wholly wrenched off, its body soaped and its nostrils filled with pepper; it was then pursued by rival factions, captured and baited at the market cross. The Duke of Devonshire, on whose manor this annual riot occurred, succeeded in suppressing the custom in 1778. Stamford, in Lincolnshire, claimed that its bull-running dated from the reign of King John. The story was that William de Warenne from the castle battlements saw two bulls fighting over a cow in the meadow below. The combat ended with one of the contestants being chased, in a fine frenzy, by butchers' dogs through the town. This scene diverted the Earl so hugely that he left the meadow to the butchers in perpetuity, on condition that every year, six weeks before Christmas, they provided a mad bull to chase through the streets. So, on the morning of November 13, a church bell would ring to call out the bullards and to warn off the frightened and infirm. Travellers on the Great North Road kept clear of the town that day, guards being posted. The bull was turned into a street which had both ends blocked, and those who wished to show their mettle did so in this corral, while the others watched from windows and rooftops. When the bull was sufficiently angered, with the aid of goads and cudgels, the barriers were removed and it was chased by men, boys and dogs. Their aim was to drive it on to a bridge and throw it in the River Witham, whence it would be pursued about the water meadows and there baited by dogs. When in sufficiently bad shape the bull was killed and its flesh distributed among the poor. Occasionally, as in 1802, the bull did not have to be killed but died of injuries.

One of the first attempts to put down the Stamford bull running was in 1788, when the mayor denounced it as contrary to religion, law and nature. The Earl of Exeter, whose seat was nearby, supported him, but the bull was run as usual; and the mayor was rudely reminded that previous holders of that office had subsidised the sport, not tried to suppress it. In the following year the mayor called in a troop of dragoons, but the officer commanding them could not convince himself of the need to intervene and, after an altercation with the mayor, dismissed his men, who then joined in the running. The custom was subsidised by the aldermen, leading citizens, churchwardens and Parliamentary candidates.

The town of Wokingham also staged a notorious baiting, though not a running. Its tradition was supposedly started in 1661 by George Staverton, a merchant who, having been treed by a bull until four o'clock in the morning, took revenge on the species by leaving funds to buy an animal for baiting every year on the day of St Thomas the Apostle. Its meat was to go to the poor of Wokingham and the money from its hide was to buy them stockings.

On a lesser scale bear-baiting also survived the eighteenth century. Bears were still bred for the purpose near London. The *Sporting Magazine* of August 1801 quoted from a Manchester newspaper a letter sent from a clergyman to a bearward:

> Parwich, near Ashbourne.
>
> William Smith,
> In about a month's time, that is on the 28th of this month, it is our Wake and if you think it worth your while to come over with a couple of bears I can only say that you shall be welcome to your meat and drink in our House and we will get you a bed somewhere in the town – and I can find a place upon my premises for your bears and I will be looking for some provisions for them.
> This place is exactly forty miles from Manchester [here follow route directions] . . . if you come you must bring a dog or two with you to run at the bears – and bring also that pointer dog that I saw in the yard when I was at your house.
> Thomas Newton (Revd)
> William Smith,
> Jackson's Row,
> Manchester.

Sometimes badger-baiting was conducted in bear-pits. John Lawrence described this creature as 'the immemorial victim of unreflecting, sottish and idling barbarity.' It was the custom

Bear-baiting
From the 'Sporting Magazine', January 1795

to send captured badgers to a 'purlieu of Sodom' near Smith-field, London, where the scum of the metropolis gathered.* Henry Alken says the custom was kept up by publicans. The badger ward secured his captive in a box in such a way that it could emerge to bite an attacking terrier. Bets were laid as to how many times in a given period a dog could draw its adversary. Alken mentions a very game badger which was drawn seventy-four times in ten minutes. When a terrier gripped the badger it was the duty of the dog handler to bite his charge in the tail or leg to make it loose its grip.† Strutt says that badgers were often baited by digging a box-like hole in the ground and then roofing it. Their tails would be 'nailed' to the ground to prevent them escaping and they were baited until they died, either from injuries or from a gangrenous tail.‡

The first Bill designed to put down bull-baiting was intro-duced into Parliament, in the first year of the nineteenth century, by Sir William Pulteney. His measure, which had the support of the then unknown Richard Martin, was strongly and ingeniously opposed by the Rt Hon. William Windham, a sophistical rhetorician whose arguments were a source of marvel to friends and enemies alike. His epitaph says that

> He was, above all things, anxious to
> preserve, untainted, the National Character
> and even those National Manners
> which long habit had associated with that character.

A member of an old Norfolk family, Windham warned potential electors of Norwich that 'a subserviency to popular notions was not to be expected from him.' A biographer said: 'He would repel flippancy and arrogance and would very keenly point his reprobation to what seemed mean or dishonourable.' As for his oratory, 'if it was not the most commanding that the House had ever heard, it was the most insinuating.'§ A less friendly appraisal of Windham came from John Lawrence:

* *British Field Sports.*
† *British Sports.*
‡ *Sports And Pastimes.*
§ Thomas Amyot: *Speeches in Parliament of William Windham* (1812).

'That man had in an eminent degree the gift of the gab; and at the same time, the pre-eminent art of confounding every subject beyond all possibility of its being developed and comprehended either by himself or others. He was the very Hierophant of confusion and his mind the chosen Tabernacle of that goddess: he had in truth been so much in the habit of shaking up right and wrong in the bag together that he had long lost the faculty of distinguishing one from the other.'†

On April 18, 1800, Windham, then Secretary at War, rose to oppose Pulteney's Bill. Bull-baiting, he said, had existed for more than a thousand years 'without having been supposed to be pregnant with any of those crying evils that are now ascribed to it.' As a schoolboy he had attended two baits and he did not think that his character had suffered. There was 'a busy and anxious disposition to legislate on matters in which the laws are already sufficient to prevent abuse.' The House should intervene only when an Act was generally and gravely called for, not to gratify petty, personal and local motives which were infinitely below the dignity of Parliament, or to furnish mankind with additional means of vexing and harassing each other. He thought the House was beginning to resemble Mr Smirk, the auctioneer in the play, who could hold forth as eloquently on a ribbon as on a Raphael.

Why, asked Windham, should they constantly strive to interfere with the few sports of the poor, when the rich had all the pleasures they needed? Magistrates opposed village 'hops' and chased away strolling players. What were the poor to do – go home and read their Bibles? 'Their sports are robust and hardy, but their tempers are not ferocious; nay, it is a fact that there is not a people in the whole world that feel a greater horror of bloodshed. Compare them with the people of France or Italy where all is suavity, sprightliness and gaiety, and let us rejoice in the difference between the humanity of their characters.' Bull-baiting, he agreed, was conducted at the expense of an animal which was 'not by any means a party to the amusement'; but, he said, 'it at the same time serves to cultivate the qualities of a certain species of dogs which afford so much pleasure to their owners as greyhounds

† *The Sportsman's Repository.*

do to others; and why should the butcher be deprived of his amusement any more than the gentleman?' He was glad that bulldogs were held in the highest esteem by the populace.

Shooting as practised by gentlemen was not less cruel than bull-baiting, said Windham. He was enough of a game shooter to know that for one bird that was hit a dozen flew off wounded; and from this he drew a typical Windham moral: 'When I hear of humane gentlemen even making a boast of having wounded a number of birds in this way, it only affords me a further proof that savage sports do not make savage people.' The poor, who were deprived of gentlemanly pleasures, might well resent efforts to curb their sports by those who had all Nature before them; those who, not content with chasing small, timid animals and winding or laming their horses, must still needs be in at the death; 'or, in other words, to gratify their ferocious dispositions by seeing the entrails torn from the animal that had been so long a victim of their cruelty.' Solemnly, Windham cautioned the House against the folly of affording the lower classes a chance to level such reproaches as these.

Sir William Pulteney, after complaining of inconsistencies in Windham's argument, pointed out that in Shropshire and other counties baiting often drew between 500 and 600 people from their work for a week; also that the bulldogs Windham admired often attacked men and women. In Yorkshire, Cumberland and almost the whole of the North bull-baiting was almost unknown, 'but he was yet to learn that the inhabitants of these counties required such amusements to sharpen their spirit and courage.'

George Canning thought that no more absurd a Bill had ever been brought before Parliament. He had not attended a baiting, but he thought the practice 'conduced to give an athletic, vigorous tone to the character of the class engaged in it and that to this hour it is permitted throughout the whole kingdom of Spain.'

This was too much for Richard Sheridan. After a protest at Windham's 'truly Jacobinical doctrine' he asked Canning whether it was bull-baiting which made the Spaniards braver than the English. There was 'a general laugh'. At a baiting, the bull was tethered to deprive it of the means of defence, 'yet this was the sport which aroused and confirmed the native courage of Englishmen!' If Windham were to attend a bait, doubtless his humane feelings would prompt him to release the bull, which certainly would be 'an effectual mode of rousing the gallant pride of a warlike populace' (a general laugh). Dropping sarcasm for the moment, Sheridan described bull-baiting as the most beastly, brutal and unworthy amusement

Defender of baiting: the Rt Hon William Windham
MP

ever devised by man; and the bulldog he thought the vilest animal in existence. 'So far from being courageous he is sly, artful and insidious, and having once got fast of a poor bull he never lets him go, no more than a placeman lets go his place.' This time, there was a 'loud laugh'.

Sheridan's blast did some good, but not enough; the Bill was lost by 43 votes to 41. *The Times* of April 25, 1800 was

entirely behind Windham. Jacobinism, it said, had increased
the rancour of the poor against the rich, and the middle class
which might have served as a buffer had been taxed out of
existence. 'A mistaken spirit of improvement and of humanity
has seconded the arts of hatred and revolution . . . It should
be written in letters of gold that a Government cannot interfere too little with the people; that laws, even good ones,
cannot be multiplied with impunity; and that whatever
meddles with the private personal disposition of a man's time
or property is tyranny direct . . . Till another person is injured
there is no room for power to interpose and it is then to redress
and not to restrain.' If it were otherwise, 'we must eat and
drink and play and sleep by Act of Parliament.' Drawing a
curious comparison, *The Times* felt it was no more immoral
for a peasant to go to a bull-bait than for a peer or merchant
to squander a daughter's portion on forced peaches and pine-
apples. It hoped that 'the same manly language' that Windham
had used would make itself heard whenever a spirit of meddle-
some legislation asserted itself.

From the failure of this Bill, baiters derived much encouragement. Clearly, if their sport was necessary to sustain the
Constitution, the more they practised it the better. In Black
Boy Alley, the occasion was celebrated with a bear and badger
bait. The owner of the pit allowed for an hour's extension, 'as
how they had got leaf from all the gemmen in Parliament,'
and the bear bore a label testifying that it was licensed by
Windham. In the following year at Bury St Edmunds, a bull,
after being goaded both in private and in public, broke loose
and spread terror. As punishment, its hoofs were cut off and
it was again baited. 'God of Nature!' exclaimed a correspondent in the *Sporting Magazine* of December, 1801, 'in what
country am I? In what part of the world do I live? . . . The
bull of St Edmund's Bury is tormented for the amusement of
Christian savages who take delight in inflicting torture. Can
the philosophic Windham, the champion of Christianity and
Social Order, stand up in Parliament and vindicate such
amusements?'

He could and he did. When another anti-baiting Bill,
supported by William Wilberforce and others, was introduced

on May 24, 1802, Windham reminded the House that the previous Bill would have gone through if he had not chanced to be present. Two great parties, he now explained, were united in their determination to reform the manners of the people, as well as to reform the Constitution: the Methodists and the Jacobins. The former, though their ultimate aims were not Jacobinical, were against all rural amusements and the 'lewd' pastimes once derided by the Puritans; 'everything joyous was to be prohibited to prepare the people for the reception of their fanatical doctrines.' Equally the Jacobins wished to give the lower classes 'a greater seriousness and gravity as the means of facilitating the reception of their tenets.' Both parties, in short, wanted the people to *read*. He understood that in the whole of the London Corresponding Society* not one bull-baiter, not one pugilist, not one man who delighted in manly exercise was to be found to give countenance to its dark, mischievous and cowardly trans- actions. The House, he felt, would agree with him that questions like this were linked to the very existence of the Constitution. If they debarred the labourer from his pleasures they would Jacobinise the whole country. Staffordshire was a bull-baiting county and it produced fine soldiers; indeed, the militia of Staffordshire were chosen to do duty about the Royal Person, a proof that bull-baiting did not corrupt morals.

Again Windham turned to the sports of the rich. What sort of people attended horse races? They were the nobility and gentry, elegant gentlemen without character, blacklegs, sharpers of every denomination, keepers of gaming tables, apprentices who robbed their masters' tills, shufflers of cards, setters at dice, lackeys, pickpockets and thieves. Hence, if bull- baiting was to be put down, gentlemen in justice must cast their eyes on their own sports.

In his earlier speech, Windham had expressed some sym- pathy with the bull. Now, he had come round to the view that the bull derived satisfaction from the engagement. If it showed no terror that was a demonstrable proof that it felt some pleasure. 'Bulls that have once been baited are more eager to attack the dogs than others and are therefore called

---

* A group of radical Parliamentary reformers.

Game Bulls. Gentlemen certainly would not deny that the dog had pleasure in the contest. In his opinion it was the least cruel of all field sports and cherished those feelings which were the best support of loyalty and the greatest protection both of the Church and State. In the French Revolution and during the troubles in our own country who were the men who committed the greatest cruelties? Not the country sportsmen. No, but the very men of war active in crying out against such sports who talked smoothly against all such horrid transactions but who, like razors set to oil, cut the keener.' Windham ended with the warning that if the Bill went through he would move to bring in a Bill to abolish hunting, shooting and all the cruel amusements of the higher classes.

General Gascoigne told the House that a friend of his had frequently boasted of the number of recruits he had raised by bull-baiting. He then made the startling assertion that the practice was one which increased the population of the country to a much greater degree than the recruiting service thinned it. This was the cue for Sheridan, who said he could well believe that bull-baiting produced debauchery in both sexes. He then told the oft-cited horror-story of the bull-baiter who, to show the courage of his elderly bitch, seized a hedging bill and cut off her feet one by one as she clung to the bull, despite which she would not release her grip.* The demonstration over, he cut her throat and sold the pups for five guineas each. This, said Sheridan, was how a bull-baiter treated the guardian of his hearth and family; 'these are some of the hopeful lessons of morality which are to be taught by bull-baiting.' Instead of making men manly and courageous, the practice inured them to acts of cruelty, and rendered them base and fit to submit to a tyrant's yoke. The Bill was lost by 64 votes to 51.

Here and there, magistrates continued to put down on the grounds of nuisance what Parliament would not put down on the grounds of cruelty. The Society for the Suppression of Vice also began to campaign against baiting and other forms of cruelty to animals. Behind its activities, no doubt, was the Hogarthian conviction that cruelty corrupted those who indulged

---

* Writing in 1725, B. L. Muralt in his *Lettres sur les Anglais* says that English bulldogs will retain their grip even when their legs are cut off one by one.

in it. It was necessary to save man from his own wickedness, while incidentally saving creatures from torture at his hands.

The Society's campaign against the bear-baiters of Black Boy Alley eventually drew on it an angry onslaught from the *Edinburgh Review* of January, 1809. Why must these 'hypocrites' pick on the recreations of a few boisterous artisans? Those interested in cruelty, said the *Review*, might care to consider the following examples:

'Running an iron hook in the intestines of an animal; presenting this first animal to another as his food; and then pulling this second creature up and suspending him by the barb in his stomach;

'Riding a horse till he drops in order to see an innocent animal torn to pieces by dogs;

'Keeping a poor animal upright for many weeks to communicate a peculiar hardness to his flesh;

'Making deep incisions into the flesh of another animal while living in order to make the muscles more firm;

'Immersing another animal while living in hot water.'

Cruelties like these, said the *Edinburgh Review*, well deserved the intervention of the law, but it was not the poor who practised them. The first was known as angling, and the President of the Society for the Suppression of Vice himself maintained one of the best-preserved trout streams in the country. Many of the Society hunted and were thus guilty of the second cruelty. The third was practised in order to produce brawn, a dish never tasted by the poor. The fourth was a method of crimping cod and the fifth was the usual method of cooking lobsters; all were cruelties indulged to gratify the tastes of high life. The *Review* continued:

'A man of ten thousand a year may worry a fox as much as he pleases – may encourage the breed of a mischievous animal on purpose to worry it; and a poor labourer is carried before a magistrate for paying sixpence to see an exhibition of courage between a dog and a bear! Any cruelty may be practised to gorge the stomachs of the rich – none to enliven the holidays of the poor! . . . Heaven-born pity nowadays calls for the income tax and the Court guide; and ascertains the rank and fortune of the tormentor before she weeps for the pain of the sufferer.'

William Windham could have put it no better.

In the year of the *Edinburgh Review*'s outburst the first society formed in Britain to defend animals issued its first (and so far as is known) its last report. A group of persons who had dined together in Liverpool to mark a royal anniversary in 1808 decided spontaneously that the benefits of the occasion ought to be extended to the brute creation, and the result was the formation of the Society for Preventing Wanton Cruelty to Brute Animals. In its report the Society said it hoped to operate by the exercise of coercion, by the boycott of cruel tradesmen, by inserting accounts of cruelty in the newspapers and by 'the diffusion of such principles and feelings as shall be incompatible with the existence of that spirit whence cruelty to animals originates.' It also hoped to award prizes for essays on such subjects as 'the best way of securing honey without destroying the bees.'* The Society was especially exercised over cruelty to horses on Merseyside and deplored the custom of cutting the heel tendons of sheep as they entered Liverpool, to make them easier to control. This short-lived society made one important point: 'There is such a thing as intemperance in benevolence; and the virtue may be degraded in the public estimation and rendered fruitless in its efforts by a union with precipitancy of judgment.' Not all animal societies have avoided this error.

* Deploring the 'absurd and ungrateful custom of destroying swarms yearly,' the *London Magazine* of September 1762 pointed out that the humane Spanish saved their bees by smoking them to the bottom of the hive with rosemary.

10

THE WILBERFORCE OF HACKS

UNDETERRED by the failure to outlaw bull-baiting, a former Lord Chancellor, Lord Erskine, tried in 1809 to persuade Parliament to accept the principle of legal rights for animals. This Edinburgh-born lawyer was described by Lord John Russell as having 'the tongue of Cicero and the soul of Hampden,' qualities which had made him an enormous fortune at the Bar (he is said to have excelled in 'crim. con.' cases). His compassion for animals sometimes led him into clashes with carters. Once, when the offender exclaimed, 'Can't I do what I like with my own?' Lord Erskine replied, 'Yes, and so can I. This stick is my own' – and beat the carter with it. In Coventry Street, London, he offered a driver a guinea for an abominably misused horse, with bones protruding through its harness. 'Why, a guinea, sir!' was the reply. 'I can work the horse three weeks longer and after that I can sell him to the slaughter-house and make £4 or £5.' Lord Erskine pursued the man and bought the horse at an unstated price.*

To old-fashioned Members, Lord Erskine's proposal seemed absurd. Parliament had only just abolished the traffic in slaves; now it was being badgered to abolish slavery for animals. When the law held human life of such little account that men and women were hanged for theft, was Parliament to rise in horror because a cow was kicked at Smithfield? Stubborn soldiers received lashes by the hundred; were stubborn horses to be left undisciplined?

Nevertheless the spirit of humanity was making sufficient

* Parliamentary Report, June 2, 1809.

progress to encourage Lord Erskine in his attempt. He drew up a Bill to protect those animals which man had domesticated. It prescribed penalties for maliciously wounding or with wanton cruelty beating or otherwise abusing horses and cattle, and Lord Erskine intended that it should discourage not only direct violence but over-loading, over-driving and racing for wagers. The preamble to the Bill, as its mover admitted, was unusual, but he wished to employ 'language calculated to make the deepest impression on the human mind.' It began:

'Whereas it has pleased Almighty God to subdue to the dominion, use and comfort of man the strength and faculties of many useful animals and to provide others for his food; and whereas the abuse of that dominion by cruel and oppressive treatment of such animals is not only highly unjust and immoral, but most pernicious in its example, having an evident tendency to harden the heart against the natural feelings of humanity . . .'

Lord Erskine moved the second reading of his Bill on May 15, 1809. On the argument that sports like bull-baiting nourished manliness and courage he said: 'I never knew a man remarkable for heroic bravery whose very aspect was not lighted by gentleness and humanity; nor a kill-him nor eat-him countenance that did not cover the heart of a bully or a poltroon.' Earlier attempts to put down baiting, he said, had not been founded on the true principle of humanity to animals; indeed, there had been too much emphasis on the diversion of servants and labourers from their masters' labours. William Windham he described as 'a person of as humane and feeling a mind as ever distinguished any man – a man, besides, of a most beautiful genius whom I have always esteemed and honoured.' The question of bull-baiting had never been fairly presented to his heart and he had got a wrong bias on the subject. Lord Erskine explained that his Bill said nothing about bull-baiting, but a bull was included in the list of animals to be protected. It would then be for the courts to decide whether baiting a bull constituted cruelty.

Lord Erskine was especially anxious to protect post horses from exploitation. The Bill was designed to punish inn-keepers who outrageously abused a horse 'rather than disoblige a mere traveller engaged in no extraordinary business, lest in future he should go to the inn opposite.' Horses drawing chaises were scourged to death; yet 'on looking into the chaises, we see them carrying to and from London men and women, to whom or to others it can be of no possible signification whether they arrive one day sooner or later and sometimes indeed whether they even arrive at all.' Too many post horses were killed by 'people galloping over our roads for neither good nor evil, but to fill up the dreary blank in unoccupied life.' Must they destroy animals to cure their *ennui*?

More shocking still, Lord Erskine thought, was the practice of buying up decrepit horses 'upon the computation (I mean to speak literally) of how many days torture and oppression they are capable of living under, so as to return a profit with the addition of their flesh and skin.' Such horses were made to pull loads which they would never have been given in their days of strength. Imminence of death brought only intensified suffering; animals incapable of further work were taken to the slaughter-houses but not killed at once for their flesh and skins in order that the market might be gradually fed. They received no food and were sometimes reduced to eating their own dung and gnawing each other's manes. Animals impounded for trespass were kept foodless during the legal wrangles for their release.

Lord Erskine foresaw the criticism that it would be impossible to distinguish between blows necessary for lazy beasts or blows of sudden temper from deliberate, cold-blooded, ferocious cruelty; but the courts, he said, settled such matters every day, notably in accusations of cruelty to apprentices. He was careful to point out that the Bill would put no money in the pockets of informers.

The comment of the Lord Chancellor, Lord Eldon, on this measure by an ex-Lord Chancellor was that he approved its object but thought it would be difficult to apply. Surprisingly, the peers gave the Bill a second reading. It suffered some whittling in Committee, where Lord Erskine took the opportunity to condemn the 'inhuman and wicked' practices of houghing and hamstringing cattle and slashing the faces of sheep intended for slaughter. He thought that despite the prevalence of cruelty to animals, Britain could show more honour, more humanity and a stronger sense of moral duty than any other land. 'There never was more purity in the mind of man than in this country and in these times,' he said.

The Commons gave the Bill a second reading, but when it reached the committee stage on June 12, 1809, William Windham, that possessor of a most beautiful genius, was waiting with a barrage of censure. No nation, he pointed out, had sought to regulate by law the conduct of men towards brutes, except in so far as ill-treatment might prejudice the rights of property. The House ought to be very suspicious of those who boasted of bringing in a new era of legislation, for the founders of new eras were liable to be led away by their splendid ambitions and to think more of themselves than of the credit of the laws or the interests of the community.

Man, said Windham, was the only creature that took cognisance of others' pain. 'Were everyone to feel with equal sensibility the pains of others as his own the world must become one unvaried scene of suffering, in which the woes of all would be accumulated upon each, and every man be charged with a weight of calamity beyond what his individual powers of endurance were calculated to support.' Would the House pass a law for the better enforcement of benevolence, meekness, mutual good-will, tenderness or any of the innumerable Christian virtues? How could the law punish a rich man who suffered a fellow creature to die in the next street for lack of a few shillings? The poor laws were an attempt to enforce charity, and what was the result? Dying paupers and pregnant women were pushed into the next parish.

Who was to lay down the standards of cruelty? Irritability might overtake a man wearied by long labour and soured by some recent vexation, or by what he thought was perverseness in his horse. Who was free from such failings? Who would report the squire for punishment because he had ridden his hunter to death or unmercifully whipped his pointer in a fit of anger? When post-horses were ill-treated, who would be punished – the post-boy, the traveller who incited him, or the owner of the horses? Ladies laughed off the cruelties of their own coachmen outside the opera with, 'Oh, to be sure it is very shocking; but then John is so very clever in a crowd! The other night at Lady Such-a-one's when all the world were perishing in the passage, waiting for their carriages, ours was up in an instant and we were at Mrs Such-a-one's half an hour before everyone else.' In such instances, was it the coachman who deserved punishment?

Windham could not let the occasion pass without a reference to the sporting cruelties practised by the higher orders who 'offer themselves gratuitously as vermin-killers to the rest of the community.' In his imagination he foresaw in the newspapers two parallel columns, one of which reported the jailing of drovers and carters for cruelty while the other described a 'glorious day's sport' in which horses were ridden to death in the field. If the Bill were passed, said Windham, Members would show themselves 'the most hardened and unblushing hypocrites that ever shocked the feelings of mankind.' The Bill ought to be entitled, not 'A Bill for preventing cruelty to animals,' but 'A Bill for harassing and oppressing certain classes among the lower orders of the people.' The House agreed by 40 to 27 to go into committee, but a few days later reversed their decision by 37 to 27, and the Bill was lost.

It was perhaps some consolation for Lord Erskine that his efforts were warmly commended by *The Times*, which so recently had deplored the attempt to put down bull-baiting. In the following year he introduced a similar measure, modified to exclude punishment of a man guilty of 'a mere act of sudden passion,' or of 'beating' an animal. But the peers were now very captious. Lord Lauderdale had discovered that he was 'decidedly hostile' to the Bill and thought the moral sense of mankind was an adequate safeguard, and Lord Ellenborough was worried at the risk of a cottager being jailed for driving a marauding pig out of his dwelling with blows of a shovel.

It was a sad setback for Lord Erskine, who revealed that he had received three trunk-loads of letters of support. One of them told how a man had killed two mares by thrusting the handle of a whip into their bodies. He withdrew his Bill, promising to try to work out some new phrasing to satisfy everyone; but he was beaten.

In 1816 it seemed that overworked stage horses might benefit from a Bill introduced by the Attorney-General, Sir

William Garrow, who had received many protests about
'enormous abuses' by stage-coach drivers. These protests were
inspired, not by compassion for horses, but by fears for human
life. With the improvements in roads in the late eighteenth
century, coach schedules had been accelerated; faced with
fierce competition, operators no longer accepted excuses for
tardy arrival. All laws against overloading were laughed at.
Sir William Garrow told the Commons on June 10, 1816, that
some stories of 'furious driving' were of a kind to freeze one's
blood with horror. As an example, two rival coachmen entering
Liverpool had flogged their horses all the way down a mile-
long hill and one vehicle ran for a considerable time on only
two wheels. When coachmen were prosecuted for 'furious
driving' the proprietors paid the fines and encouraged them
to beat the opposition again next time. Sometimes frightened
passengers demanded to be set down and to be given a post
chaise to finish the journey, but the reply was that no chaise
could be had; the contract said that the passenger was to be
taken to a certain place in a certain time. Sir William Garrow
wanted to raise the maximum penalty from a £10 fine to
three months' imprisonment. In the Lords, the Earl of Lauderdale objected that no two persons could agree on when a horse
was over-driven; mail-coach drivers were under orders to
make up time lost on one stage on the next. The Bill was lost
and coaching competition grew fiercer. That same year,
according to the *Annual Register*, a new London-to-Brighton
service was started by 'some Jews' who gave a pledge that if
the distance was not covered in six hours passengers would be
given their money back. To obviate any such risk the horses
were galloped all the way. 'This furiously-driven vehicle with
its lacerated, gasping, panting and sinking horses was the
daily spectacle of crowds of well-fed gapers,' said a correspondent of the *Sporting Magazine*. One coachman broke three
whips on a single journey and fifteen horses died in one week.
Eventually the parish officers of Newington laid information
against the operators for furious driving and the schedule was
extended by three-quarters of an hour. Little or no indignation
seems to have been voiced about the loss of horses. On any
route the travelling public could be relied on to flock to the

operator who offered to clip half an hour from the timetable; but it was on the Brighton-to-London run that competition was fiercest. The coastal 'commuter' had already arrived. William Cobbett, writing in 1823, noted that stock-jobbers were travelling from Brighton to London, spending two-and-a-half profitable hours in 'Change Alley, then riding back the same day.*

The man who, eventually, picked up the torch which had burned Lord Erskine's fingers was the voluble, erratic Member of Parliament for Galway, Richard Martin ('Humanity' Martin). He had supported Sir William Pulteney's Bill in 1800 but not until he was in his late sixties did he start to badger Parliament with his long series of measures on behalf of animals. Born to wealth, Martin played the benevolent despot in Connemara, of which he owned 200,000 acres. From the door of his castle at Ballynahinch he could drive thirty miles before he reached his gatehouse. Here he was 'unapproachable by legal process' and was said to have driven off a process-server with a blunderbuss. It is noteworthy that he was a keen follower of field sports; many of his pronouncements would shock the anti-hunting propagandist of today. Like any Irish gentleman he was jealous of his honour. In his day he duelled with the notorious 'Fighting Fitzgerald' and had the scars of several pistol shots on his body. William Jerdan, the memoirist, who was privileged to see these scars, said that Martin 'appeared to value human life at a lower estimate than the life of a dog or an ass,' qualifying this somewhat by adding: 'Dick Martin might have a gentle regard for bipeds as well as quadrupeds; but it was his special vocation to protect and preserve the latter and to care surprisingly little for thé former who, he thought, might take care of themselves.'† However, in the same year – 1821 – that he introduced his first Ill-Treatment of Horses Bill, Martin spoke vigorously in Parliament against the death penalty for forgery. He asked the Solicitor-General to consider what advice he would give to his ward at a university if a friend of that ward committed a forgery at his expense for £50 or £100. Surely the only

* *Rural Rides.*
† *Men I Have Known.*

advice was: 'If you wish to live happily in college, do not
hang your friend or companion. Forfeit your recognizance to
prosecute if you have entered into one, for no young lady of
rank and fortune will ever marry a man who has hanged his
friend and companion.' Martin said he knew many who had
prosecuted for forgery and would lament it until they died.

The Member for Galway was not too well received by the
Parliamentary reporters of his day and he clashed repeatedly
with *The Times* and the *Morning Post* ('Sir, did I ever spake in

Richard Martin MP
From a portrait in possession of the RSPCA

italics?' he demanded of the *Morning Post* editor). At Westminster he enjoyed the reputation of a 'character'. He was
passionate and garrulous, sincere and humorous. Nobody took
him too seriously, yet nobody underestimated him. Once,
when cries of 'Hare! Hare!' interrupted him, he crossed the
floor of the House to the place whence the sounds came and
with 'infinite mildness' asked who had uttered them. No one
answered, but someone pointed slyly to a City Member. 'Oh,
it was only an alderman!' said Martin, turning on his heel
and resuming his place. The House thought it a good joke.*

* William Jerdan: *Men I Have Known.*

It is probable that a pedant could never have gained the support of Parliament for a cause which many believed to be essentially ludicrous.

When he moved his Ill-Treatment of Horses Bill, Martin told a curious story against himself (*The Times* reported it, but *Hansard* left it out). He said he had seen a man abusing a horse on Ludgate Hill and had been strongly tempted to chastise him personally, but instead he paid two men five shillings to do so. Later he had inadvertently repeated this story in the hearing of the victim, who then summoned him for assault at Bow Street. The magistrate advised Martin to compromise by paying the victim £5, which he did.

Several Members who regarded the Bill as meddling legislation gave Martin credit for his motives. But when Alderman C. Smith suggested that protection should be given to asses, there were such howls of laughter that *The Times* reporter could hear little of what was said. When the chairman repeated this proposal, the laughter was intensified. Another Member said Martin would be legislating for dogs next, which caused a further roar of mirth, and a cry 'And cats!' sent the House into convulsions. Despite all this, the Commons accepted the Bill. What happened to it in the Lords, *Hansard* does not say, but at some stage it was lost.

In the following year Martin widened the scope of his Bill to include cattle and tried again. The Attorney-General, Sir Robert Gifford, opposed it and was told by its originator that he had 'placed himself in opposition to the common-sense of the whole nation.' Every preacher in London, he said, had spoken in support of the Bill. He made it clear that he would not object to a stubborn horse being beaten; but his object was to protect it from inhumane treatment. A Member complained that, as a magistrate, he would not know how to act if a post-boy were brought before him for over-riding a horse. Another Member foresaw laws to prevent the boiling of lobsters and the eating of live oysters. But this time both Houses passed the Bill, the task of steering it through the Lords being performed, appropriately, by Lord Erskine. It was now an offence wantonly and cruelly to 'beat, abuse, or ill-treat any horse, mare, gelding, mule, ass, ox, cow, heifer,

steer, sheep or other cattle.' Parliament had refused to include
the word 'bull'. A fine of 10s was the minimum penalty and
the maximum was two months' imprisonment. The day on
which this historic measure received the Royal assent was June
22, 1822.

To pass the Bill was one thing; to enforce it was another.
The magistracy of England were less enthusiastic about the
Act than its sponsor. With the object of ensuring that it should
not become a dead letter, Richard Martin went about London
gathering evidence against cruel carters, drovers and coachmen, on whom he caused summonses to be served. Legend
has it that in one of his first cases he led a maltreated donkey
into court, but legend almost certainly lies. Whatever incident
inspired this tale also inspired the song which contains the lines:

> If I had a donkey wot wouldn't go,
> D'you think I'd wollop him? No, no, no!
> I'd give him some hay and cry 'Gee-ho!'

Perhaps the first case brought by Martin was at the Guildhall,
on August 11, 1822. He had asked *The Times* not to report his
Parliamentary speeches, since its accounts did not show him
in a favourable light, but the newspaper said it would not,
presumably, incur his displeasure by reporting the court
proceedings. On this occasion Martin prosecuted Samuel
Clarke and David Hyde for savagely beating tethered horses
at Smithfield. Clarke explained that his horse was standing
'very sleepy and dull', and he admitted hitting it a few times
to make it show a little life and spirit. Hyde had belaboured
his horse with the butt of a whip whenever it held its head at
an angle other than that which he approved. When Hyde
said he was a butcher by trade, Martin interjected: 'Yes, I
perceive that. A horse butcher.' Beatings like these were an
old Smithfield custom, designed to make horses look more
marketable. The men were fined 20s each.

Sometimes Martin paid the fines himself, taking no pleasure
in punishing employees rather than employers. His appearances were often a profound embarrassment to the magistrates,
for he was intolerant of the bland ways of the Bar and did not
modify his language. In Connemara he had been accustomed,

as sole magistrate, to clap offenders in his own lake isle lock-up.
He will be seen at his most truculent in the next chapter; but
it is fair to say that Martin's court appearances alone would
have earned him Thomas Hood's tribute:

Thou Wilberforce of hacks!
Of whites as well as blacks,
Piebald and dapple grey,
Chestnut and bay —
No poet's eulogy thy name adorns!
But oxen, from the fens,
Sheep, in their pens,
Praise thee, and red cows with their winding horns!

Martin's friend, John Lawrence, whom he consulted before
drafting his famous Act, wrote of him in 1825: 'The name of
Martin of Galway will wear well; it will live in our annals
and attract posterity as a symbol of blessed compassion, where
it is most needed . . . he has actually worked an incipient and
beneficial change in the character of the London rabble. He
has not only worked upon their fears but he has even taught
them to think! And this he has effected without the usual
consequences – loss of popularity.'*

Yet it required more than Martin to enforce 'Martin's Act'.
In August of 1822 a company of humanitarians met in Old
Slaughter's Coffee-House, St Martin's Lane, London, under
the chairmanship of the Rev. Arthur Broome, to consider
forming a society to protect animals – some fourteen years after
Liverpool had pointed the way. The session at Old Slaughter's
was unproductive; but another was held in 1824, with Fowell
(later Sir Fowell) Buxton, MP, in the chair, and the result was
the founding of the (now Royal) Society for the Prevention of
Cruelty to Animals. It is noteworthy that Buxton and William
Wilberforce, another founder member, were both leaders in
the fight against Negro slavery. Three other Members of
Parliament, one of them Richard Martin, lent their support
and so did three clergymen. Broome, vicar of the church now
called St Mary's, Bromley-by-Bow, undertook the secretary-
ship. At his own expense he had already employed a man

* *Sporting Magazine*, May, 1825.

named Wheeler to gather evidence of abuses.* Although resources were meagre, severely limiting the diffusion of literature, the Society became a force to be reckoned with in the area round Smithfield. In its first year it brought nearly 150 prosecutions.

* Arthur W. Moss: *Valiant Crusade*.

11

BAITING: SECOND ROUND

IF Richard Martin thought his Act would protect bulls
from baiting, he was soon disillusioned. Optimistically, he
had supposed the courts would rate them as 'other cattle',
and some magistrates did. A contested case was eventually
laid before the judges of the King's Bench, who decided that
cows and steers became cattle at the age of two, but that the
bull at no age qualified for this description. Apparently it was
too noble an animal.

Between 1823 and 1826 Martin tried to gain Parliamentary
support for a variety of Bills designed to prohibit bull-baiting,
bear-baiting, badger-baiting, dog-fighting and monkey-fight-
ing. He also brought forward measures to control horse-
knackers. Peel, like the late William Windham, thought such
matters unworthy of legislation. He reminded Martin that they
had refused to amend the Game Laws on the grounds that
country gentlemen must have a motive for living on their
estates. While Parliament encouraged hunting and shooting,
it could not decently prohibit the amusements of the poor, or
make it illegal to encourage the antipathies of two animals,
as in baiting, when they did exactly that in fox-hunting and
hawking. Martin, however, saw no inconsistency in defending
field sports while seeking to put down the atrocities of baiting.
Gentlemen of refinement who hunted and shot were not, in
his view, comparable to the 'lowest wretches' – horse-butchers
and coal-porters among them – who could not but be corrupted
by their attendance at bear-pits. At one stage Martin pressed
for a committee to consider how far popular sports corrupted
popular morals; Windham, had he been alive, would doubtless

have urged that the committee should consider the effects of hunting on upper-class morals.

In 1825 the exasperated Peel expressed the wish that the Member for Galway would incorporate into one Bill all the objects of his compassion, but Martin felt that he was more likely to make progress stage by stage. He was twitted on many counts – for not befriending rats and oysters, for failing to petition the French King to abolish the torture of frogs, for tolerating the consumption of Strasbourg pie made from the livers of tortured geese. But he was not a man who could be twitted for sloppy sentimentalism. On one occasion he told the House he would never seek to prevent any gentleman lashing his dog into a state of discipline. 'He might whip it if he pleased from sunrise to sunset; but he must not cut it or maim it wantonly because such cutting or maiming could neither improve it as a setter nor as a beagle.'*

In 1825 Martin made some unusually lively appearances at Bow Street, where he prosecuted the promoters of a bull-bait on Hounslow Heath. Not only had the animal been torn about the face and mouth but, as Martin later explained, 'those parts which distinguished him from the minor portion of his species were actually bitten off.' At the first hearing, on June 28, a Mr Adolphus, representing the accused, made the usual complaint that the Act did not list bulls as protected animals, and argued as follows:

'It was a very old and, he believed, correct construction of law that where men, animals or things of inferior rank or kind were specifically enumerated in an Act of Parliament and the superior not mentioned at all, the latter could not be said to come within the meaning. The bull was the superior animal and yet was not named in the Act, though the cow and other inferior animals were, and he should therefore contend that cruelty, supposing it to have been practised to the bull, was not punishable under the statute.'

The representative of the Society for the Prevention of Cruelty to Animals, Inspector Wheeler, then submitted an opinion from the Attorney-General to the effect that the words 'and other cattle' were sufficient to include the bull. This

* May 5, 1825.

seems to have satisfied the magistrate. According to the *Morning Post*, Richard Martin 'took part in the conversation with all his accustomed vivacity.'

At the next hearing on July 1 Adolphus expressed the hope that he would not be interrupted by Members of Parliament or representatives of 'associated informers'.

Mr Martin: 'Well, then, I will tell you what – I am a lawyer, having been called to the Bar many years ago and I appear here as counsel for the prosecution.'

Mr Adolphus: 'Very well, that's enough. Now I know who you are and you may proceed to open your case as soon as you like.'

Mr Martin: 'Well, then, here I go . . .'

He told the court that even at Stamford bull-baiting had been stopped and the money normally collected for the purpose applied to charity (this breach in tradition did not last long). He also argued, without justification, that canine madness was being promoted by the method of breeding bulldogs.

When Adolphus contended that Wheeler's evidence was invalid, as he was an interested party liable to pay costs if the prosecution failed, Martin was stung to an unforensic outburst:

'Upon my word, you will be the cleverest fellow in the world if you can bring over the magistrates of Middlesex to decide against the current of authorities all over the kingdom for the last five years. You ought to be very fond of me for affording you an opportunity of doing as wonderful a feat. Why, you will be pronounced the most acute man in the profession and get more at the Old Bailey than you ever did. It will be one hundred and fifty guineas in your pocket in no time at all. It will come pouring in to you in hatfuls. I wish you joy.'

The reply of his adversary was: 'I shall admire your liberality when I perceive it in your manners. Any allusion to where I get my money is, in my opinion, neither manly nor liberal.'

Unworried by this snub, and unrebuked by the magistrate, Martin 'in his most vivacious manner' said that if Adolphus succeeded in his argument 'he ought to be recommended to every jail in the kingdom as the only man to bid defiance to law, precedent and everything else. If Adolphus was right every prosecution so far undertaken must be wrong.'

The magistrate ruled that the evidence could not be heard. Soon Martin resumed his attack on Adolphus: 'I tell you what, sir, if you behaved like a gentleman I would have treated you today with as much respect as if you were of the first rank of family in the kingdom; but if you will bring the manners of the place where you practise with you, you must be met accordingly.'

Adolphus replied: 'I boast not of my manners but this I know, that if I had not the misfortune to meet with you I should have escaped one corruption.'

The *Morning Post* reporter commented that the loud altercation conducted in disregard of the magistrate 'seemed to create surprise even among those who are most at home in the cock-pit and bull-ring.' Martin later apologised for his aspersions on the Bar.

While the case dragged from one adjournment to another, two more bulls were baited to death in the London area and the emasculated beast which was the subject of the proceedings also died. Wheeler received letters threatening his life. Eventually fines were imposed and the long-suffering magistrate described baiting as 'a foul disgrace'.

That summer much excitement was stirred up by a lion bait at Warwick, the first in Britain since the days of James I. The promoter was George Wombwell, who began his career as a showman with a couple of boa-constrictors and in his prime had three travelling menageries. When the event was announced the Society for the Prevention of Cruelty to Animals instructed Wheeler to protest, but the magistrates of Warwick ruled that no action could be taken until cruelty had been committed. A leading Quaker addressed a remonstrance to Wombwell, but in the words of the *Morning Chronicle* the showman 'looked at his lion and he cast a glance forward at his profits and then shook his head. The pain of the lion was to be Wombwell's profit; and between agony to the animal and lucre to himself the showman did not hesitate.'

Wombwell's trumpeters rode through scores of villages to announce the bait. There were many changes of time and place. The showman claimed that £5,000 was at stake, but only the very innocent believed him. The amphitheatre at Warwick was formed on two sides by empty warehouses and on the other sides by the menagerie vehicles. In the centre stood the lion's cage, fifteen feet square. For seats at the windows on the first three floors of the warehouses a fee of three guineas was asked, and two guineas for the fourth floor. For standing in the square the charge was half a guinea. These were very high prices for a public entertainment of the time and, as it turned out, Wombwell had to cut them.

The five-year-old lion, Nero, had been whelped in captivity in Edinburgh. He allowed his attendants to ride on his back and sleep in his cage, and towards Wombwell his behaviour was spaniel-like. The dogs were described as 'good-looking, savage vermin,' averaging forty pounds in weight; some were bulldogs and others part-bulldog, part-mastiff. Wombwell rejected one very savage dog of seventy pounds, for he had no wish to lose a lion worth £300.

The *Morning Post*'s correspondent-on-the-spot described the arrival at Warwick of numerous 'blackguards of the lowest description' and the departure from the town of the more respectable inhabitants, who feared a riot. Tradesmen shuttered their windows. This correspondent also said that the lion had been kept three days with scarcely any food and was in a most furious state, as were its adversaries.

When the dogs were thrust into the cage, three at a time, Nero seemed slow to appreciate what was expected of him. They hung, in their fashion, to his dewlap, mane and nose, but he pawed them away, roaring loudly in pain rather than in anger. Two dogs retired hurt but the third, Turk, pinned the lion by the nose at least six times. At no point did Nero try to bite his adversaries; he was content to hold them down or roll on them. After the first onset Wombwell sluiced the lion with water, the effect of which was to make the floor slippery and handicap him, so the dogs were drawn off. Angrily, a section of the crowd protested that the dogs were not beaten, so they were put in the cage again; but when the lion was obviously suffering Wombwell 'threw in the towel' and the dogs were hauled off by their hind legs.

The Times, by now strongly opposed to baiting, gave two columns to the affair, which it described as 'this extremely gratuitous as well as disgusting exhibition of brutality.' It condemned 'the torture of a noble lion with the full consent and for profit of a mercenary being who had gained large sums of money by hawking the poor animal about the world and exhibiting him. It is vain, however, to make any appeal to humanity where none exists or to expatiate on mercy, justice and retribution hereafter when those whom we strive to influence have never learned that language in which alone we can address them.'

No women had attended Nero's bait, but some were seen in the 'boxes' when, that same week, Wombwell staged a second spectacle – this time, a baiting of the lion Wallace, also whelped in Scotland, but fiercer and more accomplished than Nero. In a leading article the *Morning Post* said: 'The majestic Master of the Forest, true to his invincible character when fairly roused in his own defence, shook the vile brutes "like dewdrops from his noble main" (*sic*); thus satisfactorily proving the futility of any future attempts of the same cruel and barbarous description.' In another column, said the *Morning Post*, readers would find 'disgusting particulars' of the event – a round-by-round description with an account of the changes in the betting odds. *The Times* gave only a brief report, expressing disgust at 'the supineness of the magistracy at Warwick.'* The 'mercenary being' who staged the baits protested that the lions had received no more than a scratch or two. 'Can any man in his senses suppose that I would risk the loss of two lions, the finest ever seen in the country, for the purpose of gratifying a cruel propensity?' he asked readers of the *Courier*. In the *Morning Post* he claimed that he was 'far-famed for his philanthropic and benevolent exertions in assisting Mr Martin in strictly enforcing the provisions of his Act.'† When he died, in 1850, *The Times* conceded: 'no one probably did more to bring forward the study of natural history among the masses.'

* In Parliament on February 21, 1826, the Attorney-General said that in his view the Warwick bait was a riotous and illegal assembly and as such might have been dispersed by the magistrates.

† A long account of the Warwick lion-bait appears in Hone's *Everyday Book*.

Richard Martin lost his seat in 1826 and spent the rest of his life fighting creditors, who eventually drove him to Boulogne. Agitation against baiting continued spasmodically. In some towns the sport died out, in others it was suppressed by the magistrates. Not until 1835 was it flatly declared illegal. Joseph Pease's Act of that year laid down penalties for wantonly and cruelly ill-treating, abusing or torturing any horse, mare, gelding, bull, ox, cow, heifer, steer, calf, mule, ass, sheep, lamb, dog or any other cattle or domestic animal; also for keeping or using any house, room, pit, ground or other place for running, baiting or fighting any bull, bear, badger, dog or other animal (whether domestic or wild) or for cock-fighting.

The last battle was still to be fought. The town of Stamford had no intention of ending a 600-years bull-baiting tradition merely out of deference to an Act of Parliament; still less were the townsmen willing to be dictated to by the upstart Society for the Prevention of Cruelty to Animals, whose agents had begun to circulate among them, gathering evidence. After the 1836 bait eight townsfolk were prosecuted by the Society at the Lincoln Summer Assizes. There was intense indignation in the town and defence funds were readily raised, notably by a benefit performance of the play *John Bull*.

When the trial opened, John Rogerson, 'a London police officer sent by the SPCA,' told the court that on arrival at Stamford he went to the Carpenter's Arms, where he mingled with fifty or sixty subscribers to the baiting. They were drinking out of the horn of the bull killed the previous year. Rogerson, accused of being a spy, reluctantly paid a subscription and drank the toast of 'success to the bull'. On the day of the running he watched the bull gore one bullard and tear to shreds a red effigy with which others sought to inflame it. Once again he was accused of being a 'bloody spy' and mud was thrown in his face; a woman dragged him away to safety. The proceedings began at 10.45 and the streets were unblocked at 12.30; he did not see the bull again until 3 p.m., when its head was covered with blood and it could hardly stand. Rogerson's assistant watched it being baited in the meadows, in an enclosure with five-foot walls. Of the people taking part, he said some were drunk, some had painted faces and most were dirty and destitute.

For the defence, a Mr Hill argued that the sport was sanctioned by its antiquity and by the tolling of a church bell to inaugurate it. He urged the Society 'to restrain their mistaken but well-intentioned zeal and to trust to the labours of the press and pulpit to accomplish the abolition of that which, but for their opposition, would gradually have fallen into disuse. You may lead men where you cannot drive them – and thank God an Englishman is not an animal to be driven – neither is he to be hunted out of his pastimes.'

The jury acquitted five of the defendants, convicted three of riotous behaviour and one of assault. This result was regarded by the bullards as a victory and they planned another bull-running for the following November. This time the Home Secretary intervened, reminding the Mayor of Stamford of his duty to put down disorders. More than two hundred special constables were sworn in, at considerable expense, but as they lacked the will to intervene the running took place as usual. In 1838 Lord John Russell took sterner measures. A troop of the 14th Light Dragoons was drafted in and twelve trusted police officers arrived from London. 'The magistrates, although the interference of the Secretary of State had not been sought by them, were inclined on this occasion fully to perform their duty,' reported the *Stamford Mercury*. Aware of the 'strange infatuation' which afflicted even the supposedly respectable people of the town, the authorities enlisted very few special constables, but instead recruited twenty reliable tradesmen. The *Lincoln Gazette*'s version was that the magistrates received a 'peremptory mandate' from the Home Office to suppress 'this relic of feudal barbarism.' As the day neared the only two bulls kept for hire in the area were moved into a hotel yard under guard and constables stood at every entrance to the town to prevent the infiltration of any others. By noon of the appointed day it looked as though the bullards had been defeated, but by chance (though some said it was not by chance) a cart containing a young bull calf entered Stamford at about one o'clock. The animal had been sold by Earl Spencer and was *en route* to its new owner. Seeing their chance, the crowd seized and unloaded the animal and began to chase it. This time the cavalry chose to uphold authority and clashed sharply with a stone-throwing mob in an effort to recapture the bull. The *Stamford Mercury* said that a brewer who seized the bridle of a horse received a sword cut in the head and neck, but the *Lincolnshire Chronicle* described the victim as an elderly person hurt by a sword while trying to escape. The *Mercury* complained: 'A serious expense on the inhabitants is occasioned by the obstinate persistence in an unlawful and barbarous custom . . . It is no longer to be doubted that it can and will be put down; the Executive Government having interfered will not be baffled in making the law of the land observed at Stamford as it is observed in the rest of the kingdom.'

In the following year, thanks to duplicity by special constables, a bull was again introduced into the town, patrolled though it was by the 5th Dragoon Guards, a draft of London police and a number of horsemen who ranged the surrounding fields. A mob, at one time 4,000 strong, threw paving stones at the police. The authorities recovered the bull 'at the expense of a few broken pates' and it was escorted to a hotel yard between two columns of cavalrymen. By now, however, the town had been called upon to pay upwards of £600 for the hire of outside forces and there was a growing feeling that the money could be spent more profitably. The mayor wrote to the Home Secretary saying that if no more forces were sent into the town he would ensure that no more bulls were run. That was the end.

The Battle of Stamford has many lessons, one of which is that cruelty can sometimes be stopped by making it too expensive. How long it would have taken 'press and pulpit' to suppress the sport nobody can say; nor can anyone be sure that the end would have come sooner if outsiders had not mounted a moral crusade. The settlement was achieved in such a way as to leave the townsfolk with some illusion of having successfully defied busybodies and tyrants.

In its efforts to enforce the 1835 Act against cock-fighters, whose sport was more easily indulged in secret than bull-baiting, the RSPCA was also involved in physical strife. One of its inspectors, James Piper, died after a fracas with cock-fighters at Hanworth, Middlesex in 1838. Surreptitious mains continued to be held, often during race weeks, and occasional convictions are still secured.*

* Defending sixteen persons found at a cock-fight in a red-carpeted horse-box at Old Buckenham, Norfolk in 1928, Sir Patrick Hastings, K.C., argued that people who merely stood round and looked on could not be charged with assisting in the promotion of a cock-fight – 'You don't assist at a theatre by buying a ticket.' He said his clients, who were gentlemen of position, keenly resented the suggestion that they were doing something they knew to be illegal. This ingenious argument was rejected.

12

CHALLENGE TO THE RSPCA

THE early years of the Society for the Prevention of Cruelty to Animals were unhappy ones. In illiberal quarters, as the last chapter showed, it was classed with the Society for the Suppression of Vice as a body of meddling hypocrites employing spies and informers to oppress the poor. Within its ranks there was controversy as to whether the Society should concentrate on enforcement of the law or on propaganda, but it soon became clear that neither function was effective without the other.

John Lawrence paid tribute to the Society in the year after its inception. It was being conducted, he said, without flummery or fanatical cant, and its objectives included 'nothing to which a good, fair and hearty fox-hunter may not say Amen.'* Not all its members came into the category of good, fair and hearty fox-hunters; indeed, the Society's toleration of fox-hunting as the least cruel form of fox control led to much hiving off by impassioned humanitarians as the years went by. But Richard Martin, as already noted, was a follower of field sports and Fowell Buxton, who presided at the inaugural meeting, was so keen a game shot that the *Quarterly Review*, commenting on his memoirs, said: 'Not a word of his own intimates that he who toiled for twenty years to emancipate the Negro had ever allowed his mind to dwell for a moment on the question of man's right to inflict needless pain on any of God's humbler creatures.'†

---

* *Sporting Magazine*, May 1825.

† Vol. CLXV, 1848. His son said that Buxton was a humane fowler who never shot unless he was sure of killing, but his diary shows that he shot 500 birds in a week in a wager with Coke. The *Quarterly Review* noted that he put guns into his sons' hands as soon as they could hold them.

If it was conducted without flummery, the Society was also conducted without funds. In 1826 the Rev. Arthur Broome, its secretary, was imprisoned in respect of the Society's debts, but was released by the efforts of Richard Martin, who was in some financial straits himself. As a Church of England priest, Broome had officiated not far from Smithfield market and it was natural that the Society should devote much initial attention to that notorious area.

The next secretary, Lewis Gompertz, had a reputation for eccentricity. An inventor of talent, he designed among other things the expanding chuck for workshops and a mechanical cure for apoplexy. He was an inflexible vegetarian and believed that man had no right to make any use of an animal which was not in its own interest; and for that reason he refused even to ride in a coach. Gompertz was an active propagandist and put much energy and money into the Society, but his reward was to be denounced by a clergyman subscriber who had detected signs of Pythagoranism in Gompertz's writings. It was essential, this critic argued, that if animals were to be saved they should be saved by Christians and the ruling body agreed with him. This attitude may or may not have been the cause of Gompertz's resignation in 1832. According to his own version he frustrated one of the most active members in behaviour 'inimical to the institution', but this individual was able to summon enough support to force him out.* Both versions make sad reading. Gompertz on resigning founded the Animal's Friend Society, with the object of continuing un-interruptedly 'those operations which the Society for the Prevention of Cruelty to Animals, when united, so successfully performed.' He says that about this time several dishonest societies for the defence of animals were formed, three offenders being dealt with at the Old Bailey.

Gompertz's Society for some years outstripped in vigour the parent body. Both organisations claimed the support of Richard Martin and also of the Quaker Joseph Pease, Member for South Durham, who was to fight the next Parliamentary battles. Gompertz also started a journal called *The Animal's Friend, or the Progress of Humanity*, preceding by forty-odd years

* *Fragments in Defence of Animals.*

the rival society's *Animal World*. In this journal, in 1837, he reported a carted deer hunt by staghounds belonging to Lord Suffield, a member of the SPCA. The animal was pursued for twenty-three miles in one hour and three-quarters and, according to the *Morning Herald*, the pace was almost unparalleled for its severity, but the occasion was 'highly enjoyed by the sportsmen.' The deer died from the run. That same year he reported an otter-hunt in the Usk. The quarry was speared, but not killed, after a six-hours hunt during which it afforded 'the finest sport imaginable'; then in the evening it was released into a canal at Brecon, where it again 'afforded admirable sport for three hours without a check.' The oldest huntsmen said they had never seen any otter so full of game.

Both Societies devoted their main energies to lightening the lot of cattle and horses. Gompertz tells how sheep were driven for more than one hundred miles to the red, greasy, underground hells which passed for slaughter-houses in London. The beasts' eyes were knocked out and their legs were broken by drovers and their ears were torn by dogs. They were not allowed to drink even from the gutters. At their destination they were thrown into cellars ten or twelve feet deep, and slaughtered 'accorded to the uncontrolled fancy of the operator.' Often skinning began before life was extinct. Oxen, driven for days on bleeding stumps, and 'hunted' by Spitalfields weavers, were stunned by repeated blows with a pole-axe; then they were 'pithed' by the insertion of a rod into the brain, which had the effect of shortening the period during which the limbs threshed. Calves were bled to death to bleach their flesh, a hooked iron instrument being used to wrench the head towards the tail, thus exposing the throat.

Attempts had been made to popularise the Continental method of killing bullocks by spining them, that is, separating the spinal marrow at one of the upper vertebrae by the insertion of a small knife. It was a method which had been demonstrated by John Hunter, the surgeon, and when deftly carried out the bullock dropped senseless at once; but the knack was not easily learned, especially by those who did not want to learn it.* Slaughtermen were extremely conservative,

* Henry Crowe: *Zoophilos*.

The underground slaughter-house

From Lewis Gompertz's 'Fragments in Defence of Animals' (1852)

preferring to use the methods which had been used by Moses and Mohammed. The humane killer was many generations off.

These were dire days for the horse. Expansion of industry, the building of railways, the multiplication of highways, the re-shaping of cities – none of this was possible without horse-power. There was scarcely a tunnel, a bridge or an embankment which was not a monument to cruelty. If contractors were behind schedule, professional horse-floggers would be called in. Whereas the Greeks had spared the horses which helped to build the Parthenon, the horses which helped to build London passed, as they grew older and lamer, into steadily more callous hands. Yet the cruelties of the construction sites, caused in the main by hot temper and impatience, often in bad conditions, paled beside the calculated savagery of the horse markets. The game of beating horses to make them look lively has already been mentioned; John Lawrence confirms that the severest tortures of the whip would be inflicted on tired horses in front of 'a ring of fat-headed, unconcerned, insensate boobies.' There was another barbarous practice, centuries old: if a horse was lame in one leg, it would be deliberately lamed in the corresponding leg, so that its gait might seem natural. This was done by inserting a piece of broken glass or other sharp matter between hoof and shoe. The people of Britain marvelled, says Lawrence, that in foreign countries men could still be found to torture criminals, but did not marvel that in their own land it was possible to find 'a blacksmith beast enough coolly and deliberately to fasten a plug of iron against the exquisitely sensible quick of a horse's foot . . . We say the disgrace is national and the nation itself responsible, for were it not for the general indifference and apathy on such matters – or must we say the general interested hypocrisy and moral corruption – a few barbarous, white-livered and felonious rascals who richly deserve the utmost stretch of the *lex talionis* would not dare to perpetrate such atrocities.'*

All over London human jackals waited for dying horses to drop. In 1837 a dispute between 'journeyman horse-boilers' over the ownership of a horse's carcase was heard at the

* *The Sportsman's Repository.*

Guildhall. The animal, belonging to a market gardener, had died with a load of gooseberries in Fenchurch Street, whereupon three men rushed up offering £1, £2 and £3 respectively. 'The street keeper declared that they were all bidding against each other before the horse was a corpse. He believed that people of the trade followed a dying animal just as sharks followed a sinking ship, and like those voracious animals would lend a hand if the breath were still in the body.'

One of the men was reported as saying: 'Please you, my Lord, I see the oss fall and as I knows when a body don't intend to get up again I offers the young man a matter of 20s. Done, says he, so I goes and gets a cart for to move him away when up comes another boiler's man, and as there's a jealousy among the boilers, he offers £2 for the hanimal . . . please you, my Lord, as my offer was the first taken an't I got the best right to the oss?'

The third man said: 'Anyone as says the oss an't worth £3 it's clear he'd steal him if he could. Now, I say the oss is a big fat un, with a good smooth skin, and not one of these here hairy old trunks you will buy in Smithfield; and I offered the walue for him.' To the accusation that they were ready with knives before the animal was dead came the indignant retort: 'We never draws blood except to put a poor creetur out of his misery. No, no, my Lord, we're knackers; we arn't butchers yet, thanks be to God.' (Laughter.)

When the Lord Mayor enquired how many kites were thus employed, the street keeper said that a special watch was kept in hot weather. 'Cads' were employed 'to telegraph, as it were, the fall of every horse.' The Lord Mayor ruled that the carter should accept the best offer but by that time the horse had been removed by a fourth party.*

In 1840 the Society for the Prevention of Cruelty to Animals acquired the prefix 'Royal' (in that year a Society was also founded in Scotland). The young Victoria had become a patron before her accession and continued to take a personal interest throughout her reign; though some of her activities, like her repeated visits to Van Amburgh's animal shows, must have caused the Society some embarrassment. From roughly

* *Lincoln Gazette*, July 18, 1837.

this period the RSPCA began to lay more stress on education and propaganda, not wishing to be known purely as a prosecuting society. In 1841 it decided not to accept any money awarded by the courts but to divert such sums to charity. To punish carters for cruelty might be necessary; to reward kindly carters with medals seemed a better idea. To watch for cruelty on Ludgate Hill might also be necessary, but why not provide help there? As it turned out, the provision of trace horses on notorious inclines was not such a good idea, as carters grossly overloaded their carts in the knowledge that they would receive assistance.*

The task of educating children to kindness was a little easier than it had been in Mrs Trimmer's day, though adults still set plenty of dubious examples. New and less heartless nursery rhymes were beginning to appear, among them 'Mary Had A Little Lamb', published in 1830 by Mrs Sarah Josepha Hale, of Boston, USA. Its last verse was frankly propagandist:

> Why does the lamb love Mary so?
> The eager children cry;
> Why, Mary loves the lamb, you know,
> The teacher did reply.

About ten years later 'I Love Little Pussy', made its appearance, with this as its smug last verse:

> She shall sit by my side,
> And I'll give her some food;
> And pussy will love me
> Because I am good.†

Handbooks for governesses and nursemaids laid down that all tendency towards cruelty by the young must be firmly discouraged; not even a beetle was to be crushed in a child's presence. To indoctrinate older children, the RSPCA began to distribute tracts, to give lectures and to hold prize essay competitions. Their efforts were not eased by the circulation of such manuals as the *Boy's Own Book*, first published in 1828. Wrote the anonymous compiler: 'Whether the boy catches his sparrow in the common brick trap, ensnares a linnet to the

* E. G. Fairholme and Wellesley Pain: *A Century of Work for Animals* (1924).
† Iona and Peter Opie: *The Oxford Dictionary of Nursery Rhymes* (1951).

lime twig, secures a score of larks or finches with the clap net, or takes a nest of full-fledged blackbirds, he experiences a gratification which we have often felt but cannot now describe.' There were instructions for breaking birds to captivity. A boy who kept pouter pigeons was warned that if a bird became gorged it would be necessary to 'slit the crop from the bottom, take out the meat, wash the crop and sew it up again.' Some of the amusements listed err on the side of impracticability; as, for instance, the 'Flying Egg', consisting of a goose egg broken open, its contents replaced by a live bat, and the halves glued together again. The lesson of this book was that Nature was there for a boy's 'gratification'; that, and no more.

Not all supporters of the RSPCA were convinced that it was possible to make people humane by Act of Parliament. Vices, they said, would die out in a world being warmed with benevolence. If action was needed, it should be directed towards increasing the growth of that benevolence. These arguments were heard in many other contexts; they were a justification for taking no action against sweeps who pushed boys up chimneys. In fact, legislation in the nineteenth century did much to make people humane, if only by making in-humanity dangerous and unprofitable.

The first important Act of Parliament for which the RSPCA and Gompertz's society were responsible was the Protection of Animals Act of 1835 which, as already noted, proscribed baiting and cock-fighting. The measure, which replaced 'Martin's Act', was piloted through the Commons by Joseph Pease with very little opposition. The redoubtable Colonel Sibthorpe rose, not to weaken the measure, but to strengthen it. He asked for a clause which would prohibit 'the atrocious and abominable practice of skinning cats alive which has lately been carried on to a great extent.' Both male and female pedlars had shown a revolting talent for 'whipping off the jackets' of cats and leaving the raw remains to die or to be thrown into rivers. The Act also laid down a system of licensing for keepers of slaughter-houses; directed that all horses and cattle should be killed within three days of their reception; that they should not be worked in that period; and that they should be fed daily.

The Draught Dog

It had been hoped to include in the 1835 Act a prohibition of the practice of using dogs as draught animals, but nearly twenty years were to elapse before this was done.

The dog-drawn vehicle was a fashion copied from the Low Countries. Writing in 1820, John Lawrence said that no Dutchman would walk if he could ride and that there was not an idle dog in the Seven Provinces. Sometimes mastiffs were harnessed three, four or five abreast and drew men and goods with the speed of small horses, at full 'gallop'. Their only idle day was Sunday. Lawrence noted that the use of dogs for draught was on the increase among the labouring classes of London; and that a Monsieur Chabert had recently arrived in London from Bath with his great Siberian wolf dog which would draw him thirty miles a day in his gig.*

Draught dogs had the merit of being cheaper and more readily expendable than horses. Also, their drivers were not required to pay tolls. Despite these advantages, the fashion never spread to Scotland. When the railway age came, dog-drawn carts were used in the South of England to carry fish from the ports to the railheads. Some of them made the journey from Brighton to Portsmouth in a day, returning the next. Whereas the dogs which pulled fat Dutchmen worked on the level, those which pulled fat Englishmen were flogged up and down hills.

Humanitarians pointed out that Nature had given the dog soft paws unsuited to hard, sharp roads and that to load it with collar and harness for draught was to destroy its natural posture and balance. In the snows of Kamchatka there might be a case for dog-teams, but not on the cobbles of London. Dogs needed frequent water and found none in cities. Veterinary surgeons argued, not very plausibly, that the overworking of dogs was a cause of rabies. Many critics objected to dog-carts primarily on the grounds that horses tended to shy at sight of them; a sure sign, they said, that the practice was unnatural.

The dog-cart was defeated by piecemeal legislation. In 1839

* *The Sportsman's Repository.*

a clause in the Metropolitan Police Act forbade the use of dogs as beasts of burden within fifteen miles of Charing Cross. This rule, which angered costermongers, was inspired less by humanitarian feelings than by a desire to simplify traffic control. It resulted in the destruction of more than 3,000 dogs.

In 1843 the Earl of Wicklow, moving a Bill to ban dog-carts outside London, clashed with Lord Campbell, who saw no reason for imposing any restriction on the free use of animals by man. The Earl of Carnarvon thought the Bill was loudly called for by humanity, but the vote showed that the voice of humanity was not yet loud enough. In 1849 Lord Campbell again opposed a similar proposal. There would be hardship, he said, to aged and decrepit persons who were in the habit of being drawn by that docile, well-behaved and excellent animal, the dog. His own children delighted to ride in dog-carts. That year saw the passing of a strengthened Prevention of Cruelty to Animals Bill which made it an offence, not only to beat, ill-treat, over-drive, abuse or torture specified domestic animals, but to cause or procure such acts, thus making it possible to punish master as well as servant. But the draught dog derived no benefit from this important measure.

When another dog-cart Bill was introduced by Lord St Leonards in 1854 the Earl of Eglinton scoffed at the argument that dogs in harness frightened horses. It was impossible to legislate to please the humours of horses, which would shy at anything. He had a horse which would not pass a wheel-barrow; was this a reason for banning wheel-barrows? The Earl of Malmesbury said that in Sussex and Hampshire there were 1,500 persons earning a livelihood from dog-carts; now they were to be liable to three months' imprisonment. If owners were cruel to their dogs, why not prosecute them under existing laws? The Earl of Chichester thought that dog-carts were mostly used by bad characters; as an example, Lord Brougham told of a man who ripped up an exhausted dog and gave its entrails to two other dogs to eat. In committee, the Earl of Eglinton, denouncing the Bill as class legislation, said he knew of an honest lad who supported his mother and sisters with a dog-cart. Why did the Bill allow the use of goats as beasts of burden? 'Surely a child with a hat as large as a parasol, and a bow of ribbon as big as a sunflower, sitting in a goat-chaise, was quite as likely as any dog-cart to frighten horses and disturb the equilibrium of unpractised equestrians?' If the Bill went through, between 20,000 and 30,000 dogs would be shot immediately, 'and he would certainly recommend noble lords not to indulge in pork pies near Farnborough or Tonbridge stations for some time afterwards.' Earl Granville said if the use of dogs was stopped, men would buy the cheapest nags and donkeys and torture them as much as they liked. A donkey was unable to show the pain it was feeling, but if a man ill-used his dog he defeated his own purpose. The dog could lie down and use 'the most expressive pantomime' in appeal to the emotions.

According to the Bishop of Oxford, the town councils of Portsmouth, Southampton, Winchester, Salisbury and Newport (Isle of Wight) had already made by-laws banning dog-carts. He said ill-used dogs had been traced for distances of up to twenty miles by blood trails on the highway. It was not unusual for a dog to be driven forty or fifty miles on a hard road until it could go no further, when it would be destroyed and replaced by another. This time the Bill went through.

The Rat-Pit

The Act of 1835, which made cock-fighting and dog-fighting illegal, gave an impetus to the sport of ratting, in which dogs competed to destroy the largest number of vermin within an agreed time. Of all blood sports this was possibly the least edifying. Instead of offering exercise and fresh air it was a spectator sport conducted in the foulest air imaginable. However, it gave roughs – and not only roughs – an outlet for their savagery, while serving in a small way to keep down a too-widespread pest. Humanitarians found it difficult to work up popular sympathy for rats and the law could hardly be stretched to include them as domestic animals.

Ratting was often styled rat-hunting, but the dog did not have to hunt or even chase its prey, which had no chance of escape. Usually, the threatened rats would swarm in a heap against one side of the pit (they could be dispersed by blowing

Ratting in a London public-house

From Henry Mayhew's 'London Labour and the London Poor'

on them) and the dog merely picked up its victims one by one and broke their necks. An ill-trained dog worried the rat after killing it, or carried it proudly about the pit, a practice which brought a rain of oaths from its backers; but the well-trained dog dropped its victims immediately after killing them and went back to the heap for more, taking care not to be bitten while nuzzling out its prey. The most accomplished dogs became legends. Henry Mayhew, who described the ratting Fancy at some length, saw the stuffed body of Billy, who killed a hundred rats in five minutes. In 1848 the black-and-tan Tiny was matched to kill 300 rats in three hours and accomplished his task in 54 minutes, 50 seconds. The most sustained feat appears to have been that performed in 1862 by Jacko, who piled up 1,000 corpses in less than one hour 40 minutes. Sometimes, spectacular totals were achieved by drugging the rats with laudanum.

Mayhew said there were about seventy regular rat-pits in London and a few temporary ones. Most were associated with public-houses. When sewer rats were used the pit would smell like a hot drain, which did not prevent noble lords and titled ladies from calling in occasionally. The bites of sewer rats were dangerous, both to dogs and handlers. In its forays a dog might contract cancer of the mouth, to prevent which its jaws were washed with peppermint. If a handler's trousers were not tight, rats would run up his legs, and those he could not shake down he would pluck out of his shirt. Rats killed in a match were later collected by the dustman.

Among publicans interviewed by Mayhew was Jimmy Shaw, who claimed to have introduced ratting to London. He bought between 300 and 700 rats a week, at threepence each, from a number of families dependent on him. They gathered the creatures from hedges and ditches, notably in the Enfield area, and from warehouses and sewers. The luckier ones also received a fee from farmers and warehouse owners. Shaw had housed as many as 2,000 rats at a time on his premises, and all had to be fed on good barley meal to prevent them eating each other. Somer's Town housed quite a colony of rat-catchers, mostly sporting mechanics and costermongers. One of them reluctantly admitted having killed rats with his teeth for a wager; on the back of his neck was a scar caused by a victim which eluded his grip.*

That unfastidious organ of the sporting world, *Bell's Life in London*, carried news and gossip about ratting under the heading 'Canine Fancy'. The announcements went like this: 'Ratting! Ratting!! Ratting!!! There will be an extraordinary number of rats destroyed on Monday evening at J. Ferriman's Graham Arms, Graham Street, City Road' . . . 'J. Evans will match his dog against C. Childs of Birmingham, according to his challenge, at 15 lbs weight, to destroy 100 full-grown barn rats for £10 a side and will allow reasonable expenses to destroy in Liverpool and equally divide the pit money' . . . 'Ratting every Saturday. Best of wines and spirits. *Bell's Life* at the bar' . . . 'dogs to destroy half their weight, in a fair wire pit' . . . 'to destroy in a wire pit from twice to six times their weight' . . . 'to destroy their weight in rats, the dogs in one scale, the rats in the other' . . . 'plenty of rats will be destroyed by dogs and ferrets . . .'

One report might say 'the rats were very large and gave great satisfaction.' Another would lament that 'owing to the scarcity of vermin only four dogs competed.' Rules were strictly observed: 'Jack was disqualified through leaving four rats alive, this being one above the stipulated number'; 'the dog was disqualified for a false pick-up'; or 'the bitch was disqualified for jumping out of the pit.'

Jem Morris, a publican of Woolwich, offered 'the use of the best pit in London for gentlemen to try their dogs.' Gentlemen were a little shy at allowing their names to be used, preferring to be described as 'a sportsman well-known in the Fancy' or 'an officer of the 100th Regiment, presently quartered in Glasgow.' The Fancy were very pleased to have the support of gentlemen, which showed that the sport was not so low and debased as critics said.

In one of its early issues *Animal World*, the RSPCA organ, assured its readers that 90 per cent of rat-hunts advertised were, in fact, dog-fights. Certainly, dog-fights were still staged surreptitiously, though perhaps not quite on this scale. Occasionally a badger was baited at a rat-pit. In 1878 a beer-

* Henry Mayhew: *London Labour And The London Poor.* (1851).

seller was fined £5 at Birkenhead for allowing this to happen.
In his house, besides an iron-barred rat-pit, was an enclosure
for the badger, with a lid to admit the dog.

Defenders of ratting said it was the last sport left to the poor
man and that it improved the breed of terriers. There was no

Rat 'hunt'
From 'Animal World', August 1, 1871

cruelty in it because the rats died quickly, more quickly than
the quarry pursued by their fellow vermin-destroyers, the fox-
hunters. Without the encouragement of the licensed trade,
ratting, like trap pigeon-shooting, might have been stamped
out earlier; it decreased only when the towns shook off the

worst of their squalor. The law did not succeed in getting its teeth into the ratting Fancy until 1912, when the proprietor of a notorious forty-year-old pit at Leicester was twice prosecuted by the RSPCA under the strengthened Protection of Animals Act, 1911. For the defence, it was contended that ratting was not 'fighting', as the charge alleged, and that the pit was performing a good service by wiping out dangerous vermin at 3s 6d a dozen. After this, the sport went underground.

The Bearing Rein

Thanks to the bearing rein, Britain's reputation as the 'hell of horses' was sustained into the age of the motor car. Those who perpetuated this cruelty were not the ignorant poor but the uncaring well-to-do; and sometimes even philanthropy and piety rode behind horses fiercely trussed.

The bearing rein had the effect of arching the horse's head back, giving it a 'showier' appearance. To relieve the continual strain on its neck muscles the animal would try to toss its head upwards, scattering specks of foam, which the innocent regarded as a sign of mettle, especially if distress was accompanied by enough impatient pawing to draw curses from the coachman. Sustained use of the bearing rein impaired the circulation of the blood, distorted the windpipe and brought on 'roaring'. Going uphill, the horse was unable to lower its head for greater purchase; going downhill, it suffered restricted vision and had difficulty in recovering from a false step. The horse which grew too intolerant of this treatment would be discharged from genteel employment and find its way into the hands of a cab-owner who, although he might work it harder, would probably discard the bearing rein, since he was under less compulsion to produce a showy turn-out. Thus it often happened that the first time a horse was decently treated was after it passed out of gentlemanly service.

The vogue of the bearing rein crept in during the late Georgian years. 'Who had the honour of inventing it we know not, or even the nation whence it came,' wrote Bracy Clark, a veterinarian, quoted in the *Penny Magazine* of April 23, 1836, 'but we recollect forty years ago it was but in little use.'

It was often employed in conjunction with a severe curb bit
which was not so much a bit as an engine. Wrote Clark: 'The
sporting man formerly, and the hunting man and the traveller

'Lex Talionis'
From 'Animal World', August 2, 1875

also, used to deride as preposterous and unjockey-like these
long lever bits, or machines, both as unfair and betokening
ignorance or cowardice, or maladdress in the person using

them; and to ride 'hard and sharp', as it was called, was left alone to the butchers and their blue-frocked apprentices: but now the custom has become almost general, and even fashionably encouraged by the example of some courtly foreigners of distinction.' Clark said that much of the blame for the new fashion lay with the makers and vendors of bits 'and of those who derive a profit in recommending them, and are sharp in the plunder of their masters.'

Among the first to campaign against the bearing rein was Sir Francis Head, author, traveller, prospector and colonial governor, known as 'Galloping Head' from his hard-riding exploits in South America.* In Britain, he observed, the horse's head was reared high; in France it was left free as Nature intended; and in Germany it was tied down low. Both the English and German methods were wrong, but 'there is some science in the German error, whereas in our treatment of the poor animal we go directly against all mechanical calculation.' The Germans and French allowed the horse to use its weight when pulling, to lean against the resistance, but the English expected it to pull a carriage uphill by muscular power alone, with head held higher than Nature intended even when walking. For many years Head had noticed that, in Europe, horses pulled heavy loads with greater ease, both uphill and on the level, than in England. Occasionally an English postillion would unhook the bearing rein on a very steep hill, but animals trained in a false attitude could not readily readjust. 'That the figure and attitude of a horse working by his sinews are infinitely prouder than when he is working by his weight I readily admit . . . and therefore for the carriage of luxury where the weight bears little proportion to the power of the two noble animals I acknowledge that the sinews are more than sufficient for the slight labour required; but to bear up the head of a poor horse at plough or on any slow heavy work is, I humbly conceive, a barbarous error.'†

Sir Francis Head's writings seem to have done much to discredit the bearing rein in his generation, but by the mid-

---

* He tried to get the lasso introduced into the British cavalry 'for purposes of auxiliary draught.' (*Dictionary of National Biography*.)
† *Bubbles From The Brunnens* (1834).

Victorian years it had returned in a more cruel form. The Bedouin, or gag bearing rein, was operated by a pulley system which gave a pull of two pounds on the mouth for every pound exerted by the coachman. It caused the tongue to hang out, so was supplemented with a curb bit fitted with a hoop to hold the tongue straight. The bar of the curb passed under the tongue to bear cruelly on the most sensitive part of the mouth; and the flecks of foam the animal scattered were often tinted red.

Defenders of the bearing rein said it was essential to stop horses 'pulling' and jerking their heads up and down in congested traffic; also that it was useful when horses were 'heavy in hand' or when they had acquired bad habits, like trying to nibble at refuse. Certain animals were undoubtedly the better for a light check rein. Skilled drivers, those who had 'hands', could retain control without the aid of brutal novelties from the saddler's catalogue. Unfortunately, skilled drivers were few, though every man considered himself as skilled as every motorist does today; those who were nervous or incompetent or ill-tempered blamed their horses and trussed them like chickens. Yet the overwhelming reason for the bearing rein was not incompetence but fashion. The tightest reins were seen in the queues of carriages attending levees and drawing-rooms, or in Hyde Park. Self-made men, knowing nothing about horses, wanted a turn-out comparable with those of their betters. Coachmen and grooms supported them in their pretensions; any device which saved them trouble, or rendered unnecessary the exercise of horsemanship, was to be welcomed. They ignored the RSPCA's signs which said 'PLEASE GIVE THE HORSE HIS HEAD WHEN GOING UPHILL' and did not even slacken rein when horses stood for long periods. Horse dealers had every reason for encouraging the bearing rein, for it wore out good horses rapidly and increased turnover.

One of the most vigorous of the later campaigners against this infliction was Edward Fordham Flower, brewer, author, four times mayor of Stratford-on-Avon, who sought, like Sir Francis Head, to write it out of existence. He discerned less sympathy between man and horse among the upper classes than among the lower; and annoyed the RSPCA by saying that its members drove to humanitarian meetings behind tightly-reined horses. The RSPCA issued a great deal of anti-bearing rein propaganda, but if it had brought prosecutions they would have been thrown out. One of its correspondents in Russia ('the country of the Duchess of Edinburgh') reported: 'With plain snaffle bits the Russian coachman drives his three stallions at full gallop through crowded streets.' In Moscow there were 'incomparably powerful, docile, fast and high-actioned horses, unabused by reins, high ports, heavy lever bits, curb chains, blinkers, ill-fitting hard, heavy collars, hideous cumbrous pads and unsightly cruppers.'* Fashionable America, on the other hand, had copied the British example. In the 1870s George Angell, of the Massachusetts Society for the Prevention of Cruelty to Animals, was distributing thousands of pamphlets against the bearing rein and erecting 'SLACKEN YOUR REIN' signs on hills.

In Britain two field-marshals, Sir William Gomm and Sir John Burgoyne, strongly supported the RSPCA. Burgoyne, a veteran of the Peninsular and Crimean wars, noted in 1870 that the bearing rein had been banned for Army draught horses and that car and bus drivers were abandoning it, but it was still used by many drivers of cart horses. *Animal World* said: 'Would a carter carry a sack of corn with any more comfort or safety to himself if he had an iron bar in his mouth with a cord attached to it and his head made a fixture?'† In 1877 Anna Sewell published her *Black Beauty*, which vigorously denounced the bearing rein; she died in the following year, unaware that she had produced a humanitarian classic. Veterinary surgeons told grisly stories of 'inquests' on horses which had been maltreated by tight reins, but nobody listened. The fashion persisted into the twentieth century. Eventually, successful prosecutions for cruelty were brought by the RSPCA under the Protection of Animals Act, 1911, but by then man was transferring his cruelty to gear-boxes.

* Quoted in Flower's *Bits and Bearing Reins* (1875).
† January 1, 1875.

13

BRUTES NO MORE

IN the early part of the nineteenth century, the sentiment inelegantly described as 'philobrutism' or 'zoophily' – otherwise compassion for animals – was still being borne forward on the far-meandering streams which had their springs in Methodism and Rousseauism. It was noticeable that those who showed most concern for their fellow men tended to show most concern for animals; and usually the converse held true. Not the least factor which led to a kindlier treatment of beasts was the gradual decline in that open sottishness which led squires to boot and maim their dogs, drovers to knock out the eyes of their cattle and coachmen to scourge inoffending horses in an effort to make up time spent in tippling. The temperance movement played a strong indirect part in the fight against cruelty.

Thanks to Martin and others, animals had limited rights, but not enough to satisfy the moral and political philosophers. Echoing Bentham, John Stuart Mill in 1848 wrote:

'The reasons for legal intervention in favour of children apply not less strongly to the case of those unfortunate slaves and victims of the most brutal part of mankind – the lower animals. It is by the grossest misunderstanding of the principle of liberty that the infliction of exemplary punishment on ruffianism practised towards these defenceless creatures has been treated as a meddling by government in things beyond its province; an interference with domestic life. The domestic life of domestic tyrants is one of the things which it is the most imperative on the law to interfere with.'*

* *The Principles Of Political Economy.*

And, again paraphrasing Bentham, he said: 'The question is not whether animals understand that they are suffering or whether their sufferings are soothed by religious hopes, but whether they feel suffering.'

In 1859 came the *Origin of Species*. It was two decades since Charles Darwin had written in his diary: 'Man in his arrogance thinks himself a great work, worthy the interposition of a deity. More humble and, I believe, true to consider him created from animals.' The development of this view led to a slow shift in humanitarian philosophy. Hitherto benevolence had been a moral duty and men had talked of the 'brute creation' as totally inferior to the human creation, something provided by God for man's benefit and for that reason not to be wantonly abused. After Darwin it seemed probable that man was only the evolved head of the family and that there was no reason to suppose that the deity, if any, would accord him any preferential treatment in the hereafter, if any. Man had lost what Shelley called his 'terrible prerogative'. It was less easy to talk of the 'brute creation' and of 'dumb beasts', once beasts were seen to have the same faculties and emotions, in a diminished degree, as man. When the long theological anger had subsided, it was possible to detect a 'growing inclination, noticeable both in scientific circles and in religious, to believe that mankind and the lower animals have the same destiny before them, whether that destiny be for immortality or for annihilation.'* To the former 'brute creation', however, this philosophical shift brought little noticeable relief. Physiologists saw no reason to stop experimenting on the higher animals. Darwin himself said he could not see how physiology could be advanced without vivisection. Hunters still went to Africa to decimate the apes, their 'ancestors'. The brutal carter still beat his horse, fearing neither God nor Darwin, but only the RSPCA.

Predictably, there were sharp clashes between the Darwinians and those who still followed St Thomas Aquinas. Miss Frances Power Cobbe, whose activities as an anti-vivisectionist are described later, fought many a round with the Jesuits. Her exasperation with the Roman Catholic attitude to animals

* H. S. Salt: *Animals' Rights* (1892).

began when she was informed that Pope Pius IX had refused a request by the RSPCA to open a branch in Rome, a city by no means renowned for clemency to animals. The Pontiff's view was said to be that man owed duties to his fellow men, but none to the lower animals; therefore, while animal societies might exist in Protestant countries, they could not be allowed in Rome. In Britain, however, Cardinal Manning supported Miss Cobbe in her humanitarian causes, and, according to her, tried to change the Vatican attitude to animals. He also sought to soften the hearts of the Franciscans, who seemed to have forgotten the precepts of their founder. Miss Cobbe said she was tired of hearing St Francis's name flaunted; 'no modern Franciscan that ever I heard of has stirred a finger on behalf of animals anywhere, either from vulgar or scientific curiosity.' His successors, she alleged, never warned their flocks that cruelty was even a venial sin.*

In the works of Father Joseph Rickaby, a lecturer in Jesuit schools, Miss Cobbe found a passage which particularly inflamed her. It appeared in his *Moral Philosophy: with studious regard to the Catholic Church and to the teaching of St Thomas* (1888): 'Brute beasts, not having understanding and therefore not being persons, cannot have any rights. The conclusion is clear. They are not autocentric. They are of the number of *things*, which are another's; they are chattels, or cattle. We have no duties to them – not of justice . . . not of religion, unless we are to worship them like the Egyptians of old; not of fidelity, for they are incapable of accepting a promise. The only question can be of charity. Have we duties of charity to the lower animals?' Father Rickaby was convinced we had not. Charity was an extension of the love of ourselves to beings like ourselves, and animals were vastly below us. Man alone spoke, man alone worshipped, man alone hoped to contemplate for ever the face of his Father in Heaven. 'We have, then, no duties of charity nor duties of any kind to the lower animals, as neither to stocks and stones.'

Miss Cobbe professed herself shocked by this 'dogmatic reassertion of definitions drawn in the Dark Ages and the persistent re-erection upon these definitions of an impassable

* *Life of Frances Power Cobbe,* by Herself (1894).

wall between *persons* with rights and *things* (sentient, intelligent, affectionate *things!*) with no rights whatever.'* Zoophilists like herself did not demand equal rights for men and animals, but they wanted recognition of *some* rights for animals, one of them being a right to exemption from vivisection. 'We maintain,' said Miss Cobbe, 'that there are such vast differences between the species of animals in their descending ranks – vertebrates and invertebrates, mammals, birds, reptiles, fishes, molluscs, insects down to zoophytes and bacilli – that an analogous difference must exist in our moral relations to each class; a diminished scale of obligations corresponding to the diminished scale of sensibility; till, when the oyster and parasite stage has been reached the vanishing point of morality has been reached also. This is what common-sense assuredly dictates and what the laws and the common practice of Protestant countries accept.' Miss Cobbe pointed out that only the spiritual and moral part of man was sacred. 'There is no sufficient reason why we should consider his bodily pain of such supreme importance that we may freely inflict as much, or tenfold as much, of the same pain on an animal on the chance of learning how to save it.'

But Miss Cobbe omitted to give Father Rickaby sufficient credit for the passage which followed his dismissal of animals as the equivalent of stocks and stones:

'Still, we have duties *about* stones, not to throw them through our neighbours' windows; and we have duties *about* brute beasts. We must not harm them when they are our neighbours' property. We must not break out into paroxysms of rage and impatience in dealing with them. It is a miserable way of showing off human pre-eminence to torture poor brutes in malevolent glee at their pain and helplessness. Such wanton cruelty is especially deplorable because it disposes the perpetrators to be cruel also to man.'

Father Rickaby held that it was wanton cruelty to vex and annoy a brute beast for sport, 'but there is no shadow of evil resting on the practice of causing pain to brutes in sport where the pain is not the sport itself but an incidental concomitant of it. Much more in all that conduces to the substance of man

* *Contemporary Review*, October, 1895.

may we give pain to brutes, as also in the pursuit of science.
Nor are we bound to any anxious care to make this pain as
little as may be.' He added that 'if any special case of pain to
a brute creature be a fact of considerable value for observation
in biological science or the medical art, no reasoned considerations of morality can stand in the way of man making the
experiment, yet so that even in the question of science he be
mindful of mercy.' On this, Miss Cobbe commented: 'If it
were his object to release his students from any qualms of
conscience, any lingering natural emotion of pity for the poor
creatures on the vivisection trough, what else should he have
written?'

Cardinal Manning can hardly have been happy about the
teachings of Roman Catholic controversialists. One of them
found it necessary to say that a man had a perfect right to
kill the dog which had just saved his life; another that 'the
whole modern movement in favour of animals is a scheme of
the devil for the seduction of souls and a pestilent heresy'; a
Roman Catholic surgeon was supposed to have crumpled a
piece of paper and thrown it in the gutter, saying, 'There!
God cares as much for animals as I do for that paper'; and
a Dominican wrote that 'if animals have no rights it follows
that there is no such thing as cruelty to animals or that cruelty
to animals is not wrong' (this was regretted by a Catholic
apologist as 'a strange confusion of thought' and 'singularly
defective logic').

Cardinal Manning's personal views, as frequently expounded
by him, were as follows: 'It is perfectly true that obligation
and duties are between moral persons and therefore the lower
animals are not susceptible of those moral obligations which
we owe to one another; but we owe a seven-fold obligation to
the Creator of those animals. Our obligation and moral duty
is to Him who made them . . . In giving a dominion over his
creatures to man He gave them subject to the condition that
they should be used in conformity to his own perfections,
which is His own law, and therefore our Law.'*

Was the Roman Catholic insistence that animals were without rights a cause of cruelty in those countries under the

* Statement on March 9, 1887, quoted in Cobbe autobiography.

Pope's dominion? Miss Cobbe was quite certain it was; it had 'left the minds of millions in Catholic countries closed against the rising tide of pity and sympathy which has swelled the hearts of Protestants, Theists and Agnostics all over the civilised world.'* Others pointed out how, in Catholic countries, peasants inflicted cruelty on their employers' animals to further agrarian agitation; in Ireland donkeys and cattle were hamstrung, and in Italy cattle were collected and starved to death. The physiologists of France carried out vivisection with an unusually callous zeal, yet there were plenty of good Roman Catholics to condemn them. The general allegation was easier to make than prove. Had not England been guilty of abominations which shocked visitors from Europe? Had Englishmen and Englishwomen the right to belabour cruel carters in Italy, as they so often did? Roman Catholic apologists said that if Italy was more cruel than England that was not because of religion, any more than the fact that England was more drunken than Italy was due to religion. The same argument was used to excuse the multitudinous cruelties of Spain.

The *Catholic Encyclopedia* (1908) usefully summed up the attitude of the Roman Church: 'While Catholic ethical doctrine insists upon the merciful treatment of animals it does not place kindness towards them on the same plane of duty as benevolence towards our fellow men. Nor does it approve of unduly magnifying to the neglect of higher duties our obligations concerning animals. Excessive fondness for them is no sure index of moral worth; it may be carried to un-Christian excesses; and it can coexist with grave laxity in far more important matters. There are many imitators of Schopenhauer who loved his dog and hated his kind.'

Five years before that was published an emissary of the RSPCA was installed in the Via del Tritone in Rome and a dinner was given by fashionable Italian society in aid of animals.

More and more, blood sports attracted controversy. *Punch*, while not opposed to fox-hunting, protested vigorously from

* *Contemporary Review*, October, 1895.

its earliest years against the poultering exploits of the Prince Consort. The grounds at Stowe were the scene of slaughter on the German plan. In January, 1845, a huge force of beaters, almost stick to stick, concentrated all the hares into an open space and the guns tumbled them over at close range; 'within a semi-circle of about sixty yards from His Royal Highness the havoc was evidently greatest.' After bowling over 114 hares the Prince returned to the house and was welcomed by 'See the Conquering Hero Comes' from the Duke of Buckingham's band. Sportsmen, pointed out *Punch*, had always pretended that killing was the least attraction of sport; such feats disproved this. The Consort's aim may have been better than this verse suggests:

> Once and again Prince Albert shot,
> Once and again shot he;
> The hare that erst on four legs ran
> Now limped away on three.

Cartoons showed the Prince selling hares in the street and shooting at pheasants from an armchair. Later that year Victoria and Albert journeyed to Saxe-Coburg-Gotha, where they sat in a pavilion and watched a concentration of deer butchered in a forest clearing. The Queen found the spectacle too medieval for her taste, even after Albert's explanation that the creatures had to be kept down and this was the German method.

It comes as a surprise to find Mrs Isabella Beeton airing her views on blood sports in her *Book of Household Management* (1861). Deprecating a recent revival of falconry, she writes: 'New and nobler efforts characterise the aims of mankind in the development of their civilisation and the sports of the field have, to a large extent, been superseded by other exercises, it may be less healthful and invigorating, but certainly more elegant, intellectual and humanising.' Of hunting she says: 'It is an employment . . . requiring both art and contrivance, as well as a certain fearlessness of character, combined with the power of considerable physical endurance . . . but at best the occupation is usually accompanied with rude and turbulent habits; and when combined with these it constitutes what is termed the savage state of man . . . When a country has attained to a high state of civilisation hunting becomes little more than an amusement of the opulent.'

Perhaps the most notable controversy over field sports was that waged in the *Fortnightly Review* in 1869 between Professor E. A. Freeman, historian of the Norman Conquest, and Anthony Trollope. 'Much amusement was occasioned by the collision of these two very rough diamonds,' says the *Dictionary of National Biography*. There had been critics aplenty of deer-hunting and hare-hunting, but Professor Freeman went out of his way to befriend the fox. His criticisms of hunting, much quoted at the time, are substantially the same as those voiced today; and if the clash with Trollope occasioned much amusement it also helped people to clarify their ideas. What seems to have sparked Professor Freeman's attack was a report of a rural prosecution in which a boy was charged with cruelty by setting two dogs on a cat. His father said it seemed hard that a boy should be punished for this offence when gentlemen set dogs on hares; an observation which drew no comment from the Bench. The Professor disclaimed any false sensibility: 'As I should not scruple to ride a horse to death if there was no other way to save human life or relieve human suffering, so I should not scruple at a large sacrifice of inferior animal life to secure the life or comfort of a dog or horse,' he wrote. But sport offered no excuse for severities. 'To chase a calf or a donkey, either until it is torn to pieces or till it sinks from weariness, would be scouted as a cruel act. Do the same to a deer and it is a noble and royal sport. It is, as we have seen, a legal crime to worry a cat. To worry a hare is a gallant diversion.' And no praises were too high for the heroic sport which involved the wanton torture of a fox.

It was the custom, said Professor Freeman, for men to do what was usual in their time and place. They were able to localise their affections, befriending one animal, condemning another. Not all fox-hunters were brutes; but 'a mere fox-hunter, a mere bull-baiter, a mere amateur of gladiators can never have been an estimable character in any age.' Fox-hunting could not be defended on pesticidal grounds, since foxes were artificially preserved and even imported into

territories where they were scarce. A fox's life was held sacred
in order that it should be killed with a prescribed amount of
fright and suffering; 'if this is anything but wanton and
deliberate cruelty I do not know the meaning of words.' Even
if the hunter did not enjoy inflicting cruelty he knew it was
being inflicted for his amusement. Hunting gave exercise, but
exercise could be gained just as easily by riding after a red
herring. 'I should not think well of a butcher who took up
the trade of a butcher out of sheer love of blood and slaughter,'
he wrote. In fox-hunters in general he detected 'a certain
lawless and overbearing spirit, a certain contempt of the rights
of others and a strong intolerance of the opinions and tastes
of others.' Nor would he concede that they died a heroic
death in ditches: 'When a fox-hunter is suddenly cut off in
the midst of his cruelties I can see nothing in his end at all
resembling the end of the martyr who dies for his religion or
of the hero who dies for his country. I believe I am unfashion-
able in thinking so but I cannot help it.' Yet, concluded
Professor Freeman, 'When I look back to what has been, I
can feel glad that, at least among persons of decent character,
fox-hunting is the worst form of cruelty that I have to condemn.'

Trollope's answer was printed 'with the permission of the
Editor of the *Fortnightly Review* but not with his sympathy. The
novelist defended hunting primarily on the grounds that it
afforded healthy exercise, gave opportunities for the display
of skill and courage and enabled a man to emulate his superiors
in rank. In short, it was the most fit amusement for a hard-
worked, educated man. Few witnessed the death or wanted
to see it; they saw 'no other ostensible evidence of the animal's
destruction than a bit of fur hanging to a hound's mouth or
a bloody jaw.' Which had the worse life – the donkey or the
fox? Was it not in compliance with an instinct given by God
that the hound hunted the fox? 'We cannot doubt but that
his (the fox's) scent was imposed upon him in order that he
should fulfil his destiny to fall a prey to his pursuers.* Till
fatigue induces the fear that escape may not be achieved the
animal probably does not suffer. Then he has a sharp ten

* Another participant in the controversy described this as 'a mournful
blasphemy'.

minutes and a final half-minute of agony in his death struggle.'
Hunting the fox, in short, was salutary, noble and beneficial;
'the fox's life serves as good a purpose as that of any animal
which falls that men may live . . . as man suffers, so has the
animal to suffer his allotment of pain.'

The blood sports controversy broke out from time to time
in most of the leading journals. Every man had his own ideas
of what was legitimate sport and what was not. There were
fox-hunters who agreed with the hard-riding 'Nimrod' (C. J.
Apperley) that steeple-chasing was 'cruel and unsportsmanlike' and that the Grand National was 'disgusting'. Other
fox-hunters would despise hare-hunting on the grounds that
the quarry was too timid and afforded too brief a chase. The
hare-hunter would justify his sport over fox-hunting with the
plea that his quarry was, at least, eatable. The hunter of
carted deer would point out that he rode to recapture, not
to kill, and was mocked by the hunter of wild deer. The deer-
stalker would point out that one well-aimed bullet was more
humane than a long gruelling chase to destruction. Those who
shot driven pheasants thought it unsporting to fire at close
quarters over dogs, and those who shot over dogs condemned
the *battue*. In the main, there was rough agreement that a
sport, to be justified, must make physical demands on its
devotees. A writer in the *Cornhill* in February 1874 saw no
inconsistency in saying that pigeon-shooting was cruel while
deer-stalking and partridge-shooting were not. The two latter
sports provided health and pleasing excitement. 'The pigeon
suffers no more than the partridge but he suffers without any
man being the better for it . . . Everything that tends to make
sport physically easy tends in the same proportion to make it
morally hurtful.' It was possible to argue from this that a man
who stood up to his waist in icy water destroying duck was
performing a nobler task than one who stood on dry land
destroying partridges. The contention that field sports fostered
manliness was met with increasing scepticism. 'Is the fireman
a fox-hunter?' asked a reader of the RSPCA's *Animal World*.*
'And who shows more pluck than he does? Are the Deal
boatmen fox-hunters?'

* May 2, 1870.

Hunting was still defended on the grounds that it kept landowners on their land, gave employment to thousands, improved the breed of horses and provided the Army with chargers. But all this, in the view of the opposite camp, did not outweigh the hypocrisy of promising to get rid of a pest and then making sure that the pest was always plentiful.

14

RIGHTS FOR BIRDS

'MANY a man would shoot a bird without a pang who would hesitate to draw a trigger on a quadruped,' said *The Times* of August 1, 1870. This is still substantially true; in general, pangs only begin to be felt as the size of the quarry increases. But *The Times* noted with satisfaction that birds were 'now beginning to be regarded as fit objects for humane legislation.' The law, of course, had long been active to protect game birds, but the motive was not a humanitarian one.

At no time had birds been in greater need of protection. Never had they suffered such wanton abuse from the human race. Their foes were many and cunning: sportsmen, whether in the form of pot-hunting gentry, trap-pigeon shooters or the fast-multiplying race of 'cockney' sportsmen; gourmets, who could not look at a steak pudding unless it was preceded, or accompanied, by the tiny carcases of singing birds, which gave negligible nourishment to the already overfed; fashion designers, who ruled that women should clothe themselves in feathers; the plume and wing hunters, who recklessly supplied this demand; farmers, many of whom saw birds only as agents of depredation; dealers in cage birds; the tribe of netters, fowlers and trappers, who supplied birds for table, cage or sport; self-styled naturalists, who sought out rare birds and eggs; gamekeepers, who killed all birds which threatened the privileged creatures they reared for their masters to kill; schoolboys, who limed twigs, laid nets, robbed nests and stoned fledglings, or caught birds to sell to dealers who sold them to other schoolboys; and louts, who killed without a qualm anything that fluttered.

Shooting was fast becoming a 'democratic' sport. By mid-century the breech-loader had begun to oust the flintlock and the market was soon flooded by cheap firearms which, though they often exploded in the face of the user, were much prized by the new breed of artisan sportsmen. Every week-end, excursion trains to the coasts brought swarms of townsmen with 'Brummagem' guns to harry sea birds at close range. 'There is no doubt,' said *The Times*, 'that a great deal of murderous work against the birds is going on among us, in contempt of the laws of God and man.' On a snowy Sunday 'old and young, Churchman or Dissenter, turn out leaving the parson to edify women and empty pews and high up in the hills and down in the valleys such a fusillade ensues on the day of rest as could hardly be justified by any event short of the landing of French invaders upon our shores. This is an unmitigated evil and no attempt is made to deny it. Should nine-tenths of the birds of England deserve capital punishment it is not such a set of ragamuffins that ought to be allowed to inflict it.' *The Times* had no objection to imposing as heavy a penalty for killing a linnet without a licence as for killing a hare; but it had no great confidence that a tax on guns was the right remedy.*

This leading article was inspired by a correspondence about the massacre of small birds. The Hon. Grantley Berkeley, a magistrate of Poole, said that on Christmas Day men and boys everywhere made the roads and lanes 'obscenely dangerous' by firing at every bird within range. His gamekeeper had found a lad of eight or nine in a ditch angrily twisting tarred twine round the burst barrel of his gun, which had a hole in it big enough to admit five fingers. He knew of a church in which small shot had rattled against the window during service, causing the parson to falter. Another correspondent counted from a railway carriage thirteen shooting parties on one side of the Great Eastern Railway between Stratford and Tottenham stations. The Rev. F. O. Morris, of Nunburnholme Rectory, Hayton, Yorkshire, a naturalist and zoophilist, who was to prove a strong champion of bird life, pointed out that the French Senate had already passed laws to protect native

* October 12, 1869.

birds, in the farmers' interest, and that similar action had been taken in parts of America.

The first Act of Parliament to prevent the harrying of birds was the Sea Birds Protection Act of 1869, the story of which fits more readily into a later chapter.* This set up a close season for designated sea birds. It was followed by other Acts in 1872, 1876 and 1880, all steadily expanding the categories of birds to be allowed to breed in peace. Designed to curb the marksman and the netter alike, they were the result of campaigning by several groups of humanitarians, among them the Sea Birds Society and the Small Birds Association, with the backing of the RSPCA and the British Association; but the measures were difficult to enforce and were widely flouted. In 1889 Mrs W. Williamson, of Didsbury, started a modest Society for the Protection of Birds, which soon became a national organisation, active in the propaganda and educational fields. It obtained a Royal Charter in 1904 and today is the senior bird protection body.

The Game Battue

Meanwhile, sportsmen who shot at game birds were succumbing to the lure of the 'big bag'. Until about 1840 it had been the custom to walk up birds with dogs; then came the fashion of driving game over the guns, the excuse for the practice being the growing wariness of birds deprived of much of their natural shelter. A sportsman was now measured by his coolness and discipline in a 'hot corner' at a *battue*, almost as if he were standing in a block-house picking off murderous fuzzy-wuzzies. Old-fashioned guns still walked up their game, believing that the new system was lacking in fieldcraft, as it undoubtedly was; but apologists of driving, like Sir Ralph Payne-Gallwey, scoffed at them for failing to discern any difference between 'the art required in shooting birds flying at sixty miles an hour high overhead towards the guns and the stupid simplicity of putting a charge of shot into the tail of a pheasant flapping slowly up before the gun.' Driving, he claimed, was the neatest, most skilful and most satisfactory

* Page 187.

way of killing winged game. Moreover, it gave the birds a decent chance, because an indifferent shot was unlikely to wound driven birds.* Yet notoriously, at 'hot corners', the ground would be strewn with wriggling mounds of feathers, or with limping birds trying to bolt into the undergrowth; whether these were the victims of good or indifferent marksmanship seemed beside the point. Sir Ralph thought that so-called 'tame' birds showed as good sport as wild ones, but his critics argued that it was more cruel to maim a hand-reared bird in flight than to wring its neck in a pen. Skilled marksmen were not born, as Sir Ralph admitted. His advice to the young shot was to begin on small birds, after which 'he can be permitted to fire at pigeons (with their wings slightly clipped so as not to fly too fast) from under a flower-pot or out of a trap at a distance of fifteen yards or so.'†

The rate of slaughter was intensified first by the introduction of the breech-loader and then by the double-barrel. Richard Jefferies, the naturalist, recognised the fatal attraction of the new weapons: 'Something in the *power* of the double-barrel – the overwhelming odds it offers the sportsman over bird and animal – pleases. A man feels master of the copse with a double-barrel; and such a sense of power, though only over feeble creatures, is fascinating. Besides, there is the delight of effect; for a clever left and right is sure of applause and makes the gunner feel "good" in himself. Doubtless, if three barrels could be managed three barrels would be more saleable than doubles.' In fact, a four-barrelled gun had just been put on the market. The odds, in Jefferies' view, had become unsporting. 'When we consider how helpless the partridge is . . . before the fierce blow of shot, it does seem fairer that the gunner should have but one chance at the bird . . . Great bags of partridges never seemed to me quite right.' He sighed for the old single-barrel, the use of which called for more fieldcraft.‡

Considerations like these did not enter the minds of sportsmen like the Marquess of Ripon (Earl de Grey), who kept a detailed record of the 500,256 birds and beasts destroyed by

* *Shooting* (1889) by Payne-Gallwey and others.
† *Ibid.*
‡ *The Open Air* (1885).

him between 1867 and 1913. The birds included 79,320 grouse, 112,598 partridges and 222,976 pheasants, and among the animals were 382 red deer, 30,280 hares, 34,118 rabbits, eleven tigers and two rhino. On the whole the Marquess's quarrel with Nature was worked off against the small and unaggressive creatures. At the age of seventy he still brought down more than 100 birds in a day, which was about half what a crack shot could do when conditions were favourable. The German Emperor was a man after the Marquess of Ripon's own heart. In the State forest of Rominten, during his forty-third year, he caused a block of granite to be erected proclaiming in gold letters: 'Here His Majesty King William II brought down His Most High's fifty thousandth animal, a white cock pheasant.'*

Even the best shots by no means succeeded in killing every bird. When Lord Walsingham (Thomas de Grey) in 1888 at Blubberhouses, Yorkshire, killed 1,070 grouse in 14 hours 18 minutes he fired 1,510 cartridges. It would be uncharitable to assume that such a redoubtable performer missed completely with 440 cartridges; one must suppose, therefore, that he left a great many birds maimed.

Another Lord Walsingham (John A. de Grey, a brother of the above) published a book *Hit And Miss* (1927) which contains much in this strain: 'My first partridge I killed on the 1st of September, 1863, my second on the 2nd of the same month. On the 8th I killed four and by the end of the holidays I had accounted for 13. I did rather more execution among the hares and scored no less than 38 . . .' Obviously he felt there was a public for this kind of information, and for carefully compiled tables showing how many grouse were killed at Blubberhouses in a given number of minutes in a given number of drives; and so there was. To John Ruskin this mentality was incomprehensible: 'Very earnestly I ask you, have English gentlemen, as a class, any other real object in their whole existence than killing birds?'

The author of *Hit And Miss* said: 'The wilder and fewer the birds are that we set out to pursue, and the more difficult it is to circumvent them, the better is the sport.' This was decidedly

* Emil Ludwig: *Kaiser Wilhelm II.*

not the belief of many wealthy owners of grouse moors. Their guests included rajahs, princelings and pretenders whc looked for copious game, even as they looked for champagne luncheons *en plein air*. Still less was it the view of owners of pheasant coverts, who considered that the best way to flatter important guests was to blacken the sky with birds. If royalty was expected, pheasants were sometimes imported for the occasion. King George V, whose favourite sport was shooting, grew unhappy about the scale of *battues* organised in his honour. The Duke of Windsor has told how, in 1913, Lord Burnham invited the King to Hall Barn, near Beaconsfield, for what was to be the biggest shoot in history. It cost the deaths of 4,000 pheasants and of these the royal guest accounted for more than 1,000. But the King was remorseful on the way home, saying, 'Perhaps we went a little too far today, David.'*

It is an illuminating story and prompts the ever-topical question: 'How far is a little too far?' How many birds should the King have shot to remain a true sportsman and yet please his host? Today – if any host were willing or able to put up birds on this scale – a personal bag of 1,000 would be considered grossly excessive. What, today, is the total at which a sportsman becomes a poulterer?

The Duke of Windsor described the Burnham shoot as 'carnage' and others were using words like hecatomb and holocaust. Much criticism focussed on the hand-rearing of pheasants to 'show sport'. Some humanitarians conceded that it might be necessary to shoot over moors in order to preserve game from extinction, picking off the quarrelsome old cocks who drove away the young and were incapable themselves of breeding. Others were quite willing to leave the balance of life to Nature. allowing her rather than the sportsman to ensure the survival of the fittest. They were unhappy, furthermore, about the devices used by gamekeepers to protect their masters' birds, notably the pole-trap – a mechanical trap on a small platform on top of a pole – which brought lingering death to jays, owls and various birds of prey. Poison was also part of the gamekeeper's armoury. The *Game Rearer's Annual* for 1903 contains this bare-faced advice: 'The hooded crows

* The Duke of Windsor: *A King's Story.*

are most difficult to destroy and unless poison is used (which, by the way, is illegal) they cannot be successfully coped with. Where poison is used it is generally placed in the eyes of a dead sheep, which usually proves a fatal lure to the hoodies and the carcase can be watched from a distance to avoid mishaps.'

Both the Royal Society for the Protection of Birds and the RSPCA drew support from those – politicians, judges, magistrates, landed gentry – who saw nothing incongruous in allowing themselves to be photographed, gun in hand, behind ramparts of shining corpses. The rules of the first-mentioned body said: 'The attitude of the Society is strictly neutral on the question of the killing of game birds and legitimate sport of that character' Both societies, however, strongly opposed trap pigeon-shooting.

To owners of estates, shooting was as legitimate a source of revenue as fishing or stock-breeding. Game, they said, was just another food crop. Humanitarians pointed out that farmers did not invite sportsmen from London to slaughter their cattle, killing some and maiming others. If pheasants were necessary for food, why not wring their necks like poultry? Why kill creatures the hard way? Land-owners shrugged; they needed the sportsmen's money.

Anyone who scans the sporting journals of the Victorian years may be pardoned for wondering whether, in fact, any real standards of sportsmanship existed. Wildfowlers were still competing to see who could kill most birds with one shot. A clergyman fired his big gun on Carlingford Loch and killed sixty-one curlew, 'the cripples all escaping in the darkness'; a Royal Navy captain improved on this by destroying ninety-six widgeon with one shot and 150 plover with another; a third sportsman fired a single shot in a meadow in front of his house and accounted for seventy-eight sparrows, twelve linnets, eight yellow-hammers and four finches – in all 102 birds, 'besides several fluttering away wounded.' Whatever might be said of the depredations of cockney sportsmen, they did not slay and maim quite on this scale. In the magazine *Land and Water*, where such feats were chronicled, a writer in 1895 explained some of the niceties of the game: 'The shore-shooter loves to kill a few birds neatly and well at long ranges, while the punt-gunner ever craves after a big shot. Lively cripples are amusing enough afloat but undesirable ashore as most of them escape into deep water where they cannot be followed . . .' But not all shore-shooters were neat killers. 'Shots fired into flocks sitting on smooth hard sand or flat rocks are very deadly . . . if the shore is moderately hard they get the benefit of ricocheting pellets as well as direct hits'; a good way, it would seem, of ensuring plenty of amusing cripples.

'Tournament of Doves'

By mid-Victorian times, the shooting of pigeons from traps, a sport which in the eyes of many a Corinthian had smacked too much of idle barbarity, had grown into a national institution. It was a blood sport bereft not only of risk but of fieldcraft and physical effort; a sport which could be practised before doting female eyes in rose gardens, with Guards bands playing. This, as its critics pointed out, was not a sport handed down from uncivilised ancestors, relying on tradition to maintain it; it had taken less than a century to turn the bird of innocence into a popular gambling counter. To the marksman, actuated not by blood lust but by money lust, the bird was just an object to be tumbled out of the air at twenty-five or thirty yards' range (sometimes it was blasted with shot as soon as it was technically airborne).

The most fashionable pigeon shoots were held at Hurlingham, whence mangled birds fell dying into the grounds of the Bishop of London's palace. On their last flight they sometimes dribbled blood into the laps of ladies who had come straight from matins in Belgravia. Debutantes on their first visit to Hurlingham underwent a *frisson* or two, but quickly learned to laugh at the comedy of it all; soon they found a charm in the sight of lawns drifted with snowy-pink plumage. Even if they disapproved of the sport, it was still necessary to be seen at Hurlingham.

All over London – notably at Shepherd's Bush, Battersea, Peckham, Hornsey and Wormwood Scrubs – the gun clubs crackled. In the provinces the sport was subsidised by publicans, who did not mind whether their patrons shot exhausted birds at close range with wide-bore weapons so long as they drank plenty of beer. Rearing of blue rocks for killing had grown into a minor industry, though many inferior birds were

Dying pigeons fall into laps of admiring ladies
From 'Animal World', August 1, 1871

trapped for the purpose. After the shoot the corpses were hawked through poor streets and sold for food at twopence or threepence each.

Sometimes at a 'Tournament of Doves' the birds were wounded before they took the air. Those who transferred the creatures from basket to trap would maltreat them in order to present the marksman with an easy or a difficult target, depending on how much money was at stake and what secret instructions they had received.

The RSPCA was often attacked for failing to take action against the organisers of pigeon shoots, while pursuing villainies in rat-pits, but as the *Animal World* plaintively pointed out: 'What chances are there that Lords and Commons who actually compete in these very sanguinary contentions will pass a measure to suppress them?' There were demands that the Society should renounce all its patrons who shot at Hurlingham and if necessary form itself afresh. Some of those who accused the Society of sycophancy towards the *haut ton* were actuated more by class prejudice than by humane feelings, ignoring the feats of the 'knights of the reeking tube' at country taverns. Occasionally the RSPCA was able to bring prosecutions for the ill-treatment of pigeons before release from the trap, but evidence was hard to obtain. Inspectors, when recognised, were ordered away from pigeon grounds.

Very few newspapers were willing to defend trap pigeon shooting; oddly, some of those which condemned it most severely carried conscientious reports of matches. Women who attended the sport were accused of being a disgrace to their sex and likened to the hags who sat beside the guillotine. The *Daily News* in 1871 had a withering account of the Parliamentary match at Hurlingham, when the Commons defeated the Lords by seventy-one birds to sixty, eighty-nine birds being missed or mangled.

'The great match between Lords and Commons was shot for and twenty-two noblemen and gentlemen pitted themselves and their weapons against 220 pigeons. The noblemen and gentlemen won . . . Let it be understood that Hurlingham is above all things fastidiously select. The future King of England was among the knights who played a part in the tournament of flight. His brother the sailor prince, brown with Eastern travel and fresh from hunting fields wherein the monarchs of the forest are the game and where the element of adventure gives a dash of adventure to manly sport, did not disdain to slaughter the Fulham doves.'

There were 'huge hampers full of birds – some living, others dead,' said the *Daily News* reporter. Throughout the afternoon the number of pigeons not hit could be counted on one hand, which was due as much to their tameness as to the excellence of the shooting. In fact, the birds were altogether too languid: 'India-rubber balls lie by the scorer's seat and when neither the sudden clatter of the trap falling down nor the startling change from darkness to sunlight, nor the hoots and cries and hat-waving of the distinguished company, tempt the poor wretch to rise these balls are thrown at it by one or other of the gentlemen present.' One young nobleman 'from sheer love of the thing' had taken up his position beside the rubber balls 'and made them his department,' pelting those birds which 'either confidently or dazedly' began to walk towards their tormentors. Meanwhile the marksman would wait, weapon at shoulder, until a suitable amount of flutter entitled him to fire. The birds were picked up afterwards by a black retriever 'running on three legs as if he had been peppered by mistake.'

The opinion of *The Times*, as voiced on the same occasion, was that 'potting' at pigeons ranked below even the humblest field sport. 'To walk out of the luxurious club rooms into an enclosed lawn with awnings and covered sheds, to enjoy the strains of operatic music till one's name is called from a printed list, to receive one's gun ready loaded from a servant, to choose one's own time for giving the signal to "let go" and at last to kill or maim a bird half dazed by its sudden release is assuredly the stupidest, tamest, lowest form assumed by the venatorial art since the age of Nimrod . . .' Cruelty did not lose half its evil by losing all its grossness, said *The Times*. But there was another serious aspect: the alleged degeneracy of the upper class under the influence of wealth and luxury was a familiar theme, 'not with foreign critics only, but with domestic agitators.' Therefore the privileged class should set an example of earnest purpose and simplicity of life, instead of weakening their order and dishonouring the national character.

The *Echo* saw the danger in starker terms: 'We must have kingly kings, and noble noblemen and gentle gentlemen, or revolution will come upon us. Hitherto, with all their faults and follies, there has been enough salt in this, the *soi-disant* salt of the earth, to preserve them.' In the *Echo*'s view, the meetings at Hurlingham gave more encouragement to republicanism than all the meetings in Hyde Park or Trafalgar Square. On the theme of Parliamentary marksmen the *Christian World* said: 'The constituents of these gentlemen are gravely to blame. They ought to have known that incurable levity and frivolity incapacitate men from taking part in the government of a great nation and a mighty Empire and we cannot believe that the qualities of these pigeon-killers did not reveal themselves before they became Members of the House of Commons.' As for the peers, said this Christian organ, they were too imbecile to reflect on the evil they did to their order. Other papers took a similar line, as if to emphasise what ludicrous results can be achieved when political passions engulf simple humanitarian instincts.

The kindest comment on the Prince of Wales's performance at Hurlingham was that his wretched marksmanship showed he had not wasted his youth on this sport. In 1873, under the influence of Princess Alexandra, he let it be known that he had withdrawn his patronage of all gun clubs (in later life he supported many humanitarian measures).

So bad a press did pigeon-shooting attract in the early 'seventies that leading clubs proposed to withhold information from the newspapers; this move, however, was unpopular with their own members. Sportsmen who liked to see their feats civilly described could always turn to the *Field* or the *Morning Post*, which would tell how the Marquess of So-and-So 'stopped a three-quarter bird in good style' or 'waited very judiciously on a curving bird and scored very prettily.' The humbler fixtures were amply covered by *Bell's Life In London*, which also contained notifications of coming events ('The Editor of *Bell's Life* will be the stake-holder'). Many events were shot for 'a fine fat pig', others for 'a fat bullock', and sometimes there was the inducement 'Landlord will provide a cold collation.' From these pages it is clear that not only pigeons, but sparrows, starlings and even linnets were shot from traps. The advertising columns had announcements like this:

'NOTICE. As W. Barber, 27 Sclater Street, Bethnal Green has a large quantity of pigeons on hand, noblemen and gentlemen can have from 100 to 200 dozen of the best blue rocks on the shortest notice. Publicans for the Christmas holidays can be supplied with good flying pigeons at 12s per dozen, with traps. W. Barber can attend any ground in London at the shortest notice.'

Of one rural shoot, this newspaper said: 'The birds were supplied by a local dealer and unfortunately were of the very worst description, every kind of missile being called into requisition to get them off the traps after the string was pulled.'

Bell's Life liked to be able to report that 'everything passed off in a sportsmanlike manner,' but it was ready with censure when required. It protested at the 'extremely unsportsmanlike' behaviour of half-a-dozen armed spectators at Battersea Gun Club who shot at escaping birds before they had reached the boundary. This 'tended to destroy the harmony of the afternoon's meeting.'

In 1872 the RSPCA addressed a memorial to the Government urging it to discourage, if not prohibit, pigeon-shooting, and pointing out its inability to prosecute under existing statutes; but the Government preferred to leave the initiative to individuals. In 1883 a Glasgow Member, G. Anderson, moved his second Bill to suppress the sport, reminding the House that on the first occasion when he had recited the barbarities of pigeon-shooting a sporting Member had asked for a count, after which several of those present, including Ministers, walked out rather than listen to a 'fanatical Scotchman'. He said that blue rocks were being exterminated and household pigeons used instead, though they were still described as blue rocks. Among the trappers' tricks he listed were the wrenching out of tail feathers, touching the raw flesh with pepper or turpentine, and sticking pins in the birds' rumps. If persons objected to the removal of feathers the trapper could quietly twist the rump or squeeze the bird in such a way that it could barely fly. If he wanted a bird to veer to the right he would destroy its left eye with a pin or his finger nail. If he wished to confuse the bird completely, he would put out both eyes, or thrust the upper mandible through the soft lower one. Anderson was able to quote from a Derbyshire newspaper a report of a prosecution by the RSPCA of two men who had committed three of the malpractices he named; each had been jailed for two months with hard labour. He made it clear, however, that he opposed the sport as such, and not merely because of its attendant cruelties.

Many Members, while despising pigeon-shooting and the riff-raff it drew, opposed the Bill on the grounds that it constituted the first nail in the coffin of field sports, for the gulf between firing at tame pigeons and hand-reared pheasants was not all that wide. Sir Herbert Maxwell said that but for pigeon-shooting blue rocks would never be hatched at all. He asked Anderson 'whether, if he were a blue rock, he would accept existence under the conditions of his life being a short and happy one and violently terminated, or whether he would reject life at all upon such terms?' The country was full of sickly sentimentalists, Sir Herbert thought; they would not be content until young men proceeded forth only on the bloodless bicycle and instead of training race-horses confined their attentions to such innocent amusements as the cultivation of cucumbers. Echoing this, Colonel E. R. King-Harman described the Bill as 'a precursor of legislation under which fishermen would be imprisoned, butchers would be hung and we should all be ridden over by rampant vegetarians.'

A vigorous contribution came from Lord Randolph Churchill, who had been shocked by pigeon-shooting as practised at Monte Carlo, whither it had been imported by the English (and whither Lincolnshire blue rocks were dispatched by a London dealer). In that brilliant setting he thought the sport was 'without exception the most horrible and repulsive sight possible to imagine.' He had seen a dog run to catch a wounded bird which hovered above it. 'While the bird's fate was thus trembling in the balance the betting was fast and furious and when at last the pigeon tumbled into the dog's jaws, he never would forget the shout of triumph and yell of execration that rose from the ring men and gentlemen. Hundreds, perhaps thousands of pounds, changed hands over the dying agonies of the unfortunate creature.' A Member reminded Lord Randolph that he himself was reputed a good shot at a game *battue* and had often covered himself with glory.

The Bill received a majority in the Commons of 155 votes, but the Lords threw it out by 30 votes to 17. Lord Denham thought that pigeon-shooting was less cruel than grouse-shooting. The Earl of Wemyss said that if he were given the option of being shot by Earl de Grey or having his neck twisted by Lord Balfour he would prefer to be shot. Lord Westbury did not want to interfere with a valuable industry. Had not the gunsmiths petitioned against the Bill, pointing out that nearly all the improvements in guns over the last twenty years had been made on behalf of pigeon-shooters? Had not the sport led to the widespread use of smokeless powder? And Earl Fortescue objected to the House discussing a Bill to protect pigeons when it could not find time for a Bill to protect young girls.

When Lord Balfour moved a similar Bill the following year the Earl of Redesdale protested that 'there was nothing objectionable in a man showing his skill in the use of a gun or any other instrument, and the shooting at a bird with intent to kill it was necessary to test skill in the use of a fowling piece, as was shooting at a target with a rifle or long-bow.' The Earl of Galloway informed the House that Lord Balfour, the mover, had been one of six guns who in six days killed 8,358 head of game; the measure 'came very ill' from such a quarter. This Bill, too, was lost.

It is worth noting that pigeon-shooters were not drawn exclusively from bored aristocratic amateurs at one extreme and dissolute artisans at the other. The author of *The Life of a Country Lawyer*, Tilney Barton, says that in the 'eighties he was articled to a legal firm at Frome. One of the partners was an excellent game shot who kept his hand in by shooting pigeons, and when there were no pigeons, starlings. One of Barton's 'duties' was to catch starlings in clap nets in the Longleat woods 'for Mr Percy and his friends to shoot.'

By that time various types of artificial pigeon had been invented. One was a 'gyro-pigeon', made of metal, launched at high speed and very hard to hit. After each shoot it was covered with whiting or black lead so that shots could be recorded. The catapulted, gyrating clay pigeon, a saucer made of terra cotta, had also appeared by the 'eighties. Another device which found its way on to the market was a glass sphere containing feathers, which spilled down when hit; unfortunately, perhaps, it did not contain blood. None of these devices was liked, a common objection being that they gradually decelerated in flight, whereas birds accelerated.

Both as Princess and as Consort, Queen Alexandra used all the influence she could against pigeon-shooting, and Hurlingham stopped the sport in 1906. Elsewhere the fashion continued little abated until 1914. It was not legislated out of British life until 1921.*

'Murderous Millinery'

One of the minor Victorian figures of fun was the lady with an aigrette in her hat singing, in church: 'O all ye fowls of the air, bless ye the Lord, praise Him and magnify Him for ever.'

This aigrette, which the trade called an 'osprey' for the sake of confusion, came either from the heron's crest or from the back of the egret in the mating season. The egret was the principal sufferer; to secure its nuptial ornament the creature had to be shot, almost always when it still had dependent young. Thus each slender plume signified the death, not of one bird, but of a family. And because the plumes had a short life, one Society woman in ten years could account for a small colony of egrets.

The aigrette traffic was only part of a barbaric industry which, by late Victorian times, was ravaging the wild life of five continents. It involved a new point of ethics. Beasts were provided by Providence to supply man with food, clothing, transport and, as some said, sport; but did God intend wild creatures to be massacred in the cause of fashion? Was man entitled to seek out and slay the most beautiful creatures he could find in order to turn his women into more beautiful creatures? Was it not as wanton to kill a thousand egrets for their plumes as to kill a thousand nightingales for their tongues?

To logical humanitarians, it seemed impossible that any woman with normal maternal instincts could wish to wear an ornament obtainable only by slaughter of mother birds and starvation of their broods. To logical economists, it was grotesque that women should choose to spread death along

* *See* page 299.

the Orinoco and through the forests of India when the ribbon and lace industries of Britain badly needed their support. Yet very few women of fashion had the courage to forego this fascinating plume, which some of them prized as their own nuptial ornament; and very few men had the courage, or the desire, to forbid their wives to follow high fashion. Sometimes, in a pretence of easing her conscience, a woman would consult her milliner, who was usually able to allay any qualms: the plumes were moulted in the ordinary way; they were obtained from sea or game birds only; they were secured by a painless process; they were cleverly made from goose feathers. But the milliners lied.

The first major controversy on this theme arose, not from the slaughter of tropical birds, but from the devastation of sea birds on Britain's own shores. In the 1860s gulls were being shot, not only for their feathers, but out of mere wantonness by week-end sportsmen. Suddenly, to the voice of the humanitarian was added the voice of the mariner. Sailors and fishermen approaching the North-East coast of England in bad weather had been accustomed to rely on the cries of gulls as an indication that land was near; and evidence was produced to show that with the decrease in the number of birds more ships were running ashore on Flamborough Head, where gulls were traditionally known as 'Flamborough Pilots'. For this reason Trinity House called for action to protect sea birds. Fishermen also relied on the sight of gulls hovering over the water to lead them to shoals; and on these grounds an Act had already been passed in the Isle of Man to penalise the killing of gulls. Farmers also protested. In the East Riding they had been accustomed to see flocks of sea birds twenty miles inland following the plough and picking up grubs, but in 1868 a farmer at Filey protested that he had not seen a bird all summer on his farm, a mile from the sea. Heavy destruction of birds went on also in Norfolk, Pembrokeshire, Devon and Cornwall; but not in Scotland.

The Government showed no sign of wishing to follow the Manx example; but in 1869 Christopher Sykes, Member for the East Riding, persuaded Parliament, not without difficulty, to agree to the then novel idea of protecting certain birds in the breeding season. Since the House did not like to create precedents, he was able to show that an Act had been passed for a comparable purpose in the reign of Henry VIII.* The Sea Bird Protection Act of 1869, its terms publicised by notices posted all round the coasts, silenced the guns during the nesting season; but it did nothing to slacken the clamour for sea birds' feathers, more especially for the barred wings of young kitti-wakes. From Clovelly, where traders kept a staff for preparing plumes, boats would set out for Lundy Island as soon as the breeding season ended on August 1 and shoot down old and young birds indiscriminately at the rate of many hundreds a day. Often wings were torn off before the creatures were dead and the mangled remains were thrown in the sea, tingeing it pink. In similar fashion the Flamborough Pilots were butchered as the August dawn came up.

In the 1890s, despite two decades of criticism, the lust for feathers redoubled itself. From the humming-bird to the ostrich no bird, not even the sparrow, was safe from the milliner. Newspapers announced that 'wings will be all the rage,' so wings were furnished as required. Newspapers said that whole birds would be worn on the head, so whole birds were worn. The most notorious dress of the period was one trimmed with the plumage of eight hundred canaries; it seems to have had a mixed reception when first worn in London. Humming-bird skins were even used to make pincushion Valentines. Sometimes the heads were retained, so that love missives might be inserted in the beaks.

In the Everglades of Florida islets stank with mounds of mutilated egrets and white herons; so did the shores of the great rivers of Central and South America. The beaches of Easter Island had waist-high heaps of albatrosses. Killing fine birds in fever swamps and miasmic lagoons was an occupation which cost many a human life, but it also brought profits of up to £100 a day; so, whenever a hunter fell, another took his place. In more salubrious climes, as at Cape Cod, terns went down by the hundred thousand. In India the demand for feathers was such that men sold their oxen and ploughs in order to buy guns. The Government of India passed restrictive

* It protected the eggs of certain birds, but not the birds themselves.

laws, the effect of which was that feathers were exported as horsehair or cow-hair. Fortunately, the ostrich could be deprived of its plumes without undue pain; so, from the 1870s onwards, ostrich farming became an important industry in North and South Africa, Australia and elsewhere.

At busy periods, the dealers of London and Paris nearly suffocated under their shimmering wares. The *Field* reported in 1890 that a London dealer received in a single consignment 32,000 dead humming-birds, 80,000 aquatic birds and 800,000 miscellaneous pairs of wings. W. H. Hudson, the naturalist, described in a pamphlet a 'purple day' at the Commercial Sale Rooms in the City of London. There was a consignment of 125,000 Indian parrots which would have covered a large portion of Trafalgar Square with 'a gay, grass-green carpet, flecked with vivid purple, rose and scarlet.' Hudson cited Herbert Spencer as saying that, in aesthetic matters, women stood half-way between civilised man and the pure savage.* Another pamphleteer, the Rev. H. C. Ricketts, quoted the American Council of Ornithology: 'England alone imports twenty-five million slaughtered birds a year; Europe as a whole takes 300 million and all are made into articles of personal adornment. A single London dealer receives annually 400,000 humming-birds . . .'

Even domestic servants were able to deck themselves out in kingfisher, trogan, oriole and bird of paradise plumes. Alternatively they could wear sparrows' wings dyed yellow, blue and red. An advertisement said: 'Starlings' wings wanted, free from moth and in good condition, sixpence per dozen pairs, any quantity up to 500 pairs.'

Probably no newspaper campaigned more strongly against the plumage traffic than *The Times*. It accused women of 'wholesale, wanton and hideous cruelty,' of dishonouring their sex, of robbing Nature of her beauty without adding to their own (W. H. Hudson wrote on the incongruity of nuptial plumes on the heads of 'corpse-like' women in bath chairs in Hyde Park); it reminded them of Professor Alfred Newton's view that feathers on the outside of a biped called for the

---

'Osprey', or Egrets and Aigrettes (1894). Published by Royal Society for the Protection of Birds.

addition of tar; and pointed out that fashion, if it wished, could order that not a single feather should be worn. Other newspapers condemned cruelty on one page but announced 'wings will be worn' on another.

The clergy were much criticised for failing to denounce the rage for plumes. In the long ago, they had abused women for wearing silk, lace, ribbons and a hundred other gauds; why could they not condemn feathers? To be fair, many of them did. But for a fashionable clergyman to go into the pulpit and berate a congregation of women with birds in their hats required the fortitude of a John Knox. So familiar was the sight of feathers in church that a parson could recite the verse about God's concern for the sparrow without any sensation of hypocrisy.

It was a common belief of the Victorians that abuses could be rhymed away, as is shown by the spate of verse directed against drinking and smoking. The plight of birds slain for plumage inspired a great many emulators, amateur and professional. Florence Suckling in her *Humane Educator* cites these verses from 'Anon', who describes a woman lecturing a man for shooting grouse:

> She quoted Burns's 'Wounded Hare',
>   And certain stirring lines of Blake's,
> And Ruskin on the fowls of air,
>   And Coleridge on the water snakes.
> At Emerson's 'Forbearance' he
>   Began to feel his will benumbed,
> At Browning's 'Donald' utterly
>   His soul surrendered and succumbed.
>
> She smiled to find her point was gained,
>   And went with happy parting words
> (He subsequently ascertained)
>   To trim her hat with humming-birds.

Ella Wheeler Wilcox had a poem which told how a woman was dissuaded, by a member of an Audubon Society, from buying a hat with a bird's wing; after which the Audubon representative went virtuously home and served birds at dinner to her guests.

Women laughed at themselves, and often they felt ashamed, but they were in the grip of the same force which, more recently, has impelled them to cause millions of pounds worth of damage to other people's floors with spiked heels. If they forfeited the right to upbraid their husbands for taking part in pheasant *battues*, they also forfeited the right to lecture their sons for bird-nesting. As Florence Suckling said: 'Why should boys be ashamed of killing what their mothers wear?'

Women could always point out that officers of the Horse Artillery, the King's Royal Rifles and the Rifle Brigade, among others, wore egret feathers in their headgear. Yet nobody accused field officers of looking like salmon-flies or Hottentots. In 1898 Sir John Lubbock, president of the Selborne Society, asked the Secretary for War if he would stop the wearing of 'osprey' plumes in the Army. Mr St J. Brodrick replied that his department was trying to compose regimental plumes from other types of feather, and these efforts were eventually successful. The Viceroy's bodyguard in India abandoned plumed hats in favour of turbans.

The Court did not allow itself to be stampeded by sentiment. Princess Alexandra opposed the 'osprey', as she opposed pigeon-shooting and the bearing rein, but Drawing Rooms still danced with plumes. Professor Alfred Newton, of Magdalene College, Cambridge, one of the early propagandists against 'murderous millinery', suggested in *The Times* of February 25, 1899: 'Two little words to the proper official from the highest Personage in the land to the effect that after a certain day "no plumes" would be admissible at Court . . . and the whole aspect of the matter would be changed.'

Among the bodies which strove to limit the plumage traffic were the Royal Society for the Protection of Birds, the RSPCA, the Humanitarian League and the Selborne Society. Many distinguished writers and artists lent their aid. G. F. Watts, the Royal Academician, painted a shuddering angel standing, hands over eyes, at an altar covered with birds' wings. The plumage trade dismissed all protests as humbugging sentimentalism; the effect of legislation, they said, would be to drive the British plumage houses to Paris, and not a bird's life would be saved (Europe had independent supplies).

They denied that birds were shot off their nests or that wings were hacked off alive; they said that nuptial plumes were shed naturally, apparently into the grateful hands of dealers. For the sake of quiet, the dealers of Mincing Lane withdrew all detailed plumage advertisements and took care that no catalogues fell into strangers' hands. For an effective Act of Parliament Britain had to wait until 1921.

In America it was the Audubon Societies, named after John James Audubon, the naturalist and conservationist, which from the 'eighties onwards took the initiative against tuft-hunters; backed by Theodore Roosevelt, they also worked for the establishment of a chain of bird reservations. By 1910 three egret wardens in North America had been murdered by plumage traders.

It was odd that the parade of exotic feathers roused far more indignation than the wearing of furs from cruelly trapped animals. Furs, perhaps, were regarded as essential clothing.

Larks, Dead or Alive

On balance, it may be that the netter was a bigger menace to wild bird life than the sportsman. At migration times, as birds gathered on the South Coast, catchers by the score laid out clap nets and planted decoys. Among the latter was the braced bird, a hardy, stout-singing cock trussed by a wire which ran round the roots of the wings near the shoulder blades and under the body. To this harness was attached a string which allowed the bird to soar a limited distance. At dawn the catcher on the cliffs would wait until he saw a flight of birds – linnets, perhaps, or goldfinches – headed for France. He would then whistle, sometimes with the aid of a mouth instrument and his decoys would pipe up in reply. At the sound the leader of the flock would turn back, which was the signal to free the braced bird for a few seconds, and then haul it down again. As the flock alighted to investigate the catcher would pull the string which caused the vertical clap nets to collapse. All he had to do then was to sort cocks from hens. The cocks found their way into tiny cages in Whitechapel and Seven Dials, more than half of them usually dying in the first fortnight. The hens were killed and plucked for food if the catcher had nothing better to do. At one time a boy could trap forty dozen goldfinches in a morning on the Downs between Kemp Town and Rottingdean, but by the late Victorian years this age of plenty had passed.

There were various other methods of catching, from individual nooses and springes to birdlime. The ever-knowledgeable Mrs Beeton describes liming techniques in her *Book of Household Management*. At sunrise and sunset, she says, the catcher hiding in his cabin beside a limed tree imitates the sounds of the birds he wishes to attract. Alternatively he gives an owl's call and the birds flock together in fear of their common enemy; 'when, at every instant, they will be seen falling to the ground, their wings being of no use to them from their having come into contact with the quicklime. The cries of those which are thus situated now attract others and thus are large numbers taken in a short space of time.' Owls in turn are caught, says Mrs Beeton, by counterfeiting the squeak of a mouse.

Another way of using birdlime is described in Dr J. M. Bechstein's *Chamber Birds* (1892). The catcher, having noted a chaffinch with a good song, ties the wings of another male chaffinch together and places upon the tail a very thin forked twig, half a finger long, well limed. Almost as soon as the decoy has uttered its *fink fink* the other bird, incited by jealousy, pounces fiercely and becomes stuck.

Larks were caught both for caging and for consumption. Food larks arrived in the cities in sacks, by the thousand, to be sold by the bushel. They had long been a fashionable article of diet. On a famous occasion during the Civil War the garrison of Exeter, besieged by the Parliamentarians, had been spared starvation through the visitation of 'an incredible number of larks . . . like quails in the wilderness.' The Rev. W. B. Daniel says that in 1801 a flock of larks three-quarters of a mile in breadth and more than double in length, so crowded as to constitute an enormous curtain, passed over the western coast of Kent towards France.'*

Larks were easily taken, in a variety of ways; by dragging nets over stubble at night, decoying them into clap nets,

* *Rural Sports.*

The nest seller

From Henry Mayhew's 'London Labour and the London Poor'

setting individual nooses or twirling a piece of wood stuck with mirrors (the Italians used to manufacture elaborate silver 'mobiles' to whet the fatal curiosity of larks). Favourite hunting grounds were Dunstable and the South Downs. In 1854 it was estimated that 400,000 larks were sent annually to the London market, sometimes in consignments of 20,000 or 30,000. But Europe's appetite for Shelley's bird was even more voracious. In the winter of 1867–8, 1,255,000 larks were received at Dieppe; and Leipzig, where larks had the reputation of being fattest, took 5,184,000 a year.* Gourmets praised larks in print, but did not recommend them as a main dish. The much-quoted *Almanach des Gourmands* which was published at the start of the nineteenth century said 'the best robins and the fattest larks are hardly, in the hands of a man with a good appetite, more than a little bundle of toothpicks'; for that reason, they were best eaten *after* a meal. The author of the *Epicure's Year Book* (1869) said 'a little pyramid of larks is delightful' and he also recommended, in September, thrushes caught tipsy on the vines – 'their orgies on the grape give them a fine flavour.' Some readers objected to his advocacy of robins as a January dish, but larks were regarded as legitimate fare. In the 'nineties London was glutted with them. They hung in wreaths outside poulterers, and were recommended for club dinners. Window notices would say 'Special order: 10,000 larks, one-and-sixpence a dozen.'

Nightingales were among the easiest birds to trap but among the hardest to keep alive. It was calculated that nine-tenths of them died early in captivity. Tits, being also short-lived, were sold at a shilling a pair. Goldfinches, netted in enormous numbers in the southern counties, bore captivity better than most and their docility meant that they could be taught tricks with a minimum of cruelty. For centuries, according to William Yarrell, this bird had been selected to perform unnatural feats. He told of a Sieur Roman who exhibited performing birds at, roughly, the beginning of the nineteenth century. Of his artistes, one shammed dead, allowing itself to be held up by tail or claw without showing signs of life; a second stood on its head with its claws in the air; a third imitated a milkmaid

* William Yarrell: *A History Of British Birds* (1871).

with pails across its shoulders; a fourth went through the motions of a Venetian girl looking from a window; a fifth strutted as a soldier and mounted guard; a sixth, as cannoneer, discharged a small cannon, carrying a match in its claw, then pretended to be dead and was wheeled away in a barrow; a seventh turned a windmill; and an eighth stood unafraid among fireworks. Many older readers may recall having seen travelling displays of this kind.

Boys were not less active than men in the catching of birds. Yet, in their fashion, many youthful catchers showed affection

Bird catchers with clap nets
From Yarrell's 'History of British Birds'

for their captives. As Henry Mayhew points out in his *London Labour and the London Poor*, lads took to this occupation, not from any motive of cruelty, but because it had a certain charm and offered independence. Assuredly, it was no calling for the idle and the loutish. The boy had to rise long before dawn and walk at least seven miles to escape from bricks and mortar, and then after a day in the fields trudge back with his captives. Some remained catchers all their lives. Mayhew mentions 'Old Gilham', sixty years in the trade, who averaged one hundred birds a week, or 312,000 in his lifetime; and as his life lengthened he had to walk farther and farther each day, thanks to the outward spread of the city. Mayhew had a theory that work-people who kept birds in cages were regenerated, humanised and even refined thereby. Thrushes and linnets sang to the clatter of the Spitalfields weavers' looms. 'I have seen and heard birds in the rooms of tailors, shoemakers, coopers, cabinet-makers, hatters, dressmakers, curriers and street sellers – all people of the best class,' he writes. This fashion generally went with a superior taste and intelligence. It was otherwise with those work-people – slaughterers, drovers and cabmen – who kept dogs, generally of the 'varmint' kind, which exercised no gentle influence on their characters. As for the rich, Mayhew thought that many of them remained mere savages in their tastes and sports.

Sparrows were sold in the London streets, at a penny or a halfpenny, as playthings for children, who tied string to their legs and flew like kites. Often the kites escaped. Starlings were sold braced and were flown from sticks. There was a trade in birds' nests complete with eggs, the usual charge being a halfpenny an egg. Linnets' eggs were sold for canaries to sit on, but most nests were bought to put in glass cases. A vendor of nests told Mayhew that the parent birds often fluttered after him in protest; his inclination would have been to leave the nests alone, but he had a living to make. Some of the catchers brought back frogs from the ponds of Highgate and Hampstead for London's French colony, also buckets of snails. There was a popular superstition that live young frogs swallowed whole were 'very good things to clear up the inside.' Other creatures carried to town were leverets, bought by the well-to-do as garden pets for their children, but usually doomed to be destroyed by dogs or cats; and nests of young squirrels.

A sly race of bird 'duffers' were not satisfied with Nature as they found it. They doped song birds with hemp seed to make them more lively, which meant that the creatures died prematurely. They painted linnets yellow to look like canaries or studied the markings of tropical birds in the naturalists' windows and coloured their victims accordingly. They also applied varnish to parrots, which were brought to London in hundreds by sailors.

The stoutest-hearted linnets and finches were pitted against each other in singing matches. Their owners carried them to taverns in carelessly handled cages covered with handkerchieves. When the signal was given the bird was hung against the wall and a judge with a watch marked down the number of perfect notes uttered by each bird in a period of fifteen minutes. These contests were often advertised in *Bell's Life* – 'a leg of mutton to be sung for by linnets,' 'birds on the nail at six o'clock.' Although called upon to perform in an atmosphere which one witness described as 'foul enough to poison a well sinker', the birds usually behaved in the manner expected of them.

Other birds of unusual talent or tractability found their way into the form of exhibition known as the 'Happy Family', in which creatures whose natural instinct was to harry or devour each other all shared a common cage and lived on terms of apparent amity – bird, mouse, rat, rabbit, cat, dog and occasionally a monkey all together. The 'Happy Family' was either a mercenary outrage against Nature or a shining example of man's power to ennoble the beasts, according to viewpoint.

Dealers in birds put them into cages sometimes little larger than a cigar-box, the excuse being that this prevented them dashing themselves about in the early stages of captivity. This was also a reason for keeping them in darkness. Bechstein describes a method of training a newly taken bird by drugging it with oil of bergamot smeared near its nostrils; semi-conscious, it would consent to jump from finger to finger without attempting to fly away. Song-birds faced two forms of mutilation to improve their singing; the splitting of their tongues, sometimes on the edge of a sixpence; and blinding, with red-hot needles. In many quarters it has been vigorously denied that blinding of song-birds was ever carried out, all such tales being described as the inventions of 'shuddermongers'. Yet *Animal World*, opened almost at random, in July 1873 reports that a man was sent to prison for a fortnight in a London police court for 'sighting' a number of chaffinches with a red-hot needle; and A. W. Moss's history of the RSPCA* says that many convictions were obtained for this offence even in the present century.

* *Valiant Crusade.*

Dealers admitted that a very high percentage of birds died on their hands, but the excuse was 'I must have something to put in the window.' Their advertisements were more brisk than sentimental: 'Any quantity of jackdaws for sale! Jackdaws for pets! Jackdaws for shooting!' The least valuable birds – those which were sold in paper bags to children for a halfpenny – tended to be half-starved, since it was uneconomic to waste seed on them.

Because catchers worked in areas where they were unknown, and gave false names when detected, prosecutions for offences committed in the close season were not easy to bring. Dealers asked no questions of their suppliers. In 1873 they issued a helpful poster which said: 'Birds That May Be Caught According To Act Of Parliament: Blackbird, Thrush, Yellowhammer, Sparrow, Skylark, Linnet, Greenbird, Chaffinch, Titlark, Bullfinch, Water Ousel, Bubble and Squeak.'

15

UNDER THE KNIFE

IN the 1870s, opposition to vivisection became, for the first time, a crusade. Painfully, indignantly, the heirs of Harvey and Hunter became aware that they had powerful enemies on all sides: on the Throne, in Parliament, in sees and pulpits, in university chairs, in the republic of letters, in the press, in the shrill ranks of the New Women, and not least but most embarrassingly, in the forces of medicine. Instead of being thanked for wresting the secrets of Nature, they found themselves accused of dilettante savagery and atheism.

At this period, before bacteriology arrived to turn laboratories into menageries, experiments on animals fell into three main categories: those conducted by physiologists in pursuit of knowledge; those undertaken by pathologists fighting disease; and those performed for demonstration purposes to students.

Subjects for vivisection were usually acquired surreptitiously. At hospitals consignments of dogs and cats were received with a nod and a wink, as human corpses used to be accepted from the resurrectionists. Occasionally, hospitals advertised in the press for strays, or 'useless dogs, any breed.' It was not unknown for medical students to trap domestic animals and experiment on them with knives and poisons in their lodgings.

From its inception the RSPCA was against unrestricted vivisection, especially experiments performed to gratify an 'unprofitable curiosity'. But its members held as many views on the subject as they did on hunting and a long time elapsed before the Society began to press for legal restrictions. Lewis Gompertz was utterly opposed to vivisection unless it was for the animal's own good. The sight of 'philosophical butchers' cutting up dogs which had just licked their hands seemed to him 'morally criminal and sacrilegious in the highest degree.'* He believed that groping for truth with a knife was no different, morally, from groping for truth with rack and thumbscrews; either way, the information secured was apt to be unreliable.

Indignation against vivisectionists was fanned by reports from France of the singularly ruthless experiments conducted by the physiologists Francois Magendie (whom Richard Martin attacked in Parliament) and Claude Bernard. 'When I experiment, I have only eyes and ears; I have no brain,' Magendie used to say, not bothering to add that he had no heart. One of his feats was to dissect out the stomach of a living dog, replace it with a pig's bladder containing food, and then study the effects of emetics. In his investigations into animal heat, he inserted long thermometers by two separate routes into the heart of a living horse; and all this before the days of anaesthetics (which came in about mid-century).† Assisting him in his experiments on old war horses was young Claude Bernard, who in due time qualified for the first national funeral given by France to a man of science. Bernard's philosophy was that of his master; 'A physiologist is no ordinary man. He is a learned man, a man possessed and absorbed by a scientific idea. He does not hear the animal's cry of pain. He is blind to the blood that flows. He sees nothing but his idea.' Bernard's biographer, Professor J. M. D. Olsted, thinks it 'not unlikely' that the sights and sounds experienced by Bernard in the veterinary schools where Magendie worked led to the 'matter-of-fact attitude towards vivisection which later characterised him.' In a poetic moment Bernard described the 'science of life' as a superb salon resplendent with light which could be attained only by way of a long and ghastly kitchen. His wife was unable to support a matter-of-fact attitude towards his work, especially when it made her own kitchen ghastly with mutilated dogs wandering in and out. She and her daughters sought to offset some of his cruelties by opening an asylum for stray dogs and cats.

From about 1860 the English newspapers began to publish

---

* *Fragments in Defence of Animals.*
† J. M. D. Olsted: *Claude Bernard.*

chilling reports of experiments conducted in the veterinary
school at Alfort, Paris, where students gained in the bowels of
live horses that manipulative skill which in England was

The amputation: a study in dog-mangling by John Leech

obtained by dissecting corpses. The RSPCA was sufficiently
shocked by these accounts to send a deputation to the French
Emperor, who promised to investigate. British veterinary
surgeons also signed a mass protest. On August 8, 1863 the

Paris correspondent of *The Times* reported: 'At the veterinary college at Alfort a wretched horse is periodically given up to a group of students to experimentalise upon. They tie him down and torture him for hours, the operations being graduated in such a manner . . . that sixty and even more may be performed before death ensues.' Sometimes an eyeless, hoofless, eviscerated beast was shot if the experiments had not already killed it; at other times the students wandered off when their curiosity was satisfied and left their victim to the knacker. Earlier protests by French physicians, anatomists and animal societies had wrought some slight improvement, reported *The Times* correspondent; at Lyons the removal of the hoof was practised only once by each student. This was perhaps the most futile of the sixty experiments, since no owner would ever require his horse to undergo such an operation. Much of the Paris press shared the indignation of *The Times*, but a motion in the French Academy urging that dead horses should be substituted for live was negatived.

Among those who felt revulsion at the reports from France was Miss Frances Power Cobbe, writer and social worker, who came from an Anglo-Irish family with five archbishops to its credit. A woman 'of ample proportions, with an open and genial countenance,' she had turned forty before she began her campaign for animals (in 1862 she had been ridiculed for advocating university degrees for women). She was to become the most redoubtable anti-vivisectionist of the nineteenth century and was well hated by the ranks of orthodox medicine. Although accused of being ready to sacrifice any number of men, women and children to save a few rabbits from inconvenience, she was far from being the type of woman who would leave a legacy to a parrot. She thought the lady of fashion who handed over her child to servants while she lavished her affection on a spaniel was 'about as odious a specimen of humanity as might easily be found.'*

Miss Cobbe's first brush with vivisectors was in 1863 in Florence, where the experiments of Professor V. M. Schiff were annoying his neighbours. She framed a memorial of protest on the spot. The Professor told in his *Leçons sur la*

---

* Frances Power Cobbe, *Fraser's*, November, 1863.

Physiologie de la Digestion (1868) how he found it necessary to sever the 'nerves of vocalisation' of his dogs 'in order to prevent them indulging in noisy nocturnal concerts and thus discrediting physiological studies among the local residents.' Eventually, however, hostility drove Dr Schiff from Florence to Zurich.

The writings of Miss Cobbe did much to pave the way for the Royal Commission on Vivisection set up in 1875; but the publication which, as the Commissioners noted, 'most of all' roused public disquiet was the *Handbook of the Physiological Laboratory* published 'for beginners' in 1873 by Dr J. Burdon-Sanderson, Professor of Human Physiology at University College. It contained what the Commission described as 'severe experiments'. The author later conceded that he gave no proper definition of 'beginners' and could have done more to stress the need to use anaesthetics.

In 1874 the controversy was further sharpened by the affair of the French physiologist Magnan, who injected dogs with absinthe at a medical conference at Norwich. Some of the doctors present objected and the *Lancet* doubted whether the purpose in view justified the pain inflicted. Magnan withdrew to his native land to escape an RSPCA summons. Soon afterwards Miss Cobbe began to seek support for a memorial urging the RSPCA to press for legislative control of vivisection. Those who signed included the Archbishop of York, Cardinal Manning, the Lord Mayor of London, Lord Shaftesbury, Tennyson (whose poem *In The Children's Hospital* introduces a dog-mangling surgeon 'drenched in the hellish oorali' *), Browning, Carlyle, Ruskin (who in 1884 resigned from Oxford University when a decision was taken to allow vivisection there), some fifty peers and bishops, at least sixty medical men and several distinguished soldiers. Cardinal Manning was an asset in that few Roman Catholic leaders had found occasion to call for compassion towards animals; but he was a liability in that Carlyle refused to join a deputation containing 'the chief emissary of Beelzebub in England.' Among those who declined to sign the memorial were the Archbishop of Canterbury, Charles Darwin and Matthew Arnold.

* Curare.

Queen Victoria was known to be strongly opposed to vivisection. In 1875 she asked Joseph (later Lord) Lister to oppose the practice and received a letter explaining that animals reared for food were subjected to 'an operation involving exquisite agony in its execution,' with the object of rendering their flesh more palatable, and that horses underwent the same operation to make them more docile. By contrast, 'that which has received the odious appellation of vivisection is justified by far nobler and higher objects; not the ministering to the luxury and comfort of a generation, but devising means which will be available throughout all time for procuring the health of mankind, the greatest of earthly blessings, and prolonging of human life.' He said that all the so-called vivisections that took place in a year in Britain would, if done without anaesthetics, cause less torture than a single pheasant *battue*.

The campaign for control was further stimulated by a letter in the *Morning Post* of February 1, 1875 by Dr George Hoggan, who described his studies under 'one of the greatest living experimental physiologists.'* Nobody in the laboratory, he said, pretended to be working for the good of humanity; such a notion would have been derided, 'the great aim being to keep up with, or get ahead of, one's contemporaries of science.' When an experimenter's work was made difficult by clotted tissue the physiologist would say, 'Why don't you begin on the other side? Why don't you take another dog? What is the use of being so economical?' Dr Hoggan thought anaesthetics 'the greatest curse to vivisectible animals' because they altered too much the normal conditions of life and for that reason were little depended on; 'they indeed prove far more efficacious in lulling public opinion towards the vivisectors than pain in the vivisected.' Dr Hoggan concluded: 'Having drained the cup to the dregs I cry off and am prepared to see not only science but even mankind perish rather than have recourse to such means of saving it.'

So ably did Miss Cobbe agitate that, somewhat to her surprise, she was asked by the RSPCA to prepare a Bill to regulate vivisection. Agreement proved hard to obtain and

* Identified as Claude Bernard in Cobbe autobiography.

rival Bills were rushed up. All were withdrawn when the Government, impressed by public feeling, decided to appoint a Royal Commission. Of its six members, Lord Cardwell, the president, and W. E. Forster were vice-presidents of the RSPCA, while Professor T. H. Huxley and J. E. Erichsen represented physiology (giving rise to an unjustified taunt that Thugs had been appointed to consider the desirability of Thuggee).

The Commissioners' questioning of witnesses was thorough and fair. Charles Darwin, in a brief appearance, said he thought a ban on vivisection would be 'a very great evil' but that he would regard failure to use anaesthetics, whenever this was possible, with 'detestation and abhorrence'. He himself had never experimented on an animal. Dr George Hoggan, who had been willing to see mankind perish rather than thrive on cruelty, said he was not prepared to advocate complete abolition. He urged that all experiments be performed in halls with galleries open to the public.

John Colam, secretary of the RSPCA, offered the Commission a huge pile of horrific quotations from the writings of physiologists and others. Asked whether he thought the general tendency of the English scientific world was at variance with humanity, he said he knew of no wanton cruelty in Britain and gave vivisectors credit for using anaesthetics whenever possible; but he thought some experiments went beyond the legitimate province of science, causing pain which could not be justified even for a scientific object.

In the view of Sir William Fergusson, Sergeant Surgeon to the Queen, too many experiments were needlessly repeated. Joseph Lister, asked why physiologists were so fond of using the frog, replied: 'It is selected for its convenience, because it is so tolerant of severe treatment, and also undoubtedly largely from the fact of its being not supposed to suffer materially.' The Commissioners were not very happy about this explanation, or at the denial of anaesthetics to frogs. Dr T. L. Brunton, a lecturer at St Bartholomew's Hospital, was asked where he got the many cats for his cholera experiments and said, 'They are supplied to me by a man.' To the suggestion that they were stolen, he replied, 'I make no enquiries.' Professor J.

Burdon-Sanderson depended on his servant for his supply of animals. He complained: 'There is no proper provision in this country by which one can obtain dogs even for the most legitimate purposes and of course I am not informed as to the way in which they are obtained. They are always paid for at a proper price.'

The most unfortunate mouthpiece for science was Dr Emanuel Klein, lecturer on general histology at St Bartholomew's, and a co-author of the *Handbook of the Physiological Laboratory*. When proofs of his evidence were sent to him he made such alterations that the Commission would not accept them, and after some argument his amended evidence was printed as an appendix. In his uncorrected evidence these passages occur:

When you say that you use [anaesthetics] for convenience' sake, do you mean that you have no regard at all for the suffering of the animals? – No regard at all.

You are prepared to establish that as a principle which you approve? – I think that with regard to an experimenter, a man who conducts special research and performs an experiment, he has no time, so to speak, for thinking what will the animal feel or suffer. His only purpose is to perform the experiment, to learn as much from it as possible and to do it as quickly as possible.

Then for your purpose you disregard entirely the question of the suffering of the animal in performing a painful experiment? – I do.

In his 'corrected' version Dr Klein represented himself as saying: 'A man who conducts special research and performs an experiment has no time, so to speak, for thinking what the animal feels or suffers. If anaesthetics ought to be used, he uses them. If not he is like a man who performs a surgical operation in like circumstances. His only purpose is to perform the experiment, to learn as much from it as possible and to do it as quickly as possible.'

Dr Klein said his operations involved little pain. If, in class, he proposed to conduct an experiment without anaesthesia he always asked whether anyone objected; it was seldom that anyone did. He did not chloroform frogs – 'I do not think we have the right to regard the sensibility and feeling of a frog

as being of a very high degree.' He agreed the atmosphere
was very different in Vienna, where he had studied. In England
people were 'more disposed to take care of other people's
consciences in matters they do not clearly understand.'

Sir George Duckett, a member of an anti-vivisectionist
group, was pressed to give evidence, but declined, as he had
no personal knowledge of the practice. All he knew was that
it was 'an abomination imported from the Continent, is horrid
and monstrous and goes hand in hand with atheism. Medical
science has arrived probably at its extreme limits. Nothing can
be gained by repetition of experiments on living animals.'

In their report, the Commissioners said that a total ban on
vivisection would be unreasonable, since 'the greatest miti-
gations of human suffering' had been derived, in part, thereby;
and they agreed that demonstrations were essential to teaching.
In any event, a ban would only drive medical men to Europe,
with no benefit to the animal kingdom. The Commissioners
deplored that 'a feeling of suspicion and even of abhorrence
should have been permitted to grow up among a large and
very estimable portion of the public against those who are
devoted to the improvement of medicine and to the advancement of science.' Nevertheless, 'it is not to be doubted that
inhumanity may be found in persons of very high position as
physiologists; we have seen that it was so with Magendie.'
Because physiology was fast expanding and new laboratories
were being opened in medical schools, it seemed desirable to
take legislative precautions; and the Commission therefore
recommended a system of State licensing, 'whether for original
research or for demonstration.' One Commissioner, Richard
Holt Hutton, urged that dogs and cats should be exempted
from experiments because of their special relationship to
man.

With the publication of the Report, the opposing sides again
began to draft Bills and there was much intrigue at Westminster. In 1876 Parliament passed the Cruelty to Animals
Act, described by one Member as a gross insult to the medical
profession, which still controls experiments on all but inverte-
brate animals. It laid down that vivisection was to be conducted only by licensed individuals in licensed buildings, open

to Government inspection. Anaesthetics were to be used, unless anaesthesia would destroy the purpose of the operation; and in such experiments a special certificate was necessary. If an animal was likely to suffer pain on regaining consciousness, it was to be destroyed.

Miss Cobbe, who by now had formed a society to protect animals from vivisection, felt that she had wrought more harm than good, that Parliament had passed a measure, not to protect animals, but to protect vivisectors. Lord Shaftesbury tried to convince her that the Act was better than no Act. Soon she began to campaign for complete abolition of animal experiments and renamed her society accordingly (it is now the National Anti-Vivisection Society). In 1879 when Lord Truro introduced an abolitionist Bill Lord Shaftesbury expressed his disapproval of the 1876 Act, under which licences and certificates had been given to Dr William Rutherford, whose harsh experiments had been described to the Royal Commission. To refresh his fellow peers in the ways of science, he told a story from the writings of a Professor Goltz, a physiologist of Strasbourg:

'A very clever lively young female dog which had learned to shake hands with both fore-paws had the left side of the brain washed out through two holes on the 1st of December, 1875. This caused lameness in the right paw. On being asked for the left the dog immediately lays it in my hand. I now demand the right; but the creature only looks at me sorrowfully, for it cannot move it. On my continuing to press for it the dog crosses the left paw over and offers it to me on the right side, as if to make amends for not being able to give the right. On the 13th of January a second portion of the brain was destroyed, on the 15th of February, a third and on the 6th of March a fourth, this last operation causing death.'

One who sat listening to this story was Lord Aberdare, president of the RSPCA, who later rose to oppose the Bill, saying that his Society had never urged a total ban. He thought that if any Act needed strengthening it was the existing one which dealt with cruelty to animals in general terms; it permitted fifty times as much cruelty as the Act controlling vivisection.

In the propaganda battle, the voice of Miss Cobbe was now joined by that of Dr Anna Kingsford, or Maitland, whose self-delusive hysteria was to afford callous amusement to her enemies. In her youth she had been passionately fond of hunting, never shrinking the kill; 'I seemed to find a savage joy in seeing the dogs fasten on the fox and tear it to pieces.' But as a medical student in Paris in the 'seventies she rebelled at the experiments which went on around her. A porter explained the source of fierce screams with: 'It is only the dogs being vivisected in M. Béclard's laboratory. *Que voulez-vous? C'est pour la science.*' She refused to allow her tutor to experiment on animals, and argued incessantly with the Faculty, who admitted that many experiments were useless but said they saw no moral objection to them. One professor told her that vivisection was necessary to proclaim the independence of science against interference by clerics and moralists.

At this time Anna Kingsford was under the influence of Edward Maitland, the writer and mystic, who believed that vivisection was a demonisation of the race, a reversion to black magic. She saw Claude Bernard as the arch-demon. One day, after a bitter dispute over his methods, 'she no sooner found herself alone than she rose to her feet and with passionate energy invoked the wrath of God upon him, at the same moment hurling her whole spiritual being at him with all her might, as if with the intent then and there to smite him to destruction.' Then she collapsed. A few weeks afterwards she and Maitland reached the École de Medicine in Paris and found a notice on the closed gates saying that Bernard was dead. It was obvious to her that the 'spiritual thunderbolt' she had fired at him had done the trick: 'if it proves that I really possess such a glorious power, woe be to the torturers! God willing, what a murrain shall be among them! Oh! I will make it dangerous, nay deadly, to be a vivisector . . . meanwhile thank God the head of the gang is dead.' The official explanation was that Bernard had died from a 'poisonous effluvium' released from his experiments. Edward Maitland had moral qualms about felling opponents with spiritual thunderbolts, but Anna had now marked down Pasteur;

against him she concentrated her will with a ferocity that
made Maitland fear for her health. It seemed that she was
making some progress when Pasteur was forced by illness to
leave his laboratory and go to the Riviera for several months,
'and the average of the failures of his system, as shown by the
mortality among his patients, was largely increased.' Maitland
wondered whether it was right to rejoice in the deaths of
patients, but Anna Kingsford was sure it was – if they lent
themselves to animal experiments. Still Pasteur did not die
('What? Will not the gods smite?') but Professor Paul Bert,
a subsidiary target, did, after a great concentration of effort.
The ironic end came when, on visiting Pasteur's Institute to
obtain evidence, Anna Kingsford was overtaken by rain,
caught pneumonia and died.* As a propagandist she has her
place in abolitionist annals; but she did no good to her cause
by her plunge into the occult.

Miss Cobbe, for all her occasional excesses, was a much
more dangerous opponent. As already observed, she had many
spirited bouts with the Jesuits, who went out of their way, as
it seemed to her, to point out that man had no *duty* to spare
pain to animals. They told her that they preferred experiments
to be tried out on rabbits rather than on sick children and
quoted 'Ye are of more value than many sparrows.' To ban
experiments, they said, would be as foolish as refusing to kill
a sheep to feed a starving family. In her numberless pamphlets
and articles Miss Cobbe made telling use of quotations from
physiological works whose authors seemed to be carried on a
tide of indecent excitement. In Elie de Cyon's *Méthodique
Physiologique*, published in St Petersburg in 1876, she found a
passage which began:

'The true vivisector must approach a difficult vivisection with
the same joyful excitement and the same delight wherewith a
surgeon undertakes a difficult operation, from which he expects
extraordinary consequences. He who shrinks from going into a
living animal, he who approaches a vivisection as a disagreeable
necessity, might very likely be able to repeat one or two vivisections, but will never become an artist . . .'

* Edward Maitland: *Anna Kingsford*.

And a later passage said:

'The sensation of the physiologist, when from a gruesome wound, full of blood and mangled tissue, he draws forth some delicate nerve-branch and calls back to life a function which was already extinguished – this sensation has much in common with that which excites a sculptor, when he shapes forth fair living forms from a shapeless mass of marble.'

Angered by the use of these extracts, and by the reproduction of his engravings on posters called 'The Horrors of Science', Elie de Cyon made a scornful attack in the *Contemporary Review* of April 1883 on England's 'pseudo-humanitarian movement'. English scientists, he said, should never have lowered the flag and let a parcel of sophists try to teach them morality and humanity; professors should have resigned rather than allow police regulation of research. As evidence of his own delicacy of feeling he said: 'After having performed during the last fifteen years an incalculable number of vivisections I have never yet been able to bring myself to operate on a human being.' This French-domiciled Russian made much of the fact that among his opponents were many old maids. 'Let my adversaries . . . show among the leaders of the agitation one young girl, rich, beautiful and beloved, or one young wife who has found in her home the full satisfaction of her affections.' In France it was different. The Catholic religion gave old maids a necessary refuge, providing full satisfaction for 'the mystical and superstitious tendencies indigenous to the soil of the human mind.' But the cold formalism of the Protestant religion was very far from satisfying these tendencies. The only effect of this outburst was to give anti-vivisectionists new ammunition.

The polemical war was also carried on by the Humanitarian League, founded in 1891 by Henry Salt, among its spokesmen being Edward Maitland and Edward Carpenter. They mocked man for his cowardice in being ready to sacrifice the lower animals for his supposed gain and to cure him of the results of vicious living, for worshipping a divine Father who permitted the craftier members of the family to torture the weaker. They jeered at Claude Bernard for saying: 'Science permits us to do to animals what morality forbids us to do to our own kind.' How could Science command or forbid, any more than chemistry? Eventually came George Bernard Shaw who said that vivisection would never be crushed by argument but by 'the frankly intolerant abhorrence of all genuinely virtuous persons.'*

To trace all the vicissitudes of the anti-vivisection movement would be tedious. Societies multiplied wastefully, splitting on personalities as well as on policies. Suffragists tended to be anti-vivisectionists, and vice versa, and the movement has always had a sprinkling of spiritualists and occultists. Doctors complained incessantly of misrepresentation by women incapable of seeing pain in anything but an emotional context. The abolitionists concentrated much of their efforts on trying to exempt dogs from experiments, but dogs were rapidly losing popular sympathy because of rabies and hydrophobia scares. In the stray-infested Metropolis during the late 'seventies 'lynch law' operated. Any animal which looked sick was assumed to be in the early stages of rabies and was chased, stoned and battered until its terrified state reinforced the worst suspicions. Juries required little persuasion to bring in hydrophobia verdicts in cases of sudden death. To this hysterical atmosphere the abolitionists contributed their quota of confusion and prejudice. When the muzzling laws came in, during the 'eighties and 'nineties, they preached civil disobedience and dogs were carried from muzzling areas into non-muzzling areas for exercise. Sir Victor Horsley, the surgeon, battled angrily with 'Miss Cobbe and her lying crew,' and led medical cohorts into her meetings.† From the turmoil of those days emerged the National Canine Defence League, founded in 1891 at Cruft's Dog Show.

Thanks to the growth of bacteriology, the number of animal experiments sanctioned each year multiplied enormously, but a great proportion of them were inoculations, not vivisections in the original sense. Many of the experiments by Pasteur, Koch and other bacteriologists make unpleasant reading, but Stephen Paget is entitled to the point he made in his long defence of vivisection in the *Encyclopedia Britannica* (11th edn,

* In letter to *Daily News* quoted in *Humane Review*, Vol. IV (1903-4).
† Stephen Paget: *Sir Victor Horsley*.

1911): 'It is probable that animals kept for inoculation have on the whole less pain than falls to the lot of a like number of animals in a state of nature or in subjection to work: they are well fed and sheltered and escape the rapacity of larger animals, the inevitable cruelties of sport and the drudgery and sexual mutilation that man inflicts on the higher domestic animals.' He thought that mice in the hands of cancer researchers might be 'incommoded' by large tumours, but did not think 'distressed' was a word applicable to mice.

Through most of the Edwardian years the vivisection controversy was kept on the boil by the famous 'brown dog' case. This victim of the laboratory was first heard of in a book *The Shambles of Science* (1903) by Emelie Lind-af-Hageby and Leisa Schartau, two young Swedish women who described what they had seen as students at University College, London. The animal was used for three separate experiments, during the last of which it was killed; a procedure which, as a Home Office inspector later said, he would not have allowed if he had known about it. Those involved in the experiments denied that the dog ever suffered pain. In 1907 the International Anti-Vivisection Council persuaded Battersea Council to permit the erection in Battersea Park of a statue to the dog with the inflammatory inscription:

'In memory of the Brown Terrier Dog done to death in the laboratories of University College in February 1903 after having endured vivisection extending over more than two months and having been handed over from one vivisector to another till death came to his release. Also in memory of the 232 dogs vivisected in the same place during the year 1902. Men and Women of England: How long shall these things be?'

At first the statue roused little interest, but later in the year it became a target for medical students from University College and elsewhere. There were raids, demonstrations, protests. A London magistrate told arrested students that the inscription was perfectly legitimate; whereupon attempts were made to burn his effigy in King's College courtyard, but it proved incombustible and was thrown into the Thames from Waterloo Bridge. There were more demonstrations, more arrests. In *The Times* Stephen Paget called on the authorities to remove the statue, but the Mayor of Battersea declined to veil what he had unveiled. There was talk of making the statue the subject of a libel action. By 1910 Battersea Council had weakened and the brown dog, which was costing £700 a year to protect, was removed. A protest meeting in Trafalgar Square followed. Miss A. L. Woodward, of the International Anti-Vivisection Council, went to court in an effort to enforce the original agreement, but Mr Justice Neville declined to make the necessary order, saying of the inscription: 'It seems to me calculated to hold up the University College to public execration and to inflame the public mind against it; and to be calculated to lead to a breach of the peace.' On March 24, 1911, *The Times* reported that 'the dog has been smashed into small pieces by a smith and the fragments have been disposed of.'

The 'brown dog' case disclosed an instance of unauthorised experimentation. Others were reported to a second Royal Commission on Vivisection, which began its duties in 1906. The RSPCA strongly represented to this body that supervision by three inspectors of 46,000 experiments a year was 'totally inadequate'. In 1910 Mr Winston Churchill, Home Secretary, was pressed in the Commons to give the name of a scientist who had performed an uncertificated experiment, and to say why he had not been prosecuted. Mr Churchill replied that the experiment had involved the spaying of two rabbits under anaesthetic; the experimenter had held a certificate in previous years for this operation, but had failed to notice that his latest certificate did not permit it. When the lapse was detected from a written paper, six months had elapsed and it was too late to prosecute, even if that had been thought necessary. 'He is a distinguished man of science to whom the refusal of a licence is a very severe penalty,' said Mr Churchill, 'and I think the House will agree that in these circumstances I am not called upon to disclose his name.' The name was later disclosed, but not by Mr Churchill. Dr Christopher (later Viscount) Addison asked Mr Churchill whether he proposed to take action in respect of 'the corresponding operation' performed on male pigs, cattle and sheep without an anaesthetic; to which the answer was that there was nothing illegal in such operations if carried out *bona fide* for commercial or domestic purposes, without causing unnecessary suffering.

In its final report, in 1912, the new Royal Commission said that since the Act of 1876 four licences had been withdrawn, one for a deliberate violation, another for gross carelessness. There had been sixty minor infractions. No prosecutions alleging cruelty had been brought, either by the Home Office or by individuals. The Commission rebutted many statements by Stephen Coleridge, of the National Anti-Vivisection Society,* whom it called 'an acute and indefatigable critic supported, as he told us, with ample funds' (in 1903 he was sued for libel by one of the 'brown dog' doctors and had to pay £2,000). Coleridge had complained that the Home Office officials had made themselves 'the injudicial defenders of the vivisectors', and that their bias was evidence in the assertion by one of them that he was not appointed to be a detective.

The Commission conceded that certain claims to have derived valuable information from vivisection had been exploded, but remained convinced that valuable knowledge had been obtained, directly or indirectly, in this way, and that animals as well as men had benefited. On the moral argument, it was evidently impressed by the statement of Sir Victor Horsley, on behalf of the British Medical Association: 'To them [the doctors] the moral duty is the pursuit of knowledge and an immoral act is the obstruction of that pursuit of knowledge.' The Commissioners noted that torture, a once-legitimate means of obtaining information, had been abandoned because the means to the end could no longer be justified, and said: 'At the present time the average moral sense of Christian communities is not offended by the sacrifice of lower animals for the food, clothing, adornment and, within limits, the sport of man.' This conceded, it seemed reasonable to give man the right to experiment on living animals, provided they were anaesthetised and killed if necessary. To prohibit such experiments would be 'inconsistent if not preposterous.'

The long-drawn bitterness of the controversy did little or

* Miss Cobbe left this society in 1898 to form the more militant British Union for the Abolition of Vivisection.

nothing to help the cause of laboratory animals; rather were scientists stiffened in their determination to give no ground. Only one animal seems to have gained some small benefit. Under the Dogs Act, 1906 police may not send strays for vivisection.

The debate continues today, with much the same arguments. It is still true that not a single prosecution for cruelty has been brought by the Home Office under the 1876 Act. Humanitarian and sceptic alike join in wondering whether any other Act in history has been so scrupulously observed.*

* In 1963 the Home Secretary set up a committee under Sir Sidney Littlewood to consider whether any changes were necessary in the system of control. The number of animals used in laboratories now exceeds four million a year.

16

RSPCA FORGES ON

AFTER some fifty years' existence, the RSPCA was a potent influence in the land. Numerous overseas societies were modelled upon it, one of the more famous being that founded by Henry Bergh in New York in 1866 – the first in America. Although the RSPCA's members were often at odds on matters like hunting, vivisection and vegetarianism, the Society's policy was to advance on a broad humanitarian front, leaving the extremists to conduct their own polemics.

On October 18, 1860, *The Times*, commending the Society's work, said that in London thousands of sharp eyes made it impossible for anyone to put a galled horse to work, and that magistrates were alert to enforce 'the Magna Carta of the brute creation.' Unfortunately these remarks formed a minor part of a leading article expressing surprise that the RSPCA should have consented to accept contributions towards the founding of an institution so fundamentally preposterous as a home for lost dogs. 'From the reasonable inspirations of humanity to the fantastic exhibitions of ridiculous sentimentalism there is but a single step,' lamented the leader-writer. The scheme was the inspiration of a lady of Islington who was shocked at the number of starving strays in London. Her proposal was that if valuable dogs remained unclaimed they should be sold to defray the costs of the home; and that 'common-bred dogs' should be given to any persons who might require a useful dog on promising to take care of it. *The Times* detected class distinction here: 'The King Charles owns an enchanted life – the turnspit or mongrel may be turned into sausage-meat without a tear over its untimely grave from the Lady of Islington.' In any event, the newspaper said, dog thieves took good care that no valuable dog should ever be lost. No doubt, it added, the home would be divided into male and female compartments, 'for is it not founded by a Lady of Islington?' In other organs, wags suggested homes for mice and butterflies. Unstifled by mockery, the Lady from Islington, whose name was Mrs Tealby, went ahead. The first home was established in Islington and it later became the well-known Battersea Dogs Home.

The protests would have been even shriller if a proposal had been made to open a home for stray cats. This creature was still something of an outcast. Although the public showed fury towards dealers who skinned cats alive, lesser cruelties roused no great concern. The cat's subsequent rise in esteem is said to have come about at a time when the public mind was obsessed with thoughts of bacteria and rabies; then, the cat's manifest cleanliness may have helped to lift it into favour.* It remains to add that, in 1886, when a Miss Lindo had the idea of opening a Home of Rest for Horses (which still survives at Boreham Wood) she, too, drew on herself much ridicule.

When the Society launched its journal *Animal World* in 1869 the editor, John Colam, listed the main reforms which faced it. These included: the erection of public abattoirs; more humane methods of slaughter; abolition of the slow bleeding of calves; protection of sheep from the shearer in cold weather; abolition of dog muzzles; improved horse shoes; abolition of 'barbarous instruments of torture' used in game preservation; discontinuance of pigeon-shooting clubs; a ban on the offering of rewards for destruction of small birds; improvement in the construction of roads; abolition of the bearing rein; appropriate harness for draught animals; suppression of experiments on animals for science when accompanied by torture; anaesthetics for animals; improved laws for the protection of animals; and better treatment of cattle in transit.

Slaughtering was left almost wholly to private enterprise, which meant unsupervised butchering in cellars, but belated

* Morus (Richard Lewinsohn): *Animals, Men and Myths.*

efforts to copy the French lead in founding well-appointed public abattoirs were being made in mid-century (for example, at Edinburgh and Islington). Whether cattle died painlessly or not depended on the skill of the slaughterman. The traditional pole-axe required 'a skilled hand and a resolute heart.' Its use could be learned only on the living animal; a beast felled by irresolute apprentice labour suffered Dante-like tortures.

Perennial efforts were made, by the RSPCA and other bodies, to devise more humane ways of killing; even dynamite and the guillotine were tried. Shooting with a rifle was too dangerous at close quarters. Benjamin Franklin had suggested that electricity might be used, but no serious experiments were made on these lines until, about 1869, Dr (later Sir) Benjamin Richardson at the Royal Polytechnic Institution harnessed what was then 'the largest electrical instrument ever made,' a series of twelve Leyden jars boasting ninety-six square feet of surface. With its aid he killed various small animals and rabbits, but the method, besides being cumbrous, was unsatisfactory and dangerous. He then tried narcotic gases, but these were either too slow or contaminated the flesh. Dr Richardson was more successful in devising lethal chambers for destroying unwanted pets.

The main problem in pole-axeing was to aim the blow accurately at a beast excited by the sight and smell of blood. This was particularly difficult when the 'pole-axe' consisted of a steel wedge, held by an assistant, and a heavy mallet. Bruneau, a Frenchman, and Baxter, an Englishman, both designed cattle masks which contained a species of interior punch. At the other end of the punch, outside the mask, was a knob. If this was struck hard and squarely, the animal subsided instantly. In theory the mask prevented the animal from seeing what was happening, but in practice it often heightened the animal's fears. Siegmund, a veterinary surgeon of Basle, devised a variation of this mask which employed, instead of a punch, a small pistol to fire a bullet through the brain. It has been called the prototype of the humane killer, though that weapon in its familiar form did not arrive until early in the present century. To all new methods of killing, the trade was stubbornly resistant, alleging that they damaged the flesh, or were impractical, or were too expensive, or were more cruel than existing methods.

The Jewish method of ritual slaughter, which involved throat-slitting without preliminary stunning, was the focus of strong criticism, as it still is; but death from quick bleeding was not necessarily more cruel than death from an ill-wielded pole-axe. Undue suffering was often caused by the operation of casting the shackled bullock, that is, throwing it to the ground with the aid of ropes; it was a feat which could take up to ten minutes and sometimes resulted in a broken leg. When cast, the animal's head was twisted back with chains and lever until the sometimes dilatory Shochet arrived and half-severed it with a very sharp knife. Much of the flesh was sold on the Gentile market. Bills are still introduced into Parliament in an effort to reform this practice, but they rarely make any headway.

Gentiles who condemned ritual slaughter (which at least was dignified by a prayer) were often content to eat the flesh of calves which had been bled to death by non-Jewish slaughterers, possibly over a period of days. In many areas this practice was being put down and the RSPCA secured numerous convictions; the luckier calves were now stunned before their throats were cut. But in the trade's eyes, if not in those of the epicure, well-bleached veal was more delicate and wholesome. Butchers who were prepared to risk prosecution would stab the calf, partly bleed it, then plug the wound with tow. They would then feed the dying animal gruel as a heart restorative and bleed it again, kicking it or twisting its tail if the blood was slow to flow. Rather than risk eating the product of such ingenuity many persons refused to touch veal.

The idea of anaesthetising smaller animals before slaughter had been considered but rapidly dropped on the grounds of expense. Sheep rarely qualified for preliminary stunning; they were killed by inserting a knife into the neck and sometimes were skinned when less than half-dead. At Halifax in 1872 a butcher who was fined for skinning a sheep alive was said to have impaled it with a fork to hold it in position. Pigs had their throats cut while fully conscious; at least they were no longer whipped to death.

Those who spent their days killing cattle were commonly supposed to have hardened hearts and corrupted morals, though this did not prevent virtuous citizens from eating the results of their labours in a refined atmosphere of soft lights and music. Occasional efforts were made to save the souls of slaughtermen. About 1892, according to Edward Maitland, there was a great gathering of London butchers under the presidency of the Rev. Charles Spurgeon, when the hymn 'There is a fountain filled with blood' was selected as peculiarly appropriate and sung with fervour. There was talk of remonstrating with Spurgeon but he died and 'passed to the Master Butcher'.*

It was one thing to refine methods of slaughter, but another to cut down the innumerable cruelties on the road to the slaughter-house. This road might be many thousands of miles long, for the animal which was knocked on the head in London came, as likely as not, from the Argentine pampas or the plains of North America. It might have been hauled hungry aboard a tossing vessel by a steam winch with ropes attached to its horns and goaded by spiked sticks. It might have been the lucky survivor of a great tempest, fortunate to reach land and not to have been smothered, lamed or disembowelled when whole deck-loads of animals were thrown together in heaps. In the latter half of the century live cattle were even imported to Britain from Australia, but fortunately the death-roll in ships from Queensland was high enough to discourage the traffic, or to enforce higher standards if only to avoid loss of money. In 1866 a Select Committee on the Trade in Animals recommended the enforcement of ventilation, disinfection and the provision of proper accommodation. The Board of Agriculture laid down regulations, but the shipping interest in Parliament was always strong enough to ensure that sentimentalism did not run riot.

The trade from both Americas was abominably conducted in its early years. Herds were driven from the Rockies for seven or eight days to the railheads, where they were beaten

* Edward Maitland: *Anna Kingsford*.

and goaded into wagons by yelling men armed with heavy
steel-spiked saplings. In the train there was no room to lie
down, if only because the floor space was crowded with
smaller animals like sheep and pigs. On the long hauls there
would be rest stations where the beasts would be clubbed out
of the waggons to recuperate and clubbed in again. It was
accepted that an animal would lose ten or fifteen per cent of
its weight on the passage east. In 1871 a consignment of cattle
reached Chicago from Brigham Young's farm in Utah with
a shrinkage of 'only 250 pounds a head'. About 6 per cent of
cattle and 9 per cent of smaller animals died in transit,
representing 600,000 animals a year (this included the
thousands thrown into the great rivers from cattle boats).
Sometimes whole waggon-loads of animals would be found
frozen solid. Those cattle destined for the New York market
arrived half-starved, fevered, pierced with holes, bruised,
ulcered and variously diseased. In 1869 the Cattle Commissioners of that city said: 'There was revealed . . . such an
amount of reckless barbarity toward animals and of criminal
indifference on the part of many who furnish meat to con-
sumers that one almost wonders why the city has escaped a
pestilence.'* Thanks to British regulations, cattle bound across
the Atlantic enjoyed better conditions at sea than on land,
though bad weather could quickly turn the decks into a
shambles. Shipowners were quick to point out that cattle often
put on weight during the ocean passage. Then came disembarkation, more goads and the red uproar of the slaughter-
house.

On the short Irish run, conditions were sometimes worse
than on the Atlantic. Skippers showed no inclination to alter
course for storms and there seemed little point in feeding and
watering doomed animals. Cattle from the Orkneys and
Shetlands sometimes had no food from the moment they left
their byres to their arrival in the mainland market, and precious
little then.

In the end, it was refrigeration, not regulation, which put
an end to the miseries inseparable from long-distance transport
of live animals. Henry Bergh estimated, about 1870, that to

* George Angell: *Essay on Cattle Transportation in the United States* (1872).

transport thirty-two live steers weighing 20,000 pounds from Indianapolis to New York, with average shrinkage, cost $1,210; to transport the dressed meat in a refrigerated wagon cost only $100. The frozen meat trade gained impetus everywhere in the 'eighties and humane Britons made a point of asking for 'frozen' meat. On the other hand, those who were 'satisfied with nothing but the best' made a point of asking for 'home-killed'. When the twentieth century came in Britain was still importing half a million cattle annually from North America. The introduction of canning also played its part in cutting down cruelty; it would be foolish to pretend that animals died peacefully in Chicago, but the length of their ordeal was limited.

The castration and spaying of food animals, supposedly to improve their flesh, was a subject on which not all humanitarian minds were eager to dwell. In 1887 the British courts were called on to decide whether the doctoring of female animals involved cruelty in law. John Fermor, of Sussex, was charged with cruelty to five sows, which had been spayed in the usual manner, uterus and ovaries being removed through an incision in the flank. Five veterinary surgeons gave evidence that the operation was of no benefit, because the sow's flesh deteriorated only when the animal was in heat and there was no need to kill it at that time. The magistrates held that the operation caused pain but dismissed the charge. In the Queen's Bench Mr Justice Day said Fermor agreed that the operation had caused pain and might have constituted torture, but cautery of a human was open to the same accusation. Cruelty could arise only in an act done for no legitimate purpose, and which the person performing it knew could not be justified. Sows were spayed in the belief that it increased their weight and development. Mr Justice Wills said the point was whether the act was done for a lawful purpose, and not whether in the opinion of the tribunal the practice was a good one. 'The belief may be erroneous,' he said, 'but we must be careful that we do not try to teach new, though perhaps improved views, on matters within the area of fair scientific discussion by means of criminal law.' One of the veterinary surgeons had described spaying as barbarous and unnecessary but had admitted performing 4,000 such operations in a year; this witness, the judge thought, could have had no grounds for complaint if he had been prosecuted, convicted and severely punished. There was no evidence to show that Fermor had shared this witness's view. In the records of the Queen's Bench the case bears this remarkable summary: 'A person who with reasonable care and skill performs on an animal a painful operation which is customary and is performed *bona fide* for the purpose of benefiting the owner by increasing the value of the animal is not guilty of the offence of cruelly ill-treating, abusing or torturing the animal even though the operation is in fact unnecessary and useless.'

The case does not, perhaps, show the veterinary profession in too happy a light. In fact, veterinary surgeons were now contributing powerfully to the welfare of animals and much of the work of the RSPCA depended on their counsel and assistance. For centuries veterinary science, like medical science, had stagnated; Britain's first veterinary college was not founded until 1791, long after those at Lyons and Alfort. Farriers and 'cow-doctors' were accustomed to apply such rough remedies as they knew and the difficulty now was to put them out of business. Right through the nineteenth century farriers and blacksmiths were to be found burning the insides of horses' mouths with hot irons to cure them of lampas, an ancient but imaginary disease which was only a harmless swelling. Often veterinary surgeons were persuaded to 'burn out the lampas', knowing that if they refused it would be done more barbarously by a farrier. For similar reasons they nicked and docked horses, practices against which they could perhaps have made a stronger stand; but some compromise was inevitable until popular ignorance was broken down.

In its prosecuting role, the RSPCA commanded such respect that *Bell's Life* complained, in 1870, that people were afraid to pursue or even dig out badgers for fear of getting 'a roughing up by the SPCA people.' Magistrates less readily dismissed charges than of old, but there were still some who offended the Society's sense of fitness. In 1870 Sir Robert Carden at the Guildhall said that when he looked in the face of a lady charged with cruelty to her horse he was sure she must be innocent. 'Policemen should henceforth be admonished to proceed against ill-looking persons only,' said the Society's journal, 'since it would be a better guide to success at the Guildhall than the clumsy routine of legal proofs. It will be a source of satisfaction to good-looking persons that they run little risk of punishment at the hands of Sir Robert Carden.'*

It was not always easy to secure convictions for cropping dogs' ears, a practice resorted to by promoters of dog-fights and also by breeders anxious to improve on Nature. The 1835 Act was the authority under which charges were brought and sometimes won; oddly, cropping of horses was not regarded as an offence. Sir Edwin Landseer was a fierce critic of cropping, refusing to paint animals which had been so treated.

Prosecutions became something of a gamble when there was no clear precedent for a conviction. The year 1870 offered the unusual spectacle of Spanish bull-fighters being prosecuted in an English court. These proceedings arose from the staging of an imitation bull-fight in the Agricultural Hall, Islington. All bloodshed was to be excluded from the performance which, in the words of the *Daily News* of April 2, was 'not to be more genuine than the eel-pies for which the neighbourhood of the Agricultural Hall is famous.' The matadors were old, the bulls were young – 'almost sucklings and of an abominably good temper' – and the horses were made of wicker. Red rosettes slapped on to the bulls' hides with gum failed to arouse them; nevertheless, the matadors 'leaped actively out of the way of nothing and escaped from no peril whatever with extraordinary daring.' Perhaps the greatest cruelty inflicted, said the *Daily News*, was on the audience who paid high prices to see a bad farce. There were cries of 'twist his tail' and other incitements, as a result of which the promoters eventually decided to ginger up the performance. The red rosettes were applied with one-inch spikes instead of gum; the matadors' staves also had spikes masked by rosettes; and the animals were peppered with steel-tipped spears which they tried in vain to shake out. The new tactics angered not only the bulls but John Colam, secretary of the RSPCA, who jumped down into the ring

* *Animal World*, November 1, 1870.

followed by others and grabbed the matadors' staves. The
Spaniards 'yelled vehemently', roughs in the audience hurled
abuse at Colam and the interventionists did well to escape
unscathed. Seven Spaniards were fined at Clerkenwell for
taking part in a cruel performance. Had they been Englishmen,
said the magistrate, he would have jailed them.

Critics sometimes alleged that the RSPCA chose to proceed
against the humble rather than the well-to-do, that it harried
the poor man trying to earn a living while winking at the
cruelties of fashionable sport. In 1871 the Society stirred up
controversy by prosecuting two whippers-in of Lord Middleton's hunt on a charge of over-riding their horses. The
proceedings were brought at Norton in the East Riding.
Before any evidence was called two magistrates prudently
withdrew on the grounds that they themselves might be
prosecuted for the same offence next week. It emerged that
the horses left their stables at eight a.m. and died at the
roadside about six p.m. having pursued four foxes and covered
about fifty miles of heavy country. At one point they had
been 'revived' with gin and water at a farmhouse.

Albert Darley, a hunting man and magistrate, explained
in evidence the niceties of over-riding. It was cruel, he said,
to ride a horse to death, but if one rode it until it was so far
exhausted as to die a quarter of an hour afterwards, that was
not, in his opinion an act of cruelty. This was just the sort of
sturdy common-sense the bench had hoped to hear, and they
dismissed the charges amid applause.

The press was less impressed by Darley's logic. According
to the *Daily News*, the moral was: 'If your horse means to die,
dismount within fifteen minutes of his death and you may
defy the Society.' *Reynolds' News* said: 'As the case was adjudi-
cated upon by a bench composed mostly of fox-hunting squires
or their friends, and as the incriminated parties were servants
of a nobleman who is master of the fox-hunt, as a matter of
course the summons was dismissed . . . This is "justices'
justice" with a vengeance and out-Herods every display of
folly, caprice or incompetency the lengthy roll of magisterial
dereliction can exhibit . . .' The Darley argument, said
Reynolds, could preserve a man from being charged with

murder if the victim he battered with an iron bar did not die until fifteen minutes had elapsed. The *Saturday Review* thought that when over-riding was suspected the masters and not the men should be prosecuted.

The sporting press, however, was delighted with the outcome of the case. In the *Sporting Gazette* indignation was expressed that the funds of the charitable had been squandered on 'one of the most unwarrantable and unjustifiable prosecutions ever brought in a court of justice'; and *Sporting Life* jeered at the discomfiture of John Colam's 'mawkish old maids and lachrymose humanitarians.' The *Morning Advertiser* asked sarcastically how the Society proposed to regulate the pace of hunting. The time was coming, it feared, when even rat-killing and pigeon-shooting would be banned, and a true Englishman would have no option but to emigrate.

The Middleton case had a salutary effect, for 'hard runs' were thereafter discouraged. Six years later the RSPCA, with some boldness and perhaps some trepidation, served summonses on Her Majesty's Whips for allowing a hind to be worried in water by the Royal Buck Hounds (the lacerated hide was retained as a souvenir by the Society). Apparently no effort was made to rescue the animal or call off the hounds. The magistrates threw out the summonses on the grounds that the deer was not a domestic animal.

In its educational role, the Society was active on many fronts. Not its least success in the 1860s was to persuade clergymen to hold an Animal Sunday, the example being set by Dean Stanley, Dean of Westminster. A great propaganda campaign, involving meetings and demonstrations, was concentrated on carters, drivers and coachmen; those who could read were given handbooks on the care of the horse. But the cruelties which horses underwent were not caused by their drivers alone. The Society agitated against the practice of 'paving' roads with sharp flints and leaving the horses to tread them down; also against the operation of brakeless omnibuses, the animals being expected to stop or slow the vehicle by muscle-power. A long-standing reproach was remedied – in London at least – by the installation of drinking-troughs for

horses and cattle. The body responsible had begun by pro-
viding fountains for human beings, but in 1867 it became the
Metropolitan Free Drinking Fountain and Cattle Trough
Association.

To reward conscientious workers for the cause, the Society
introduced a Queen's Medal, John Colam being its first
recipient. The initial design for this award had featured a

Water for man and beast
From 'Animal World', July 1, 1870

variety of domestic creatures, but not a cat. Queen Victoria
detected the omission and drew in a cat with her own hand,
being anxious that everything should be done to abate the
prejudice against this creature.* The Society offered prizes for
improved methods of killing, notably in the shape of more
humane traps and snares for rabbits.

In 1870 for the first time women began to take a directing
hand in the affairs of the RSPCA. The Ladies' Committee
formed in that year was founded by Miss Angela (a year later,

* E. G. Fairholme and Wellesley Pain: *A Century of Work for Animals.*

Baroness) Burdett-Coutts, following a suggestion by George Angell, the American humanitarian. The Baroness was one of the Great Victorians and well deserves her tomb in Westminster Abbey. A daughter of Sir Francis Burdett, she added the name Coutts in 1837 when the major share in Coutts' Bank was left to her. As the richest heiress in England she drew much attention at the Coronation of Queen Victoria, of whom she was a close life-long friend. Declining all early suitors, she administered her own fortune, supporting almost every philanthropic cause from ragged schools and the housing of the poor to female emigration and the Flower Girls Brigade. It was said of her that 'no other woman under the rank of Queen ever did so much for the Established Church.'* To the RSPCA her tall, serene, black figure brought enormous prestige, and its Ladies' Committee became a body of great strength and influence.

The Committee concentrated on propaganda, in schools, in the press and among carters and drovers, who now received their good conduct awards direct from the Baroness. One driver who was sacked because he refused to commit an act of cruelty was presented with a bound volume of *Animal World* and, one hopes, another job. In 1885 the Baroness and Sir Walter Gilbey inaugurated London's annual cart-horse parade, which became so popular that entries had to be limited to one thousand.

It was a Victorian belief that essay-writing, if not ennobling in itself, helped in the clarification and strengthening of ideas. Carters and drovers could not be set to this task, but schoolchildren could. In a short space the prize essay contests started by the Ladies' Committee achieved a popularity hard to credit in this sophisticated day. By 1889 one thousand schools were competing, to the tune of 40,000 essays. It became a task for royalty to present the prizes at such centres as the Crystal Palace, the Albert Hall or Alexandra Palace, which were the scenes of gigantic, but always decorous, beanos. Even in the twentieth century the essay competitions continued to gather momentum; the total submitted by London schools

---

* *Dictionary of National Biography.*

alone in the RSPCA's jubilee year verged on the quarter-million.*

Soon after the Ladies' Committee was formed, the idea was conceived of recruiting the young into a humanitarian movement of their own. The temperance reformers had already shown the way; since the 1840s there had been Bands of Hope, the young members of which pledged themselves never to touch drink. Why not similar groups of youngsters pledged never to harm animals? In the 'seventies the first Bands of Mercy† began to appear. The credit for originating this movement is generally given to Mrs Catherine Smithies, of Wood Green, whose husband helped to found *Animal World*. Soon Bands of Mercy were being formed in the Dominions and in America and by 1883 the organisation was formally linked with the RSPCA. The children listened to readings and lectures; they sang 'All things bright and beautiful'; they learned innumerable poems with names like 'Dobbin's Friend', 'Hide, Birdie, Hide', 'Jessie to her Dead Robin', 'Don't Rob the Birds of Their Eggs, Boys', 'Only a Cur' and 'Boys Don't Throw Stones'; they took part in tableaux and parades, each member carrying one of the letters which spelled out 'A Band of Mercy'; and they qualified for medals. Mostly the organisation was run by women, but clergymen and even squires were co-opted to deliver readings. Mrs Florence Suckling, an active pioneer of the movement, outlined numerous exercises for Bands of Mercy in her book, *The Humane Educator*. There was a play which began with Mrs Percy rebuking some young girls for gushing over a hat with a bird on it. Sarah Jane, the maid, was so ashamed that she decided to empty a water jug down the gun of Mr Quickshot, the pigeon-shooter, and dip all his cartridges in warm water. The barrels burst in his face. The girls told him that 13,848 goldfinches were sent to London from Worthing in a single year and that a pair of sparrows in one week could destroy 4,000 caterpillars. Alice suggested that if Mr Quickshot really must shoot he should join the Rifle Volunteers; and Mr Quickshot had the grace to admit that there was force in

---

* E. G. Fairholme and Wellesley Pain: *A Century of Work for Animals*.
† Now the Animal Defenders movement.

their arguments. When Sarah suggested that hats could be trimmed with artificial birds, Mrs Percy exclaimed, 'My dear, the idea is as bad as the act!' It seems improbable that plays like this had any effect on the Mr Quickshots of real life; but they may have helped to bring up a new generation with a distaste for 'murderous millinery'.

The Band of Mercy movement spread many legends about

A Victorian hero: Greyfriars Bobby guards his master's grave
From 'Animal World', May 2, 1870

faithful animals, the most famous of these being Greyfriars Bobby. In 1858 a labourer called Gray died and was buried in Greyfriars Churchyard, Edinburgh. Afterwards his dog was found on his grave and, though often dislodged, always came back. A restaurant-keeper fed him every day. The Lord Provost exempted Bobby from the dog tax and gave him a collar inscribed: 'Greyfriars Bobby. Presented to him by the Lord Provost of Edinburgh, 1867.' When the dog died in 1872 the curator of the churchyard found him a grave near his master. Finally a fountain was raised in Bobby's honour by Baroness Burdett-Coutts.

It was an unusual lantern lecture which did not feature a picture of Greyfriars Bobby. Other slides might show 'Old Shepherd's Chief Mourner' (also a dog) or 'Alpine Mastiffs reanimating a Distressed Traveller' or similar works by Landseer; perhaps pictures of Cowper and his hares, or the Earl of Shaftesbury or even the Duke of Wellington. The Duke was a Band of Mercy hero because of the way he befriended a boy whom he found crying over a tame toad. No one, the boy explained, was willing to look after his pet when he went to boarding-school, so the Duke undertook to do so. He sent five letters to the boy reporting on the toad's welfare, one of them reading:

'Field-Marshal the Duke of Wellington is happy to inform William Harris that his toad is alive and well.'

Strathfieldsaye, July 27, 1837.

When the boy returned for his Christmas holidays, his pet was safely enjoying its winter sleep.*

No soldier had a better claim to figure in this gallery of honour than Sir Charles Napier. In the fierce Indian heat, while men died round him from apoplexy, he shared his tent with his charger, Red Rover. Angrily he fought against the over-loading of baggage camels, which were supposed to carry no more than 350 pounds. 'Yet I have seized and weighed the loads of many camels on the march which have passed 8,000 pounds,' he wrote.†

It had long been a taunt, though seldom a deserved one, that persons who were eager to prevent cruelty to animals did not care about cruelty to children. In 1884, in curious circumstances, the RSPCA helped to form the National Society for the Prevention of Cruelty to Children. In New York, Henry Bergh, pioneer of America's animal welfare societies, was asked to intercede on behalf of 'a little animal' suffering at the hands of a brutal woman. The little animal turned out to be a child. Bergh rose to the challenge and successfully prosecuted the woman for cruelty to an animal. After this

* Florence Suckling: *The Humane Educator.*
† Rosamond Lawrence: *Charles Napier.*

many similar cases were brought and a special society was formed in New York to protect children. The RSPCA, informed of these events, decided that a similar organisation ought to be started in Britain and the necessary steps were taken by Lord Shaftesbury and the Rev. Benjamin Waugh.*

It is unlikely that the English courts, which had ruled that bulls were not cattle, would have decided that children were animals.

In the propaganda field, a new campaigning body began to assert itself from 1891 onwards: the Humanitarian League. Its object was to advocate humane principles from a strictly rational standpoint. The League was founded by Henry Salt, Ernest Bell, the publisher, and others and remained active until 1919. While humanity to animals was perhaps its major preoccupation, it was concerned also with prison reform, the abolition of corporal and capital punishment, workshop sweating and so on. Salt, a former master of Eton College, kept open house for Fabians, rationalists, reformers, mystics and intellectuals of all stamps, a frequent visitor being George Bernard Shaw ('we were Shelleyans and Humanitarians,' the playwright wrote). According to Stephen Winsten,† Salt was anxious that the League should not become a depository for sentimental indulgences and false enthusiasms, and this is evident from the general tone of the *Humane Review*, the League's organ. The reviewer of Florence Suckling's *Humane Educator* complained strongly that 'the treatment of animals in verse has been almost as bad as their treatment in actual life.' He quoted Martin Tupper's appeal to boys to be kind to beasts:

> I wot your lot is somewhat rough,
>   But theirs is somewhat rougher;
> No hopes, no love, but pain enough,
>   And only sense to suffer;
> You men and boys have friends and joys,
>   And homes and hopes in measure –
> But these poor brutes are only mutes,
>   And never knew a pleasure.

* A. W. Moss: *Valiant Crusade.*
† *Salt And His Circle.*

'It would be impossible,' wrote the reviewer, 'to cram into eight lines a more appalling concentration of good intentions, bad poetry and worse thought.' To hedge off animals as dumb and senseless, he said, was to ensure that they would be treated accordingly. He much preferred 'the great, breezy, healthful utterance of Whitman':

I think I could turn and live with animals, they're so placid and self-contained,
I stand and look at them long and long.
They do not sweat and whine about their condition,
They do not lie awake in the dark and weep for their sins,
They do not make me sick discussing their duty to God,
Not one is dissatisfied, not one is demented with the mania of owning things,
Not one kneels to another, nor to his kind that lived thousands of years ago.
Not one is respectable or unhappy over the whole earth.*

Though its approach was primarily intellectual, the League was ready to lodge protests and send deputations, as for example when three of its members called on the Shechita Board to protest at Jewish methods of slaughter. And it did not spurn the emotional aid of Lady Florence Dixie, a one-time 'female Nimrod' anxious to atone for the deer whose throats she had cut.

A feature of the century was the tendency of the naturalist to become an observer – and later a photographer – rather than a killer. For too long Nature had been studied in the stuffed trophy. Richard Jefferies, Henry Thoreau and Ernest Thompson Seton were among those who set the new fashion. Each began by killing the creatures he loved, but – like Sir Edwin Landseer lining up a stag – found it harder and harder to pull the trigger. Thoreau's advocacy of sitting and watching wild creatures inspired a certain amount of derision. Asked by the puzzled people of Concord why he did not shoot a bird if he wanted to study it, he replied, 'Do you think I should shoot you if I wanted to study you?' In *Walden* he wrote that of late years he had found he could not fish without falling a little in self-respect. He helped to shoot a moose but the

* *Song Of Myself* (1855).

operation was 'too much like going out at night to some woodside pasture and shooting your neighbour's horses.'

In their writings and sketch-books the new race of naturalists roused the curiosity of new generations in *living* creatures. Nature books for the young became an industry. Boys' papers dropped their articles on home taxidermy and gave instructions in nature photography instead. Not all the new writers represented animals behaving as animals and many of their works were blatantly sentimental, or anthropomorphic; but the general result was to spread affection and respect for wild creatures.

Naturalists, hunters and humanitarians alike worried about the threat of extermination which overhung many species. Pleas to preserve Nature's 'precious heritage' for generations unborn came ill from sated sportsmen with guns under their arms; but the most ruthless agents of extermination were the bullies of commerce, armed as often as not with clubs. The last pair of great auks was taken in 1844, sole survivors of once-great Atlantic colonies, defenceless as cabbages; the last quagga died in a zoo at Amsterdam in 1883. Clubbed, speared and gaffed with peculiar brutality in lands beyond human habitation, the fur seal came within an inch of extinction; even the foetal furs were torn from the womb. The greed of sportsmen in Africa had led to systems of control and licensing. In America bison had once been so numerous that a man could ride past the same herd for more than a day. From about sixty million they had been cut, by the century's end, to a bare thousand and only an insignificant part of their flesh had been used for meat.

The fight to conserve dying species, by the setting up of reserves and sanctuaries, falls outside the scope of this book; but the emergence of a conscience which could rebel at extermination, even when it could not always rebel at cruelty, was a development of the first significance. In some, the conscience was scientific, in others religious; and in a few with time to think the revolt was one of simple disgust against the enterprise which could dispatch the equivalent of a cutting-out expedition to a remote coast of ice in order to flood the market with seal-skin trunks.

17

HUNTING: BUCK HOUNDS AND BEAGLES

IN the 1890s, opponents of 'blood' sports began to grow militant. Like the anti-vivisectionists, they were sometimes a source of embarrassment to the RSPCA, to which body many of them belonged. On ethical grounds, the RSPCA opposed hunting, but was not prepared to attack fox-hunting until some less cruel alternative form of fox control could be devised. It deplored the pursuit of carted deer and still kept a wary eye on the Royal Buck Hounds.

Much of the criticism against blood sports was conducted by, or with the backing of, the Humanitarian League. Henry Salt, its founder, was aware that reform could come only by instalments, so he selected his targets with some care. In his view the 'worst and most demoralising' form of hunting was the pursuit of tame or captured animals which were taken and hunted over and over again; and the most notorious addicts of this exercise were the Royal Buck Hounds, supported by the taxpayer. If this 700-year-old institution enjoying the highest patronage could be discredited and disbanded, then similar hunts would have no option but to disband; or so it seemed to the Humanitarian League. Whether the hunting of carted deer was really the most suitable sport to attack may be doubted. Its supporters could argue that while they performed no pesticidal function they did not seek to kill: why pick on a 'blood' sport in which no blood was shed, save by misadventure?

The Royal Buck Hounds had already attracted a good deal of derision, not merely because its members pursued dishorned deer in and out of barns and railway waiting-rooms, but because the mastership was a political appointment; 'sometimes a Conservative minister chased the stag, sometimes a Liberal,' says E. F. Benson.* It was also mocked because it attracted social climbers. According to Lord Randolph Churchill in a Commons debate in 1883 its ranks consisted of 'the counter-jumpers of London – that class of persons who were dominated by the generic term of 'Arry,'; and it was known in the East-end as ''Arry's 'Ounds'. But a Member protested that 'there were many gentlemen in the Metropolis who could not enjoy sport in any other form than by following the Queen's Buck Hounds.' These remarks were made during a debate on an unsuccessful Bill designed to prohibit the hunting of captive animals or the shooting of trap pigeons.

Nearly a score of hunts pursued the carted deer, their 'wonderful chases' being described in detail in the *Field*. 'Our deer today was an untried Irish hind and the glorious uncertainty as to whether she would run well or not added to the enjoyment,' wrote a correspondent of the Dragoon Guards Stag Hounds in 1896. The hind took to a road which she was reluctant to leave, ran alongside a railway, then took 'a bad line' of country and shook off her pursuers. 'The Master decided to leave her out, which we hope will improve her travelling capabilities.' A week later, when the Dragoon Guards released another Irish hind from the 'Black Maria', the creature took refuge in a cemetery, whereupon 'hounds were stopped and taken home.' In a 'grand run' of the Mid-Kent Stag Hounds the deer was lost after three hours forty-five minutes. 'We have left her in an awful country,' said the Hunt's correspondent, expressing the pious hope that 'we may once again take her safe.'†

The campaign to discredit the Royal Buck Hounds was waged, with Salt's encouragement, by the Rev. J. Stratton, Chaplain to Lucas' Hospital, Wokingham, who in his youth had hunted the fox. The deliberate cruelties which had once disfigured the hunt – allowing young hounds to pull down old

---

* *King Edward VII.*

† More successful were Surtees' Surrey stag-hunters who, 'by selecting the proper animal, could ensure a finish at any place they most wished to dine at.' – *Jorrocks' Jaunts and Jollities* (1838).

and deliberately lamed animals – had been discontinued, and deer which showed 'surliness' or reluctance to run were no longer beaten or otherwise abused. Apart from the risk of mauling from ill-trained hounds, the likeliest causes of injury were fence stakes and barbed wire. Tactfully, the hunt had dropped its Easter custom of decking the quarry with ribbons, since this only emphasised its tameness, but not every stag was so tame that it could be handled without the use of 'body armour' and a two-handled shield. It was widely assumed that the dishorning of stags was to protect the hounds, but a correspondent of the *Field* explained on January 23, 1892: 'The practice of reducing the extra length of horn is for the benefit of the deer as they cannot get hung up in the woods nor can they injure themselves in the Swinley Paddocks' (where the royal deer were kept).

The Rev. J. Stratton began his campaign with letters to newspapers and followed up with a pamphlet *Cruel Sport: Some Facts Concerning the Queen's Buck Hounds* (1891), a copy of which he sent to Queen Victoria. It produced a letter from Sir H. F. Ponsonby who said: 'I do not wish to enter into discussion upon a subject with which I have nothing to do. But I may observe, though probably you are already aware of the fact, that the Queen has been strongly opposed to stag-hunting for many years past.' Later approaches to the Queen brought the reply that this was a matter on which she could take action only on the advice of her ministers.

In 1893, when the Chancellor of the Exchequer was asked whether the Government would abolish the Buck Hounds, he said the question was a very difficult one and would require 'mature deliberation'. Next year another Bill to end the hunting of carted deer, along with rabbit coursing, was unsuccessful. About this time there was much indignation when a stag of some repute called Guy Fawkes, hard-pressed by the Buck Hounds, disembowelled itself on a fence which it had not the strength to clear, and was finished off by huntsmen.

Sometimes Stratton walked twenty miles a day gathering evidence; he also employed an ex-inspector of police. If they hoped to uncover spectacular atrocities they were disappointed. Mostly, investigations showed that the quarry, on being turned out, ran for refuge to sheds or buildings. People of position declined to talk about the Hunt's activities, not wishing to denounce their neighbours, and the humbler classes were also anxious to give no offence. Stratton received a good many abusive letters and once shots were fired at his house, after which he bought a revolver. At Wokingham, for long a main-stay of bull-baiting, a meeting was held in defence of the Buck Hounds. In 1894 the Sporting League was formed, having as its object 'the protection, support and improvement of all legitimate sports, pastimes and recreations.' But Stratton went on engineering resolutions, memorials and petitions, gathering signatures, organising deputations. Throughout he made use of a quotation from an article which had found its way into the *Field* on September 3, 1892. The writer equated the hunting of carted deer with bull-baiting and said that 'nothing but the prescription and aegis of royal patronage have saved it from being consigned to limbo.' He argued that if anyone were to capture badgers, aniseed them and turn them out in the open with five minutes' start of a scratch pack of terriers there would be an outcry; and yet the badger was better able to defend itself than 'the dishorned buck of modern stag-hunting that "soils" in a river or shelters in a cowshed; and the badger is no more wild in nature than the park-reared deer.'

In 1896 John Colam, secretary of the RSPCA, quoted this passage in a letter to Lord Salisbury and the *Field* of November 28 announced: 'Perhaps the time has arrived when we ought no longer to refrain from explaining that the article in question . . . does not represent the views of this paper. The article should have been declined and returned to the writer, the sentiments being quite opposed to the line the *Field* has always taken, but by an oversight the article was inserted during the absence of the departmental editor.' The Rev. J. Stratton must have been well aware that the article did not express the viewpoint of the *Field*, which had been freely chastising him; and his use of the quotation, in all the circumstances, was open to criticism. The issue which contained the *Field*'s explanation also carried this admission: 'We repeat that we do not seek and never have sought to exalt the hunting of the carted deer to the position of the highest form of sport, but because it falls short of the ideal it does not follow that it is attended with all the barbarities alleged against it by Mr Stratton' (this presumably explained why the *Field* also carried reports of pigeon-shooting).

The defenders of carted deer-hunting were able to exert strong pressure in Parliament when the Cruelty to Wild Animals in Captivity Bill was discussed in 1900. Lord James of Hereford explained that the measure – the first to offer any protection to wild animals – was intended chiefly to protect beasts in menageries, and had nothing to do with stag-hunting or rabbit-coursing; but the peers would not pass the Bill until a clause exonerating those two sports had been written into it.

When Edward VII acceded, a Parliamentary Select Committee was appointed to make economies in the Royal Household and it decided to save £6,000 a year by abolishing the Buck Hounds, in which the King had no interest. The Committee does not seem to have been opposed to blood sports as such, for it toyed with the idea of recommending a pack of royal fox-hounds, but thought it would be wrong to subsidise a specific sport with public money. So, ostensibly on the grounds of economy, a Conservative Government ended an institution which had survived from Plantagenet times.

Was this really a victory for humanitarian propaganda? The Rev. J. Stratton and the Humanitarian League considered that it was. But if they thought the disbandment of the Royal Buck Hounds meant the end of hunting carted deer, they were soon disillusioned. In 1910 the controversy flared up again when the undergraduate Master of Cambridge University's so-called drag hunt was charged at the instance of the RSPCA with ill-treating a carted hind. During the chase the animal was injured on barbed wire, and took refuge in the yard of a railway gate-keeper, where it was struck and otherwise mishandled in an effort to make it run again. Instead, it fell dead. A majority of magistrates decided that as the chase was in progress at the time the prosecution must fail; if the animal had been abused before or after the chase they would presumably have convicted. The Senior Proctor, who seemed to have little knowledge of how undergraduates amused themselves, complained that the RSPCA was merely out for publicity; but the University undertook to prevent a recurrence.

With the Royal Buck Hounds out of the way, the Humanitarian League turned to other hunting targets, including (in Charles Kingsley's words)

> Those heroes bold in leather breeches,
> Who leap o'er five-barred gates and ditches,
> The perils of the field to dare
> To hunt that furious beast, the hare.

The League chose to concentrate its fire on the beaglers of Henry Salt's old school: Eton. This policy afforded better publicity and showed that the League was not afraid of assaulting the bastions of privilege.

It was a century and a half since Eton boys had battered a hamstrung pig to death in Weston's Yard; dog-fights, duck-hunts and badger-baits were a distant memory. A College drag hunt had been formed but appears to have lapsed. At this time Eton was the only great public school to hunt the hare (today a number of schools have packs of beagles). Under the opening barrage the College maintained a contemptuous silence, but in 1902, after a memorial signed by distinguished citizens had been widely quoted, the governing body replied that whether or not beagles were kept was a matter for the Headmaster's discretion. A curious aspect of the controversy was that both the Headmaster and Provost were members of the Windsor branch of the RSPCA and were re-elected each year despite expressions of displeasure from the parent body. To the Humanitarian League the Headmaster, Dr Edmond Warre, eventually wrote: 'I have never been given to understand that the Society has condemned the hunting of animals. If it does, ought it not at once to enlighten its subscribers upon this point so that they may not be contributing to its funds under a false impression?' His own view was that the hunt was neither cruel nor demoralising. The contrary opinion was expressed, less temperately, by the writer of a prize essay written for the League, who said: 'If, in the years to come, these boys, as military officers, have imposed on them by the policy of their rulers the odious task of massacring a virtually unarmed rabble, under circumstances that resemble sheep slaughter rather than warfare . . . they may be the better able to subdue their otherwise invincible repugnance by the useful preparatory training furnished by these quite analogous sports.'*

Dr Warre relaxed so far as to express regret at the language used in the *Eton Chronicle*'s beagling reports, which told how dogs which 'thoroughly deserved blood' succeeded in 'breaking up' a quarry so exhausted that it was 'absolutely stiff' or 'so done that it could not stand.' Not that respect for a brave adversary was lacking: 'one gallant old Jack hare stood up before the pack for two hours twenty minutes before he was rolled over.'

It was not the fate of Jack hares that caused most concern, however. By 1906 sporting circles had grown critical of the Eton practice of hunting hares in late March, when does were liable to be heavy with young. The new headmaster, Canon E. L. Lyttelton, said that if heavy hares were started, they were never run; but despite his denials, pregnant does were chased. A group of twenty-four women, including Miss Christabel Pankhurst and Mrs Bramwell Booth, addressed a letter to Canon Lyttelton saying: 'It seems that the hunting of a creature so timorous and defenceless as the hare is at best but little calculated to foster those qualities of manliness and courage which it is so desirable to develop in the youth of our nation; but to hunt the female hare at a time when she is handicapped by the burden which Nature imposes on her would seem to be not merely contrary to the spirit of true sportsmanship but positively demoralising and degrading to all who consciously participate in it.' The signatories expressed the view that if the education committee of a council school encouraged boys to hunt heavy hares there would be a big outcry. Ouida, the novelist, considered that 'the very discussion whether the hares are heavy or light seems insupportably brutal.' In 1907 Canon Lyttelton was able to tell importunate correspondents that the hunting season at Eton had been cut back, but he maintained that to ban the beagles 'would do more harm than good.'

* *The Eton College Hare Hunt*: Three Prize Essays (1904).

A piquant feature of the campaign was the appearance, in 1907, of a hoax publication entitled *Beagler Boy*, apparently dedicated to the task of saving Eton's noble sport from extinction. It was the work of Henry Salt and another Old Etonian, George (later Sir George) Greenwood, MP for Peterborough. In Salt's words, it contained 'the most idiotic balderdash and fustian that could be collected in defence of beagling.' Referring to unworthy attempts to discredit the Britannia (Royal Navy) Beagles because the boys had killed a three-legged hare, *Beagler Boy* said: 'A hare with only three legs would be regarded by some persons as insufficiently equipped for the chase; but to these fine sanguine young fellows, already trained to be equal to any emergency and to "make a little go a long way", even a three-legged hare is the means of providing true sport.' Alluding to Herbert Spencer's opposition to beagling, the conspirators pointed out that he was neither an Etonian nor a sportsman – 'surely that is reason enough to disqualify Spencer's opinion.' The tongue-in-cheek nature of *Beagler Boy* was not detected by many of those to whom it was addressed, and it was received, both within and without the College, with acclamation.*

After much persuasion, Henry Salt persuaded his friend George Bernard Shaw (who had been incensed by rabbit-coursers on the Hog's Back near his home) to write in condemnation of blood sports. This he did in an introduction to a volume of essays, *Killing For Sport*, published in 1914. Pretending some bewilderment, he said: 'I know many sportsmen and none of them are ferocious. I have known many humanitarians and they are all ferocious.' He claimed to be an advocate of the hunting of children during certain months, so that they would be well fed and preserved by sportsmen and the survivors would make a better nation. The essence of his philippic was that he could understand men killing for profit, hatred or revenge, but not for the sake of passing the time and being a good fellow, which was 'to behave like an idiot or a silly imitative sheep.'

* H. S. Salt in *Cruel Sports*, April, 1928.

18

TEARS FOR THE ELEPHANT

THE activities of the big game hunter did not escape the notice of humanitarians. To 'open up Africa with a rifle' might be a necessary task, but how much of the shooting was essential, how much was wanton?

The big game hunter's motives varied widely. All too often he was a trophy collector pure and simple. He might have personal reasons for wishing to attest his skill and courage; he might even be the traditional jilted lover seeking moderately dangerous distraction. Sometimes he was (or called himself) a naturalist, sometimes an ivory hunter, or a skin trader or a scout for zoos and circuses, or a combination of all these; in later days he was a game warden, shooting to cull. At his best he was to be found stalking and destroying man-eating carnivores which terrorised villages. At his worst he was an exhibitionist who, merely to exercise his marksmanship, littered the landscape with corpses of harmless animals, and who took no pains to finish off his wounded.

The big game hunter prided himself that, even if he did not risk his life daily, he went through a wide range of manly discomforts, with a fair chance of dying in delirium on the floor of a Kaffir kraal. But often he faced little more risk, and little more hardship, than did those princes of Europe who achieved such enormous bags of unaggressive creatures in Bohemia. The safari, in the early twentieth century, was already being organised in such a way that the hunter merely had to take out the appropriate licence, hire the guides, pull the trigger and pay the bills. In this way a man who had been in Africa for six weeks could knock down, for amusement, great beasts which had been there for sixty years, and bring home their feet for waste-paper baskets.

In the early days of the rifle a hunter required to have some of the skills of the naturalist to approach his prey; but as rifles improved in range and 'stopping-power' the risk to the hunter grew steadily less and the excuse that man was pitting his craft against that of the quarry wore thinner. Even the fiercest jungle animal had no defence against the high-velocity expanding bullet, the effect of which has been described thus:

'The impact causes the bullet to expand. Often it breaks into pieces or else takes a mushroom shape, the head with its tremendous velocity dragging and catching with its edges the flesh and viscera; it often happens in the case of delicate animals that upon leaving the body it makes a hole as big as the crown of a hat.'*

Even before the rifle was invented, sportsmen had been freely exercising their skill on the wild life of Africa. The Rev. Christian Latrobe, who published in 1818 *A Journal of a Visit to South Africa*, tells of a 'pleasant ship's companion' named Buck with whom he remonstrated on the outward voyage for shooting at albatrosses and other sea birds 'without any prospect of profiting by their death.' His pleas were 'pronounced overstrained' and disregarded. After visiting missionary settlements, Latrobe again met Buck, who announced that he had been to Saldanha Bay with a hunting party which had shot 106 antelope. Hardly any of these had been required for food; most 'were left miserably to perish in the wilderness, killed or maimed, merely to gratify the momentary vanity of being a good marksman.' This passion for killing, in Latrobe's view, sprang from 'those inordinate desires which for a time seem to suppress all proper feeling even in a heart otherwise benevolent and kind.'

Frederick Courtenay Selous, hunter, ivory trader and self-styled 'sportsman-naturalist', who lived by his gun in Africa in the 1870s, conceded that some people might consider his game records 'a terrible record of slaughter.' What critics overlooked, he said, was that a hunter was often accompanied by 'a crowd of hungry savages' all dependent on him. Save

---

* Edouard Fou: *After Big Game In Central Africa* (c. 1901).

by providing copious meat, he could obtain no guides, no corn or other necessities. In one period of four months Selous killed forty-two elephants, a colleague accounted for fifty and his Kaffirs for nearly forty more. He used large-bore duck guns firing a round bullet of four ounces; on one occasion, a twice-loaded gun kicked him into the air. After shooting ten elephants in a week, Selous wrote:

'It seems dreadful to slaughter so many of these huge creatures merely for their tusks; for if there are no bushmen or other natives about the carcasses are abandoned to the hyenas and vultures. But *il faut vivre*. Ivory is the only thing obtainable in this country with which to defray the heavy expenses of hunting; and if you depend on your gun for a living, as was my case, it behoves you to do your best when you get a chance.'*

The hunters who supplied zoos operated widely in the Sudan, shipping back their captives from Egypt; but the mortality on the journey to Western Europe sometimes exceeded 50 per cent. Carl Hagenbeck, the zoo and circus proprietor, tells how a zoo ship would leave Africa with a hundred nanny goats on board to give milk to the young giraffes and baby animals; afterwards the goats would be slaughtered and fed to the carnivores. It is clear from Hagenbeck's account that the highly organised zoo trade, with its hippo-pits and baboon-stations (to which muzzled baboons were carried in tight cocoons of cloth) involved a considerable degree of suffering. He describes the 'barbarous spectacle' of a zebra round-up in Abyssinia, where two thousand soldiers would encircle a herd and drive it into a river bed, then lash the animals for hours with whips until they were thoroughly exhausted and broken in spirit, when they were fettered and taken away.†

Almost every book by a big game hunter contains routine expressions of regret for bringing death to noble creatures; but the regret is rarely strong enough to dissuade the pursuer from pressing on to kill more. Here are two characteristic passages, the first being inspired by the painful death of an elephant:

* *A Hunter's Wanderings In Africa* (1881).
† *Beasts and Men* (1909).

The Prince of Wales (Edward VII) slays an elephant in Ceylon

'Such a spectacle is enough to make the most hardened hunter feel remorse. It seemed to me that I had done a bad action. Several times have I said to myself upon seeing these splendid animals suffer that I ought to place my rifle in the rack for ever.'*

The second is inspired by the shooting of a zebra:

'This was the first time I had seen these beautifully marked animals in their wild state, so I selected the largest, and as I was quite close to him he dropped in his tracks stone dead. When I stood over the handsome creature I was positively sorry for having killed him.'

In that last quotation the most revealing word is 'so'. Here is beauty, 'so' let us destroy it. The writer was the author of *The Man-Eaters of Tsavo* (1907), Lt-Col J. H. Patterson, DSO, a courageous shot who, at dire personal risk, wiped out a number of marauding lions which had acquired a taste for human flesh. Here is another passage from his book:

'As our train sped onwards through the level uplands we saw a fine ostrich striding along parallel with the line, as if having a race with us. Dr McCulloch at once seized his rifle and by a lucky shot brought down the huge bird; the next and greater difficulty, however, was to secure the prize. For a time the engine-driver took no notice of our signals, but at last we succeeded in attracting his attention and the train was shunted back to where the ostrich had fallen . . .'

To the game hunter of this period, it was as natural to shoot animals from a train as to expect the train to stop while the trophy was lugged aboard.

Occasionally a hunter tried to analyse what Latrobe called the 'inordinate desires' impelling him to kill. The explanations were never very convincing, and the least convincing perhaps was that offered by a British Member of Parliament, Sir Henry Seton-Karr, whose especial pleasure was to shoot stags, elks, reindeer and bears. When he brought down his first stag in Norway he at once felt 'that feeling of satisfied desire which always follows a hunter's skill, but which logically is out of all apparent proportion to the actual object attained.' He continues:

* Edouard Fou: *After Big Game in Central Africa.*

'Only those who have experienced it can realise the strength of the hunter's lust to kill the hunted, though they may find it difficult to explain. It is certain that no race of men possess this desire more strongly than the Anglo-Saxons of the British Isles . . . Let us take it that in our case this passion is an inherited instinct – which civilisation cannot eradicate – of a virile and dominant race and that it forms a healthy natural antidote to the enervating refinements of modern life.'*

Sir Henry was of the school which held that it would be a perversion of Nature to thwart the hunting instinct, proper though it might be to tame other savage passions. Nothing was to be put into the sportsman's way. Sir Henry was capable of writing: 'It remains for some English or Norske millionaire to buy up and depopulate the isle of Tusteren in order to turn it into a perfect and most sporting natural deer forest.' He was aware there had been criticism of the practice of turning land into deer forest but was not concerned to justify this policy, since 'sportsmen can well be trusted as a class to look after themselves and their own pursuits.' He himself would continue to hunt 'shamelessly and without apology.' In *My Sporting Holidays* he tells of his bloodthirsty moods after 'black days' in which no beasts fall; he is jealous of other men's trophies; and he exclaims: 'How the incidents of the death of each noble stag dwell in one's memory!' Yet, in the midst of gloating, doubt breaks through: 'Why is it, by the by, that the size and beauty of wild stags and other big game arouse in certain individuals this lust to kill?' Put a civilised man in sight of a fine head, says Sir Henry, 'and he will straightway be seized with an inordinate desire to slay the animal in question.' Moreover, 'this desire will increase in direct proportion to the size and beauty and difficulties and exertion entailed in its pursuit.' But the only explanation Sir Henry can offer is the one he has already given; to which he adds that 'the pursuit and slaughter of wild game is a perfectly natural, healthy and widespread trait of humanity, even necessary in some cases, for health and happiness.'

These observations would merit less attention if Sir Henry had not been a Member of Parliament. In both Houses there were numerous sportsmen who thought, consciously or un-

* *My Sporting Holidays* (1904).

consciously, along these lines; and they took care to emasculate any Bill which seemed likely to prevent virile Anglo-Saxons from pursuing health and happiness by slaughter.

Ernest Thompson Seton, the artist-naturalist, who grew to prefer the camera to the gun, recalls how in childhood he was 'gripped in a wild animalism that was as surprising to us as it was ancient in our blood.' One day he speared a number of hens for no reason he could explain and was well beaten for it. As a youth he stalked deer and knew the quivering excitement of 'buck ague'. Eventually he shot at a moose and 'away we ran on the trail like wolves fairly gloating over the continual jets of blood.' This time regret at killing 'for the sake of a passing thrill of triumph' caused him to make a vow – 'that so long as they are threatened with early extermination I will never again lift my rifle against any of America's big game.'* This was not a vow to abjure shooting altogether; it was the resolution of a naturalist rather than a sportsman.

But for the skill of the taxidermist, much slaughter might never have been undertaken. Sportsmen sent their trophies home to the firm of Rowland Ward, whose *Sportsman's Handbook* advised on the preparation and cleansing of trophies (No. 2 Taxidermine to rub into the pelts of pachyderms, No. 3 for birds, and so on). The Rowland Ward who compiled the fourth edition, published in 1888, was the third of the line. He notes with pleasure a decline in the use of high-calibre weapons with bullets which smash and tear. 'The true sportsman,' he says, 'seeks rather an exercise of his skill and courage than the silly vanity of copious butchering.' A camera was now part of the hunter's equipment, which meant that 'an animal may be photographed in its surroundings just as it fell'; and with a little resource the animal could even be photographed in its surroundings as it lived.† The firm of Rowland Ward was ready to turn animal products into 'innumerable articles of domestic utility,' which included making not only waste-paper baskets but liqueur-stands out

---

* *Trail Of An Artist-Naturalist* (1941).

† Modern tourists with film cameras demand to take pictures of animals charging, which often means that the hunter standing by with his rifle must kill in 'self-defence'. – J. A. Hunter: *African Hunter* (1954).

of elephants' feet. The 1888 *Handbook* says: 'It may sometimes fall to the lot of the traveller to secure an albatross,' meaning that the traveller often felt the urge to go up on deck and shoot one. Such a sportsman might not know what to do with 'his unwieldy and not very rare specimen.' The *Handbook* therefore points out that, if he does not wish to preserve the bird whole, the tubular wing bones will make excellent pipe stems and the big webbed-feet can be fashioned into beautiful tobacco-pouches or work-bags for ladies.

Not every savage head dispatched to a taxidermist had been shot in the wild. Sir Garrard Tyrwhitt-Drake, the menagerie owner, had a standing request from a well-known crack shot to let him shoot any animal which had to be destroyed. This sportsman was rich and brave enough to go on safari, but apparently had no time to do so; however, on receipt of a telephone call, he would always find time to arrive at the zoo with a battery of expensive rifles to shoot a lion, a bison, or even a hyena for his collection.* Carl Hagenbeck says that once when he was faced with destroying a rogue elephant, a member of the Rowland Ward family offered to find a sportsman willing to pay £50 or so for shooting it. Hagenbeck was eager to cut his loss, and a Mr W. duly arrived at Hamburg with an appropriate arsenal. At the appointed time the elephant was tethered to a wall, but the sportsman did not turn up. When he was fetched it appeared that his sporting ardour had deserted him; nevertheless, he would not allow anyone else to shoot. 'After further delay,' writes Hagenbeck, 'I at last proposed to the embarrassed hero that the animal should be hanged, and to this he gave his consent.' Six men pulled on a rope and the animal was dead in less than a minute. 'Thus ended one of the strangest tragi-comedies I have ever seen.'†

---

* *My Life With Animals* (1939).

† Hagenbeck's *Beasts And Men* has a photograph captioned 'Strangling a Sick Elephant'. It shows the beast lying on its side and several men pulling on a rope. This may well have been a more humane method of execution than that described in *The Times* of March 2, 1826. An elephant from the Exeter Change menagerie in London was killed by 'repeated discharges of musketry, the noise of which, together with the agonised groans of the poor beast, being distinctly heard in the Strand, caused . . . immense crowds to assemble.' Offers of one or two guineas to see the protracted death throes were declined, on the grounds of danger. – See *London in the News*, by William Kent.

Pig-sticking, while not strictly a form of big game hunting, may be touched on here. It was an obsession with British officers in India, where it evolved from the earlier sport of bear-sticking. Its addicts regarded it as vastly superior to fox-hunting. Instead of forty hounds chasing one fox, one man pursued one quarry which was perfectly capable of ripping him open if he was thrown. This 'purifying risk' was held to justify the sport. Sweepstakes were organised with the prize going to the rider who achieved 'first spear', that is, who first drew blood. Under the rules, this rider was supposed to pursue the quarry to the death. In major contests like that for the Kadir Cup eagerness to claim 'first spear' led to hasty, superficial mutilations which were followed up by spear after spear, until the dying animal sat back on its haunches and was run through efficiently, or was shot. On such occasions the purifying risks were less easy to discern. Those whose trophy was the 'glittering tush' grudged fox-hunters their enormous literature and gradually built up one of their own. A typical sentence from a book of memoirs is this: 'That was the first pig I ever dipped steel into, and I felt elated at fleshing my maiden spear, though I had yet to learn the triumphant delight and rapture of taking a first one. I examined the fallen enemy with feelings of great interest and gratification . . .'*

The sport was not without its rules. The writer of the foregoing mentions a colonel who used to stop the leave of anyone who killed a sow 'unless she was in proper condition and had no squeakers at her tail.' A rule of the Calcutta Tent Club was that anyone who speared a sow paid with a dozen of champagne. In some clubs, shooting a pig brought expulsion.

In their cups, pig-stickers sang fustian like this:

> See how he flashes his fiery eye,
> Ready to cut, to thrust, to die!
> A boar that will charge like the Light Brigade
> Is the bravest brute God ever made.

* Captain J. T. Newall: *Hog-Hunting in the East* (1867).

and

> We envy not the rich their wealth,
>   Nor kings their crowned career,
> The saddle is our throne of health,
>   Our sceptre is the spear.
> We rival, too, the warrior's pride,
>   Dress stained with purple gore,
> For our field of fame is the jungle side,
>   Our foe – the jungle boar.*

One of the least inhibited pig-stickers was Sir Robert Baden-Powell. He describes the sport as 'manly and tip-top' and says it offers 'a taste of the brutal and most primitive of all hunts — namely the pursuit, with a good weapon in your hand, of an enemy whom you want to kill . . . you rush for blood with all the ecstasy of a fight to the death.'†

In 1908 Sir Robert founded the Boy Scouts, whose code enjoins kindness to animals.

* Major Charles van der Byl: *My Fifty Years of Sport* (1937).
† *Pig-Sticking or Hog-Hunting* (1889).

19

CROCKS FOR EXPORT

A MEMBER of Parliament watching a procession of horses bound for the slaughter-houses of Belgium noticed among them a pony with an identifying tape on one fetlock. He was told that the animal was a family favourite on which all the owner's children had learned to ride and which had spent its last days pulling a mowing machine on the lawn. The purpose of the tape was to notify the slaughterman that the pony's hoof was to be returned to the family as a memento of its fidelity.

The export of old horses, which yielded such bizarre stories as this, was much on the public conscience in the early years of the present century. Most, but not all, of the animals were work-worn and decrepit, or misfits of some kind. To pasture them all would have been impossible; to kill and bury them would have been a waste, so long as an export market existed. It was a traffic which was heightened, to some extent, by the coming of the motor car. Though the petrol engine ended centuries of misery for the draught horse, the fate of the horses made redundant was unpleasant. In winter the trade was swollen by farm horses which had helped with the harvest and were cheaper to sell than to feed. But every kind of horse, sooner or later, found its way on to the Channel ships, not excluding State Coach horses, mayoral horses, hunt horses and Army chargers (after the 1913 Yeomanry training 1,500 temporarily unfit horses were sold for prices ranging from £7 to £16). Costers, when the price of vegetables rose, sometimes had to dispose of animals whose food cost twice as much a day as their own meagre rations. Coachmen and grooms, ordered to take horses to the nearest slaughter-house, did not always resist the temptation to sell them into slavery instead.

Shipments of old horses to Belgium, Holland and France began to multiply in the late Victorian years. Most of the animals were slaughtered for human food, but those with a week or two's work in them were required to discharge their last debt to man on Flanders farms. The trade was conducted from numerous ports and precautions were taken to shield the sorriest beasts from the public gaze. Nevertheless, the RSPCA prosecuted many dealers who tried to ship manifestly unfit beasts. In 1898 the Ministry of Agriculture made its first attempt to regulate the trade, but enforcement was inadequate. The stumbling procession of British horses winding over the Belgian *pavé* became one of the saddest sights in Europe; notoriously, it gave the veterinary students of Antwerp a chance to study every kind of equine infirmity.

Strong and perennial condemnation of the traffic appeared in the press, notably the *Daily Mail*. In 1910 a ship which had weathered bad storms on the way from Hull arrived at Antwerp with thirty dead horses, of which seventeen had to have their throats cut on board. The secretary of the RSPCA, Captain E. G. Fairholme, was robbed of his camera as he photographed the bloody disembarkation and had to be given police protection. His Society had already secured more than 700 convictions for attempting to ship unfit beasts. In that year Parliament passed a Diseases of Animals Act, introduced by George Greenwood, stiffening the earlier regulations; but it still did not give power to stop the export of animals which might suffer, not only on the voyage, but on reaching Europe.

In 1914 an Act was passed, not without heavy opposition, to prohibit the export of a horse worth £10 or less. Colonel William Hall Walker (later Lord Wavertree), who moved the second reading, was a famous sportsman and breeder whose Minoru won the Derby for Edward VII. He was at pains to put both sides of the case. Some 50,000 unwanted horses, he said, were being exported every year; to have buried them in England would have meant running the risk of plague. Deplorable though it might seem, the Continental market was of real benefit to Britain. Colonel Hall Walker was proud that we had sold one thousand donkeys cheap to Belgium to take the place of draught dogs and thought the Government should stimulate this trade by rearing donkeys on waste land in Wales and Ireland. He then informed the House:

'Very bad horses are used for making sausages. When these sausages are six months' old they are sold at tenpence per pound and are used in foreign restaurants in the East-end. When they are two years' old they are worth more money and are sold at 3s 6d per pound in first-class restaurants in London, and they are wrapped up in silver paper to give them a more dignified appearance.'

It was thus possible that the family which requested the pony's fetlock (the anecdote was told by Colonel Hall Walker) might have eaten some portion of its carcase two years later.

To the Colonel's argument that the Chancellor of the Exchequer could afford to hire more inspectors out of the £3,000 a year he made from the horse traffic, the President of the Board of Agriculture replied that his inspectors were already exceeding their powers under the 1910 Act. When Walter Long argued that hunts could make good use of dead horses, Sir John Rolleston told of a hunt horse he had seen put up for auction. For twenty illness-free years it had been ridden by master, huntsman and whips. As the auctioneer said, no pace had been too fast for it and no day too long. This pride of the hunt was knocked down for £5 and went to be stabbed in Belgium. 'The Spanish owner who sends his old horse to the bull-ring is a more humane man than the British owner who sends it to a horse repository,' said Sir John Rolleston.

Much of the agitation leading to the 1914 Act (which was rendered inoperative by the war) was stimulated by the single-minded Miss Ada Cole, who secured a gruesome film of the horses' ordeal, from 'sausage boat' to abattoir. In 1919, after spending much of the war in German custody, she again attacked the horse traffic. So did the RSPCA, from which Miss Cole later broke away to found the International League for the Protection of Horses. In 1921 the Minister of Agriculture expressed horror at the revelations by one of his own veterinary inspectors whom he had sent to report on the trade. There were campaigns to raise the minimum value of horses for export, or to tax the trade heavily, and these raised angry protests from dealers and breeders. The Continental market showed great reluctance to accept carcasses, or dressed meat, the demand being for 'freshly killed'. Gradually the traffic dwindled, but it was still going on when the Second World War broke out. In more recent times agitation has focused on the export of Irish horses to Europe.

Decrepit horses sent for slaughter had this advantage: their sufferings were visible to the onlooker. Out of sight, in the coal mines, totally cut off from their natural environment, laboured an army of horses and ponies some 100,000 strong whose miseries were as difficult to assess as they were easy to exaggerate. When horses were freely belaboured in the public streets it seemed improbable that ponies underground were handled with exemplary gentleness; but evidence of ill-usage was hard to obtain. The ponies were taken below ground when they were considered to be mature and rarely came up again until they were unfit for haulage work. Some showed terror at the noises and tremors of the workings, dashed their heads on the walls and kicked out at all who tried to placate them; these had to be rejected. Even tractable horses often damaged their heads and eyes in narrow workings which changed their contours under stress. A conspicuous cause of wastage among ponies was 'double-shifting', that is, using the animals on two shifts in twenty-four hours, often on punishing gradients. Sometimes loaded tubs broke away and overran the animals which were supposed to be pulling them.

In 1887 a Coal Mines Regulation Act had laid down rudimentary rules about the employment of pit ponies; they were not to be used, for example, in roads too small for them, or when they were unfit, and miners were forbidden (largely in their own interests) to ride on the animals' backs. It was the duty of mines inspectors to watch over the ponies' welfare; the owners refused to allow RSPCA inspectors underground. Gradually allegations of inhumanity towards pit ponies grew to such volume that the Home Secretary referred them to the Royal Commission on Mines of 1910. One of the leading accusers, Francis A. Fox, admitted to the Commission that he had greatly overstated his case, that he had used 'flamboyant language', that his claim to have received complaints from colliers all over England was 'conventional exaggeration' and that the atrocities he cited were extreme and not typical. The Commissioners considered that miners were 'an eminently humane class of men, as ready to deal considerately with the animals worked by them as they were to risk their own lives in saving one another from danger.' The ponies, in the Commissioners' view, mostly worked in equable and warm temperatures and were not overworked. Of blind ponies, they said: 'If it were forbidden to employ them at all in a mine they would have to be sent to work on the surface, under even less favourable conditions, or else shot.' Most of them were treated kindly and appeared physically well. For these reasons they thought that blind ponies should still be allowed to undertake suitable light work in mines, 'but only when led and treated with special kindness.'

However, Parliament was persuaded by J. G. Butcher (later Lord Danesfort) to forbid the employment of blind ponies. When the Coal Mines Bill of 1911 was being discussed he explained that they constituted only one per cent of the equine labour force and rarely worked more than two days a fortnight. If not led, they walked into obstructions, and if led the lads who guided them were always being lamed. Less sentimental Members pointed out that blind ponies were peculiarly qualified to work in darkness and could not be frightened by sudden lights. Sir A. Markham, speaking for the industry, said he had known stone-blind ponies to be worked underground for twenty years with never a mark on them.

The Coal Mines Act laid down other rules governing the use of pit ponies: no animals under four years of age were to be allowed underground; all were to have proper stables, suitably ventilated; there was to be one horse keeper to fifteen horses; and records of hours worked were to be kept. Ironically, the year in which miners were vindicated saw pit ponies used as hostages in an industrial quarrel. When miners struck in a group of Welsh pits, a number of ponies were brought to the surface but others were left below, and the strikers refused either to tend the fires which operated the ventilation machinery or to allow rescuers to go underground.

In one pit the animals were saved by the manager and helpers who worked from Sunday night to Wednesday morning to keep the ventilation going, during which time the ponies were without food and water. At length the strikers' committee relented and 320 horses were found alive but weak.

Relief for the pit pony could come only from mechanical haulage, which did not begin to arrive in effective form until the 1930s. Impatient humanitarians were invited by the Pit Ponies Protection Society (founded 1927) to order their coal from non-pony pits, a list of which was kept. The Society has tried to abolish double-shifting and it wants to set eleven years as the maximum period to be served underground.*

The year 1911 also saw the passing of an improved Protection of Animals Act which consolidated and extended many earlier measures, and under which a great many RSPCA prosecutions are still brought. It was introduced into Parliament by George Greenwood. This time the law extended 'captive animal' to include any 'bird, fish or reptile', thus rendering illegal the skinning of eels alive and the threading of living creatures as bait for fish in the Waltonian manner (other forms of live baiting are, of course, still practised). Under the new Act magistrates were given power to deprive a person of any animal to which he showed cruelty. They were also empowered for the first time to punish for sins of omission. Increased penalties authorised by the Act – for example, six months imprisonment instead of three – had to be cut back in the following year when juries showed a reluctance to convict. There had been hopes of a ban on gin traps, which had been the subject of much protest, but those who set them were now required to inspect them at reasonable intervals. Hunting remained unaffected. It was still legal to nick and dock horses and crop the ears of dogs, though the Kennel Club, gingered by Edward VII, now excluded cropped dogs from the show bench.

* In 1962 the National Coal Board still had 6,471 pit ponies, more than half of them in the old-fashioned mines of Durham and Northumberland. No other West European country has so many. In 1960 there was a wastage of 1,444 animals, or about one in six; of these, 834 were destroyed because of disease, old age or infirmity and 183 were killed by, or destroyed after, accidents. A Government forecast in 1962 was that pit ponies might be eliminated by 1972.

Again in 1911, George Greenwood tried to interest Parliament in a Humane Slaughter Bill, the first of many unsuccessful ones. Captain G. L. Derriman, a former officer in the Grenadier Guards who became secretary of the RSPCA in 1905, had designed a humane killer which consisted, in essentials, of a .45 revolver attached to a long shaft, with a trigger at the end of the shaft. It fired a soft bullet which flattened on striking the animal's skull and made a big enough hole to permit pithing of the brain. Captain Derriman's attention had been drawn to this problem when, in the South African War, he had to kill trek oxen with a revolver.

Soon afterwards various types of captive-bolt pistols were devised, one of the most successful being named after Christopher Cash, who financed and encouraged many experiments; but whatever the principle the slaughtermen raised objections on the usual grounds. Through the years the RSPCA spent huge sums in an effort to popularise the use of the humane killer, both at home and in Europe. Its efforts were reinforced by other bodies, notably the Council of Justice to Animals and the Animal Defence Society (which built a model abattoir at Letchworth). The public were urged to buy only the flesh of animals which had been humanely killed, a course more easily recommended than practised. In 1929 Scotland gave a lead by making compulsory the preliminary stunning of cattle and sheep, but not pigs. During the following year a similar Bill for England was lost in a political upheaval. Lt-Col T. C. R. (later Sir Thomas) Moore tried again in 1933, some thirty million animals having been slaughtered by the old methods in the interval. With difficulty, Lt-Col Moore steered the Bill through. It enforced stunning of cattle and, if electricity was reasonably available, of pigs, but not sheep. The anomalies have since been tidied up.

An extraordinary, even chaotic, number of animal welfare organisations flourished in the present century. Some were formed to combat specific injustices or to champion specific creatures, notably dogs, cats and horses, but never rats or fish. Among the more specialised objectives was the succouring of old war horses, in Europe and the East (Mrs Geoffrey Brooke's hospital for animals in Cairo commemorates this campaign). Many welfare societies overlapped, like the anti-vivisection bodies, and not all co-existed amicably. Some of them, regrettably, over-simplified or over-sentimentalised the issues, or held out hopes improbable of fulfilment; a few operated, with some stridency, in fields in which no reliable facts could be obtained, enlisting the aid of the more popular newspapers. A redoubtable body was the National Canine Defence League, which campaigned against the unreasonable chaining of dogs and helped owners to fight destruction orders (the right of appeal was won in 1938). There were societies run by various churches, societies to pray for animals, societies to put down unwanted animals, societies to enlist the sympathy of children towards animals. The impact of many of these organisations is impossible to assess; a few of the more excitable ones may have done more harm than good by stiffening the opposition. But all this does not mean that the hearts of the campaigners were in the wrong place or that their basic motives were in any degree suspect. Animal welfare is the total of the efforts of little-known people working often with great single-mindedness and devotion; if some of them are cranks, so were most of the great reformers.

Among organisations which caught the public imagination were those which, instead of crusading against cruelty, concentrated on reducing animal suffering, whether caused by cruelty, apathy, ignorance or poverty. Our Dumb Friends League, started in 1897 and now absorbed in Blue Cross, gradually built up an admirable network of clinics, hospitals, homes for dogs and cats, fields of rest for horses and much else. In 1917 (an unpromising year) Miss M. E. Dickin, shocked by the suffering of pet animals in the London slums, opened a free clinic in a Whitechapel cellar, where a clergyman was already destroying stray cats in a lethal chamber. This was the start of the People's Dispensary for Sick Animals, an organisation which at the time of writing has eighty-four permanent and twenty-four mobile dispensaries, and five hospitals; it treats about a million animals a year. Miss Dickin at various times extended her activities to countries like South Africa, Rumania, Greece, Bali, Morocco and Tangier. In one land or another her workers were confronted with such enormities as animals mutilated in feuds, horses with nails knocked into them, half-skinned mules, donkeys with nostrils slit to stop them braying, cats dropped into tar and cats killed by being given fat-impregnated sponges to eat. They confiscated goads and cruel devices innumerable.*

In a different field, a timely development was the formation, in 1938, of the Universities Federation for Animal Welfare, which grew out of the University of London Animal Welfare Society (1926). Both owed their origin and inspiration to Major C. W. Hume, soldier, scientist, philosopher and humanitarian. The first aim on the Federation's prospectus was 'to enlist the influence of university men and women on behalf of animals, wild and domestic.' It was made clear that the approach would be realistic and objective, 'with a maximum of sympathy but a minimum of sentimentality.' The Federation was anxious to avoid the error of fitting the facts to a preconceived policy. One of the first problems it tackled was that of inhumane trapping; it took over the campaign against 'cruel furs' initiated by Major Charles van der Byl in 1909 and issues a 'white list' of furs obtained by humane methods. It has explained how crabs should be killed and has stimulated experiments to humanise whaling. Suspecting that certain electric killing apparatus used on unwanted pets was less efficient than it seemed, the Federation carried out, and sponsored, elaborate investigations; its fears proved to be well-founded and new specifications for electrocution equipment were laid down.* The Federation has also published works on the care of laboratory animals, its policy in this field being to cultivate humane opinion among experimenters instead of piling odium on them in public. At times, 'animal lover' has come near to being a pejorative term; but UFAW gave it a new dignity.

* M. E. Dickin: *The Cry of the Animal.*
* Major C. W. Hume: *Man and Beast* (1962).

20

PERFORMERS ALL

THROUGH the nineteenth century zoos had been multiplying everywhere. They were regarded as a valuable source of enlightenment and recreation for the working classes; and the most famous of them was the Regent's Park Zoo which opened in 1829, by which time the Tower menagerie – where the public used to present their live pets to the lions, as late as in Regency times – had petered out.

Carl Hagenbeck was a pioneer, at Hamburg, of the open-type zoo, in which animals had plenty of space for exercise. Bars were replaced by ditches and undercut rocks. But for every well-run zoo there were a hundred cramped and shabby menageries where beasts suffered every kind of abuse, inflicted stealthily or openly.

Whether confinement, of itself, constitutes cruelty has been the subject of endless and, on the whole, profitless debate. Humanitarians are accused of assuming that animals think like human beings, who in the main do not regard regular meals as a compensation for loss of liberty. Sir Garrard Tyrwhitt-Drake has argued like this:

'Take the case of a primitive native. I venture to think that if he was offered freedom with its attendant hunt for food and family worries against confinement in an enclosure with warm sleeping quarters, one or two wives and plenty of good food and drink and no worries, he would choose comparative confinement . . . still more so is it with an animal.'*

The fact is that we simply do not know how animals feel on this question. Probably the free-roaming type resent captivity

* *Beasts and Circuses* (1936).

more than others, but that is about as far as we can go. A proposal to abolish zoos, which logically would mean abolishing also the bird in the cage and the goldfish in the bowl, would receive negligible support from the public.

It is probable that the high mortality rate in many zoos last century was caused, not by ill-treatment or neglect, but by a mistaken emphasis on keeping the animals warm, to the exclusion of fresh air. Sir Peter Chalmers Mitchell, who became secretary of the Regent's Park Zoo in 1903, said his hardest task was to convince keepers and others that cold air was not the first evil; much more important than warmth was access to the open.*

Intense and even virulent controversy went on over the ethics of presenting live rabbits, goats and mice to the snakes and larger carnivores. Charles Dickens attacked this practice on the grounds that it not only terrified the victims but was demoralising to the spectators; and indignant Darwinians objected that often the animals consumed were higher in the scale of Nature than their devourers. Defenders of the practice said that no more cruelty was involved than when a thrush killed and swallowed a snail; that it was blasphemous to criticise or try to alter the ways of Providence; that for certain snakes live diet was an absolute necessity; and that to deprive them of their natural diet was a manifest act of cruelty. This debate was raging when Sir Peter Chalmers Mitchell joined the Zoo. The snakes were no longer fed in public, but it was well known that live animals were presented to them behind the scenes; ladies and gentlemen sometimes dined at the Zoo and watched the feeding afterwards, by financial arrangement with a keeper. Sir Peter was not convinced that the act of presenting animals with their natural prey was so cruel as to bring obloquy on those who countenanced it, or to require prohibition. Nevertheless, to allay criticism, he began experiments to see whether snakes could be persuaded to eat freshly killed prey; and with patience and persuasion this proved possible in all but a very few instances. Other zoo-keepers were less successful.

The training of captive animals to perform tricks was a

* *Centenary History of the Zoological Society of London* (1929).

practice which, through the Victorian reign, had come in for steadily mounting criticism. 'Surely it is neither unjust nor inhuman to admire the perfection to which the sagacity of animals may be brought,' wrote a reader of the old *Sporting Magazine*. This point of view was widely shared; and in so far as sagacity was fostered by patient means, no objection could be sustained. But how much patience was used? It was well-known that bears were taught to dance by making them step on hot plates to the sound of music, or by tying hot plates to their feet. They were also taught other performances by trussing them up and then gradually slackening the rope; if, instead of performing as desired, they tried to attack the tamer the rope would be tightened and the creature clubbed. Eventually the bear found it profitable to give the required show of 'sagacity'.

'The subduing of wild beasts, as men have learned from Van Amburgh, is merely the result of merciless thrashing when they are young,' explained *The Times* of August 24, 1869. 'The application of the heavy cudgel, the iron bar or the red-hot ramrod on the tender limbs gives an impression which the threatening glance of him who wields these weapons keeps for ever fresh in the brute's memory.' Isaac Van Amburgh, a Kentucky-born tamer and showman, had enjoyed world-wide notoriety for his success in disciplining savage creatures with a crowbar, which he called the 'silent system'. In Ephraim Watts' biography* of this supposed friend of animals it is hard to distinguish fact from fable, but the brutality of his methods is evident enough. 'He considers that all wild beasts are cowards at heart and that it is only their immense strength and ferocity which have gained them the undeserved reputation of courage,' writes Watts; 'you have to face them boldly and show them now and then what you can do, and it's all over with their terribleness.' Van Amburgh had power in his eyes as well as his crowbar; 'they have a cold whitish appearance and would resemble a dead ghost's only that they continually move in a quick circle and seem to visit all places at once.' As a boy he set out to subdue a famous wild boar and 'struck him a dreadful blow with a crowbar across the spine

* *The Life of Van Amburgh* (1838).

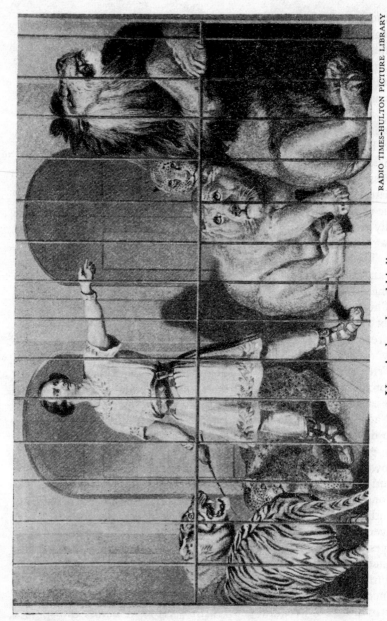

Van Amburgh and his lions

and thus commenced his moral education.' In similar fashion he 'saluted' a large wild bear and 'after a certain period occupied in the necessary preliminaries' led the animal into captivity. In a tiger's den 'he introduced himself with his crowbar and continued presenting his card until the tiger crouched down in one corner and expressed himself happy to make his acquaintance.' The man with the cold white eyes said he was willing to face a pack of hyenas with a crowbar, provided he had a wall behind him; but he would not take on a rhinoceros – 'you could not communicate any information through his hide.' In defence of his art, Van Amburgh cited *Genesis*; man was given dominion over all the beasts and it was therefore contrary to Holy Writ for man to flee from a tiger. In Britain Van Amburgh made his first appearance at Astley's Royal Amphitheatre in 1838 and later filled the Theatre Royal, Drury Lane for 115 nights. The young Queen Victoria paid six visits to the show and Landseer was called in to pay tribute to him on canvas. Yet praise for Van Amburgh was not unstinted; in many, distaste was aroused not only by his industry in battering lions till they lay down with lambs but by his proposals to fly wild animals in balloons or submerge them in diving-bells. The trainer felt that his services to Britain were inadequately recompensed by the award of a silver crowbar from the staff of the Theatre Royal, even though this weapon had been potently magnetised by three German barons.

When Carl Hagenbeck began to train lions in the 1880s the methods of Van Amburgh were still in vogue. Hagenbeck considered such ways were not only cruel, but stupid and ineffectual. What was the point of beating the intelligence out of a beast? Why not enlist its loyalty? He thought the secret of success lay in the careful selection of intelligent beasts and rejection of the intractable. Others had argued on similar lines, but Hagenbeck was able to set a practical example. Gradually the use of the hot iron was dropped and the lion with burned whiskers and charred chops became a rarity; but the public still expected to see a spectacle featuring all the apparatus of violence and excitement, with the tamer apparently maintaining control by firing blank shots in the animals' faces. Writing in 1909, Hagenbeck says 'Obedience which in former days was due to fear is now willingly paid by the animal from motives of affection. The period when unfortunate animals were driven to jump over a bar from dread of a whip or a red-hot iron – a disgrace to the humanity of man! – is gone by.' Yet the autobiography of a beast tamer published nearly fifty years later contains assurances like 'in this profession, someone has to be afraid, the lions or the tamer' and 'Javanese panthers are not to be tamed with lumps of sugar.' The author, Alfred Court, agrees that 'patience and gentleness are at the foundations of training cats,' but insists that 'energetic and instant correction is as indispensable as caresses if you intend to get results.' He describes several affrays with violent carnivores, notably with a man-eating Bengali tiger ('It was my turn to be brutal and brutal I was . . .').* No man can be criticised for defending himself violently against a violent beast; the point is whether compelling such creatures to perform in a ring is a necessary exercise of man's dominion.

Sir Garrard Tyrwhitt-Drake holds that the system of training is not cruel, though individuals may be. Wild animals are not taught unnatural tricks, he says. Dogs and monkeys can be made to perform back-somersaults, but not horses. He tells of a well-known Continental trainer who tried for eighteen months to persuade a horse to walk on its front legs with its hind legs in the air, but without success. If the trainer had succeeded, 'wonderful as the feat would have been, the ordinary public would not have appreciated it at one-hundredth part of its difficulty as a trick.'† The reader may wonder what other preposterous feats have been, and are being, attempted, by patient methods or otherwise.

A campaign to give legal protection to performing animals achieved limited success in 1900 with the passing of the Cruelty to Wild Animals in Captivity Bill. This measure was introduced shortly after an episode in which two elephants at Crystal Palace ran amok, one killing its keeper and escaping to devastate the vines and shrubberies of a member of the Government. Lord James of Hereford explained that as the

* *Wild Circus Animals* (1954).
† *Beasts and Circuses.*

law stood a man could inflict on a wild animal any cruelty short of maiming, as in the training of menagerie animals. As amended and passed, the Act imposed a ban on abusing, infuriating, and teasing an animal in close confinement or when pinioned or restrained. This law did nothing, of course, to stop the exhibition of animals cruelly trained in other lands.

Jack London's novel *Michael, Brother of Jerry* (1917) reveals the animal training methods still employed in America early in the present century. 'Cruelty as a fine art has attained its perfect flower in the trained-animal world,' he wrote. His story is about an Irish terrier Michael who is passed from one trainer to another in an effort to discover whether he will make a hoop-jumper, plate-spinner, goalkeeper, pony-rider or 'dog Caruso'. They attempt to teach him 'the double flip, the dream of all dog trainers.' This involves jerking him up by a chain on the collar and at the same time tugging his hindquarters under, forward and up, the process being expedited by a well-timed blow with a stick under the lower jaw. The story describes how a Shetland pony is made to 'kiss' the man seated on its back; in fact the pony turns its head for this apparent purpose when a long pin is thrust into its shoulder. A mule bucks violently when mounted because the weight of the man in the saddle drives a spike into its back.* Lions are made to jump and roar by luring them on to electrically charged buttons. A tiger is taught to sit in a chair with the aid of ropes and tackle, clubs, prongs and blank cartridges, finally emerging as an educated tiger. There is also the 'monkey band', with each member 'a helpless marionette compelled by unseen sticks and wires, poked and jerked by concealed men, to move and act throughout an entire turn.'†

Jack London made the point which many humanitarians had long been stressing: that animals had to be in a state of intimidation if they were to perform on schedule. No allowance

---

* According to Lord George Sanger's *Seventy Years a Showman* this effect could be achieved by using a pin in the training period; later the animal would respond to a tap of the finger.

† A variation on this theme was Lord George Sanger's Madame Stevens, the pig-faced lady. Madame was a brown bear dressed in women's clothes, with face and paws closely shaved to reveal white skin. Strapped in a chair, she was prodded with a stick to make her grunt answers to her demonstrator.

could be made in the ring for temperament. He expressed the hope that people would get up and walk out of theatres which featured animal acts; and a number of clubs were formed whose members pledged themselves to do this.

After World War One controversy over performing animals became so heated that the Government was inspired to action. A Select Committee was set up to consider such questions as whether cats were ill-used when made to push perambulators on tight-ropes, whether elephants enjoyed sliding down chutes into water tanks, and not least, what happened to canaries when 'vanished' by conjurors.

Evidence of ill-treatment of performing animals was difficult to obtain. It was usual for RSPCA inspectors to attend, in plain clothes, all entertainments which included animal acts and afterwards to inspect the performers. This afforded a check on the use of animals in poor condition but not on harsh methods which might be used to make them perform to time-table. Inspectors were not allowed on stage before the performance on the grounds that their presence might disconcert the animals.

Those who gave evidence of cruelties included retired stage performers who said that if they had spoken out earlier they would have been black-listed. A circus proprietor strongly hinted that hostile evidence was to be expected from those whose pride was wounded by seeing their names in smaller type than animals. Much of the testimony concerned acts committed a long while before and lacked corroboration: an unco-operative bear hit on the snout with a log of wood, feline aerialists tossed into the wings in disgrace, a lion's head hauled down by a windlass to the floor so that the animal could more conveniently be beaten, elephants lashed or prodded with hot irons. One witness spoke of seeing the members of a monkey orchestra lying about exhausted after the protracted prodding endured in their 'performance'. Another, an RSPCA former inspector, told of a fine of £5 imposed on the owner of a 'Great Sousa Rooster Orchestra' whose birds, tightly laced into their uniforms, suffered from sores and collapsed when released. Such evidence was offset by that of theatre managers, menagerie owners and others who said that cruelty had become rare and that any offenders were dropped from the bill.

The RSPCA witness was sharply handled by one member of the Committee, who seemed surprised that the Society could produce records of only ninety convictions in thirty years. Was this sufficient reason, the inspector was asked, for putting scores of performers out of business? 'Yes, in the circumstances,' replied the inspector. He said he could not prove that it was cruel to make an elephant stand on its head, but that cruelty must be involved in training it to do so.

One stage witness caused a stir when he alleged that a well-known illusionist killed a canary every time he 'vanished' it. The cage, he said, collapsed and disappeared up the man's sleeve, the bird being crushed; and the witness claimed to have seen blood dripping from the illusionist's sleeve. In some wrath, the illusionist in question sought permission to demonstrate to the Committee a trick which, he said, had already been performed at no cost in canaries before Edward VII, George V and the RSPCA. The Report of the Select Committee says:

> *The witness produced a canary in a cage*
> *The witness then performed the vanishing canary trick*
> *The witness withdrew.*

It had been agreed that the secrets of tricks were not to be publicly disclosed. All that emerged from discussions of this sleight was that the bird had been removed with great rapidity from one place to another. A member suggested that this was enough to give any bird a heart attack, but the illusionist said he had used the same bird four times nightly for a year; when his canaries died, they did so from colds or asthma. It appeared, however, that less talented conjurors were vanishing canaries in collapsible cages up their sleeves, apparatus being sold for that purpose; and the Select Committee condemned this practice.

Canaries were one problem, chimpanzees were another. Sir Peter Chalmers Mitchell, of the London Zoo, argued that it was 'monstrously wrong' to train these animals for public exhibition, that they were 'almost hysterical' creatures and that a 'chimpanzee in a temporary rage is not a convenient animal to deal with' (the chimpanzees which held a tea-party at the Zoo merely fooled about, under no time-table pressure). The Select Committee was sufficiently impressed by this evidence to recommend that the training and performance of chimpanzees and anthropoid apes should be banned.

Other recommendations were: that the training, exhibition and performance of large carnivores should be controlled by a committee of supervision, drawn from all interested parties; that all trainers should be registered; that representatives of local councils and officers of the RSPCA should have access at all times to training places; that there should be powers to ban foreign acts; that existing penalties for cruelty should be increased; and that the use of cruel appliances in conjuring tricks should be banned. On the whole the Committee thought that training methods had greatly improved and that the best results were obtained by kind and patient treatment. It saw no harm in performances by sea-lions and seals, which were 'in accordance with natural proclivities.'

Few of these recommendations were heeded by Parliament. The Performing Animals (Regulation) Act of 1925 did, however, lay down that trainers should be registered and that local authorities should be able to send officials into training quarters. Lord Danesfort tried with the backing of the RSPCA to persuade Parliament to enforce a ban on the training of apes and the larger carnivores. During the debate on his 1930 Bill the House of Lords, never at a loss for specialists, heard a maiden speech from Lord Auckland, who said he had owned and trained almost all kinds of carnivorous animals. Although he had listened to trainers boasting of the brutalities they had inflicted, he still thought it possible to train animals by kindness alone. Many of the foreign trainers in Britain who indulged in such dreadful abuse of their animals did so because 'it generally takes anything from one to two years to train a lion with kindness and the trainer has neither the patience to do this nor the money to support the animal during that time.'

Lord Danesfort's Bill passed through its main stages but did not reach the Statute Book. When he reintroduced it in 1933 he added bears to the list of animals to be excluded from exhibition, on the grounds that they were exceptionally hard to train without cruelty or danger.* The Earl of Kinnoul described a variation of the traditional way of teaching these animals to dance; they were put in a tub with a metal bottom over a slow fire, and when they tried to get out were bludgeoned with a club. Lord Jessel opposed this Bill, as he had opposed the earlier one, insisting that there was insufficient evidence of abuse and that any such measure would cause 'tremendous injury to a large number of people' and deprive children of harmless amusement. According to Lord Chesham, the management of the Tower Circus, Blackpool (where in 1928 a free-for-all involving ten lions, seven bears, two tigers, a puma and two dogs was broken up with hoses), had tried to do without wild animals but had been forced to restore them; and at Olympia it was impossible to show a profit without them. This time the second reading was lost by one vote.

Meanwhile circuses were being industriously picketed by the Performing Animals Defence League (founded 1914), which also encouraged the public to pledge themselves to walk out of places of entertainment showing animal acts. Captain Edward T. MacMichael, director of the League, had a brush with Lord Lonsdale, who combined the presidency of the Mills Circus with a vice-chairmanship of the RSPCA, which was opposed to animal acts. Lord Lonsdale thought his interest in circus animals was beneficial rather than otherwise to the cause. The League has offered £500 to any person who under its supervision succeeds in training any hitherto untrained animal to perform circus tricks to a time-table by kindness.

A new form of animal entertainment which roused strong controversy was the Wild West rodeo staged at Wembley in 1924; an incongruous form of spectacle, as some thought, for a British Empire Exhibition. The RSPCA opposed the event, and its advance criticisms were made the reason for refusing facilities to its inspectors. According to the promoters, Charles (later Sir Charles) Cochran and Tex Austin, the rodeo was a genuine sporting competition. It had three main classes: riding

---

* His Bill coincided with a ruling in Nazi Germany that no more licences were to be issued to gipsies to train performing bears. Many of the surviving bears were in very bad shape.

'outlaw' horses, 'bull-dogging' or steer-wrestling, and steer-lassoing. In the first class the rules laid down that the rider was to use only one hand on the reins, and not change hands; to hold the reins six inches above the horse's neck; and not to pull the horse's head. In bull-dogging the cowboy rode alongside the steer, leapt on to its back and wrestled it to a standstill; or in other words, he gripped its mouth and nostrils and twisted its head round until it had no option but to lie down. In the lasso contests, conducted against the stop-watch, the horseman cast his rope round the neck of a running steer, then threw it off its feet by tangling the rope in its legs and riding his horse away at a tangent; as the horse kept a strain on the rope the rider dismounted and tied up three legs of the steer, rendering it helpless.

Eighty thousand people applauded the first performance, but the roping of steers came as a shock. The press said it was an unpleasant sight to see animals violently thrown and dragged along the ground, and urged the withdrawal of this feature. *Sporting Life* thought the lassoing was a direct challenge to the British idea of fair play; the pursuit of domestic animals in an area from which there was no escape was comparable to coursing rabbits in a field with all the bolt-holes stopped. In the face of criticism, it was announced that no more steer-roping would take place in public but that, in justice to the eighty cowboys who had travelled 5,000 miles to Wembley, it would be staged in private. Following reports that steers' legs were being broken, Captain E. G. Fairholme of the RSPCA urged the Prime Minister to stop these private contests 'in the name of humanity.' The RSPCA then took out a series of summonses against Cochran, Tex Austin and various cowboys, alleging cruelty, and also applied for a summons under that section of the 1911 Act which dealt with keeping premises for fighting or baiting animals, the Society's argument being that wrestling was fighting. In Parliament the Home Secretary said that no more roping contests would be allowed. The promoters then introduced a modified form of lasso competition in which the cowboy's end of the rope was attached to the horse by a piece of string, which broke as the rope tightened, the steer remaining on its feet.

Before Hendon magistrates, prosecution witnesses told of such incidents as a thrown steer ploughing the ground with its horns, and another being chased from the arena with a broken leg and then shot. Tex Austin, when questioned by Sir Henry Curtis-Bennett for the RSPCA, agreed he had been prosecuted in America by 'a bunch of people' like 'these people here,' but the charges had been dismissed. He did not think the steer with a broken leg suffered pain. When Sir Henry asked, 'Then it was quite happy with its broken leg?' the reply was, 'I never asked it.' For the defendants, Sir Edward Marshall-Hall said that if his clients were convicted then the managements of Sandown Park and Liverpool Racecourse must also be guilty. He deplored the fanaticism the case had evoked.

The magistrates, like the country, were divided. They decided in favour of the defendants by six to five, for which they were 'warmly applauded'. In the view of *The Times*, the decision was one to satisfy most Englishmen. It blamed the use of tan on the floor of the stadium for much of the trouble. 'If men and animals are not to be allowed to take risks together,' it said, 'then the Grand National must never be run again and hunting as well as steeple-chasing will have to be abandoned.' The cowboys had 'handled horses and cattle as they have never been handled in these islands before' (which was what the critics were complaining about) and it would be a pity if they went home feeling unappreciated.

Rodeo performances that year were not confined to Wembley Stadium; improbable though it seems, they were staged in music-halls. At Poplar Hippodrome amateurs were invited to ride a half-bred Hereford steer, with a prize for the contestant who remained longest on its back. One night the curtains parted, and the steer emerged from a gate at the back with a rider astride, slipped on the stage matting and hurt its head. It lay there for some time, then it was kicked, its tail was twisted and it limped off. In the ensuing prosecution, the charge was of causing cruelty to a steer by allowing it to be used in an unfit state. A veterinary surgeon said the animal had been dishorned within an inch of the head; even the bony frontal protuberances on each side of the head had been cut

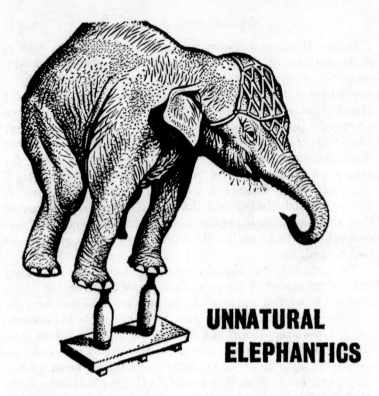

UNNATURAL ELEPHANTICS

This noble beast was not born for such a pitiful existence. To be made to look ridiculous. To be made to perform unnatural antics just to raise a laugh. To spend dreary days in captivity and to be jolted on dark journeys from town to town.

You and your children see his kind only in the gaudy circus ring. You are not allowed to see training in progress—nor is the R.S.P.C.A. The R.S.P.C.A. rightly campaigns for the banning of all performing animal acts and implores *you* to help by abstaining from attendance at such performances.

REMEMBER THE
RSPCA

You can become a member of the R.S.P.C.A. by subscribing £1 per annum or a life member for a donation of £20.

Send to: R.S.P.C.A. (Dept. STL), 105 Jermyn Street, London, S.W.1

From a press advertisement by the RSPCA, 1963

through. Another veterinary surgeon did not think the animal was suffering pain in the performance. The cowboy said he had bought the steer from the Wembley stock and dishorned it himself. In his view a steer could be dishorned and ridden the next day. He was fined £20.

There was talk of legislation to prevent rodeos, but this did not materialise until ten years later, following reports that Tex Austin proposed to stage a new entertainment at the White City. Sir Robert Gower, chairman of the RSPCA, introduced a Bill which he thought would conform to 'the almost unreserved conscience of the nation.' One Member, T. E. Groves, feared that the measure would mean the end of an act which had fascinated thousands – that of the boxing kangaroo. 'It is a perfectly simple and amusing turn which involves no cruelty,' he said. Lt-Col R. V. K. Applin told him that the Act did not affect boxing with animals; 'the whole point of a boxing kangaroo is that you do not touch him except to hit him on the nose.'

The Government left the Bill to a free vote and it was passed. From that date it became an offence to throw an unbroken horse or untrained bull with ropes or other appliances; to wrestle, fight or struggle with an untrained bull; and to ride or try to ride any horse or bull stimulated by the use or a cruel appliance (as, for example, a cinch rope pulled tight round its genitals). And Englishmen still retained the right to hit a kangaroo on the nose.

The rodeo which the promoters of this Act had hoped to prevent was held at the White City but was sparsely attended and vigorously picketed. If there was any suffering involved in the horse-riding contests, observers thought, it was incurred by the human, not the animal performers. Tex Austin lost heavily and returned to America in some dudgeon.

Meanwhile, fairground operators devised perverse new ways of exploiting animals, one of them being to drive a lion round a 'Wall of Death'. Was this, in law, cruelty? At Oxford, police banned the performance; at the Nottingham Goose Fair it was exhibited, then stopped. The RSPCA tried to prevent any repetition of the act elsewhere and eventually, in 1932, brought a prosecution at Loughborough. Evidence showed that the lion normally occupied a cage in the middle of the pit. After a preliminary display by a motor-cyclist it was made to sit in the bucket seat of a car with its body across the bonnet and head hanging over the side. The car did not mount the vertical wall, only the slope at the foot. On this occasion the lion was sick, reluctant to move, and devoid of all spirit. A veterinary surgeon testified that it was suffering from carbon-monoxide poisoning and had a heart ailment; in his view it must have been subject to great nervous strain. The exhaust of the car was so sited that fumes were emitted into the face of driver and passenger. The driver said he had given the performance for seven years and that the lion had made its first ride when nine months old. He was fined £5 with £11 4s costs. Had the lion not been sick (in fact, it was mortally sick) it is unlikely that cruelty could have been established.

The cinema industry also came under fire for pandering to cruel instincts. In the early 'thirties there were a number of films which set out to feature nature in the raw – lions tearing at zebras and wart-hogs, crocodiles being shot, one snake swallowing another, a hippopotamus plunging down a cliff and exhausted game being pursued by cars and aeroplanes. In the view of some educational authorities, nature photography was being abused in order to satisfy bloodthirsty appetites. Criticism was also levelled at Wild West and battlefield pictures in which waves of horses were dashed to the ground. In 1935 the British Board of Film Censors set up a consultative panel on which the RSPCA was represented, but local authorities had power to overrule the Board's decisions. Two years later Sir Robert Gower, with the support of the Film Censor and other bodies, introduced into Parliament a Bill to prohibit the production or exhibition of films which involved suffering to animals. It appeared from the debate that some criticism was misplaced, for rubber horses and mechanical elephants had been employed more often than was suspected. But this raised the question: if the illusion of cruelty was created with the aid of dummies, did that excuse the result? One Member said that in battle scenes horses were ridden into trip wires to make them fall. If this were done, said Geoffrey Lloyd, Under-Secretary for the Home Office, it would be 'a most dastardly form of cruelty'; but he pointed out that the producers of a film showing the Charge of the Light Brigade had taken legal action against a magazine which accused it of using this device. One or two peers seemed afraid that the Act would prevent the cinema showing a fox-hunt, but it was made clear that such events as hunts and the Grand National would be exempt. This being understood, the Cinematograph Films (Animals) Act was admitted to the Statute Book.

The reference to the pursuit of game by cars and aeroplanes is a reminder that, even in Britain, aviators were not above using their machines for 'sport'. In 1927 the *Field* described, with disapprobation, how test pilots on the Yorkshire shores of the Humber had taken up wildfowl shooting. The pilot would intercept a formation of ducks as they flew from the breeding-grounds to the stubble fields, then pursue and gradually overtake them, being careful not to make contact for fear of damaging the propeller. On being overtaken the ducks would execute a quick about-turn which brought them within range of the passenger sitting with a shotgun in the rear cockpit. A motor boat was supposed to retrieve the dead and wounded. Those who indulged in this sport, said the *Field*, deserved no more praise than 'the gallant fellows who, a year or so ago, used motor cars to ride down gazelle in Mesopotamia.'* Today the law specifically bans the pursuit of a bird in an aeroplane, a prohibition which, without this explanation, would seem incomprehensible.

Animal societies praised one new form of entertainment: the pursuit of the 'electric hare' by greyhounds. This, they thought, would wipe out the cruelties of coursing, but they were wrong; if anything, the popularity of coursing increased. In 1926 the first electric hare in Britain 'ran' at Manchester. It was not the first mechanical hare, for as Brig.-Gen. A. C. Critchley has revealed, greyhounds pursued an artificial prey near the Welsh Harp, Hendon in 1876. The track was a straight one of 400 yards and the hare was operated by an unseen windlass. However, the idea failed to become popular. It was revived by a farmer in Oklahoma in the mid-1920s and then Brig.-Gen.

* R. N. Rose: *The Field* 1853–1953.

Critchley took it up.* Arguing that the new sport represented an advance in humanity, he sought to persuade C. P. Scott, editor of the *Manchester Guardian*, to award a coursing cup; but this move was frustrated when a worldly member of the staff informed his editor that greyhound racing enthusiasts were primarily gamblers.

* Brig.-Gen. A. C. Critchley: *Critch!*

21

HUNTING: 'SHOULD CONTINUE'

B ETWEEN the world wars, the cry against hunting grew shriller. Whether this was part of the general revulsion against blood-letting, as some have argued, is debatable; there is no evidence that countryfolk pursued their traditional sports with diminished relish. Criticism came mainly from the towns and much of it from Socialists, whose humanitarianism was not always innocent of class prejudice.

The Humanitarian League had died out in 1919, but in 1926 one of its former members, Ernest Bell, in conjunction with Henry B. Amos, started the League for the Prohibition of Cruel Sports (not to be confused with the later National Society for the Abolition of Cruel Sports). Its object was to do for wild animals what legislation had already achieved for tame. In fox-hunting counties like Leicestershire, and stag-hunting centres like Taunton and Minehead, the League's rallies and meetings became the focus of tumult. Horn-blowing, yelling and the singing of 'John Peel' greeted the League's speakers at Brackley, Oxfordshire in 1930; and when those on the platform rose to sing 'O God Our Help' the audience rose to throw rotten eggs. Police cleared the platform and saw the speakers home. Such episodes, unthinkable in any other century, soon became part of the English way of life.

The League Against Cruel Sports (as it became known) published a journal, *Cruel Sports*, which criticised the RSPCA for its toleration of fox-hunting, and attacked the Church for sheltering behind the RSPCA. It fulminated against the 'blooding' of children, especially royal children, and the holding of juvenile meets; it censured the Government for slogans

like 'Come to England for the hunting'; commended farmers
who denied their land to hunts; queried the patriotism of
masters of foxhounds who said they would leave England if
hunting was put down; recorded affrays like that at Minehead, in 1928, when three Army officers at a hunt ball threw
a reporter* in the sea and, when he struggled out, threw him
in again; combed hunt reports for references like 'every horse
was done at the finish' or headlines like 'A Wonderful Hunt.
Triumph of Welsh Pack. Seven Hours Run. Distance At
Least 45 Miles' (*Morning Post* January 29, 1929); exploited to
the full every report of a stag chased over a cliff or out to
sea; and diligently collected the more unguarded statements
of sporting writers.

In the opposite camp the editor of *Shooting Times* did his
best to persuade his readers (who probably needed no persuasion) that field sports were a bulwark against decadence.
Sportsmen and athletes between them kept the torch of
chivalry alight; in Newbolt's words, they formed the 'brother-
hood that binds the brave of all the earth.' Love of field sports
was 'a basal law of Nature'; people might not like these basal
laws 'but you have got to accept them and work upon them
as a foundation if the human race is to progress onwards and
upwards.' The issue of April 9, 1927, in which this philosophy
was expressed, contained the passage: 'There is a wonderful
glamour about our early days with the gun; nothing quite like
it ever seems to colour the experience of our more mature
years. That is one reason why our boys should begin early
with the gun. Let us not deprive them of the golden memories
of boyhood, when the blood runs hot and enthusiasm has not
had its keen edge dulled.' The writer made the point that a
sportsman was to be judged not by his skill but according
to whether his 'heart was right' and he obeyed the unwritten
rules.

Lord Willoughby de Broke, author of a standard work on
fox-hunting in the 1920s, held this view: 'If there be anyone
who is temperamentally opposed to sport, and would injure it
if he could, he is hardly worth considering. His whole outlook
would probably be anti-social and un-English in whatever

* Mr E. A. Hemingway, later chairman of the League.

rank of life he is to be found.' No one, in Lord Willoughby's opinion, was too good to be a master of foxhounds. His book contained no un-English sentimentality about fox cubs: 'When the hounds run into their cub it is probably wise not to take him from them. Let them tear him in pieces while they are angry and thus learn the habit of breaking up their foxes properly while the huntsman excites them by horn and voice.' Bag foxes were still used by many hunts, but Lord Willoughby disliked the practice: 'a mounted man in livery carrying a fox about the country in a bag is not an edifying spectacle; and to eat a fox out of a bag on the way home does not do hounds any good.'*

An authority on beagling, Captain J. Otho Paget, presented critics with this passage: 'In hunting, whether it be of fox or hare, every follower should identify himself with hounds' aims and give his entire sympathy to them. If he allows himself to sympathise with the hare his pleasure in the chase will be neutralised and he may as well go home at once.'†

The RSPCA did not stand back and leave the cause of hunted animals to the League Against Cruel Sports. In 1930 it backed an abortive Bill by Lovat Fraser which would have outlawed deer-hunting. Two years later it took out a summons against the Master of the Mid-Kent Stag Hounds alleging cruelty towards the carted deer Bridget, which had been chased into the English Channel. Bridget avoided the first attempt at recapture but was taken next day by the Hythe lifeboat after much swimming and wandering. 'Poor old Bridget,' the hunt secretary was reported as saying, 'she's a great pet. We would not lose her for anything. These deer cost us up to £20 a week.' Though Bridget was a 'great pet', the Hunt denied strongly that she was a domestic animal, as the RSPCA alleged; legally, she was a captive wild animal, and as such could be hunted. The Hythe bench were unanimous that no cruelty had been caused and the King's Bench dismissed the Society's appeal. In *Punch* of July 27, 'A.P.H.' expressed surprise that the gallant hunt had given up at the water's edge: 'Is it less noble to be drowned at sea than to

* *Hunting the Fox* (1920).
† *The Art of Beagling* (1931).

break your neck in a ditch? Surely the whole hunt – hounds, horses, horn-blowers and all – should have charged across the beach and followed Bridget out to sea.' In 'A.P.H.'s' view there was scope for a Mid-Kent Man Hunt. Offenders would be sentenced to 'one year's imprisonment and to be hunted three times by the So-and-So Man Hounds.'

The popular newspapers, reflecting the prejudices of their mainly urban readers, were almost all hostile to field sports, as they still are. But often they overplayed their hand. Country dwellers tended to grow indignant at the suggestion that they were primitive savages or that they were cowed by landlords into allowing hunts to ravage their land. Hunting was more popular in rural areas than townsmen cared to believe. Deer, foxes, hares, rabbits and badgers all had to be kept down and the traditional methods of doing so were regarded as not less humane than the townsmen's proposals for indiscriminate shooting and poisoning. The countryman could not see why he should be expected to go about the work of control with a long face, taking no pleasure in a healthy gallop over the fields; and in the main he had no higher opinion of the agitators who came out from the towns with leaflets and placards than he had of those who threw bottles and litter into his fields. In short, he saw no reason why the townsman should be the guardian of his conscience.

The ceaseless propaganda against hunting led, in 1930, to the founding of the British Field Sports Society. This body contends that hunting is the only efficient and humane method of control which does not threaten extermination; that it is a delusion to suppose that, in the absence of hunting, foxes would live to a serene and peaceful old age; and that a fox killed by hounds dies almost as quickly as if by a bolt from a humane killer. Not the least of the Society's tasks was to persuade sportsmen to close their ranks, to stop sneering at each other's sports, to refrain from uttering, publicly, such sillinesses as 'the fox enjoys being hunted' and to refrain from giving the press reports capable of being 'misunderstood'. If much of the arrogance for which fox-hunters were notorious has dwindled in the last thirty years, the credit may perhaps be divided between the British Field Sports Society, which has discouraged acts of provocation, and the League Against Cruel Sports, which has ever been on the look-out for them.

In 1949, for the first time, controversy over field sports caused embarrassment to a British Government.

The Government was a Socialist one. Among its stalwarts were many who had long campaigned against hunting on humanitarian grounds and who now felt honour-bound to try to suppress it by legislation. If the Government could not be gingered into preparing the necessary Bill, there were plenty of private Members willing to do so.

In the first ballot for private Bills, during the 1948–49 session, seven out of twenty-three successful Members brought forward measures affecting animals or birds. Of two anti-hunting Bills one was designed to prevent the hunting of deer, badgers and otters, and the coursing of hares and rabbits; the other, to suppress fox-hunting. The former measure, fathered by Mr Anthony Greenwood, was taken up by Mr F. Seymour Cocks, MP for Broxtowe, who was successful in the ballot.

News of this two-fold threat quickly stirred up anger in the rural areas where Labour's support was weak; there were threats not only to change party allegiance but to let food production slide. The Government went to some pains to quench the zeal of Mr Cocks' supporters. Was it worth losing tens of thousands of votes for a non-political principle? Mr Cocks emphasised that his Bill specifically excluded fox-hunting and would still permit the countryman to flush a hare with hounds on the open hillside. But the countrymen of Britain were sceptical; obviously, they said, if deer-hunting was outlawed fox-hunting would be next on the list. Soon rural Members of Parliament were being subjected to heavy pressure from constituents, and not all the protests were organised ones. Miners arrived at Westminster to lobby for coursing and found the place full of farmers (the National Farmers Union opposed the Bill). In the Westerham and Edenbridge areas of Kent fox-hunters, otter-hunters and beaglers, rallied by the British Field Sports Society, blew horns of protest and demanded that 'freedom of choice should be left to the individual.' Mounted fox-hunters also sounded their horns in Piccadilly and Regent Street, raising echoes even in Soho where hunting horns had sounded centuries before. In twenty weeks the British Field Sports Society obtained more than a million signatures of protest.

The RSPCA backed Mr Cocks' Bill with two reservations: if deer were no longer to be hunted, there must be ways to prevent inhumane methods of destruction; and there must be power to kill 'rogue' badgers. To the National Society for the Abolition of Cruel Sports this attitude seemed inconsistent. Why could not the RSPCA oppose fox-hunting with the same reservation as for deer-hunting? The view of *The Times* was that it was a serious step to interfere by law with the wishes and pursuits of a large section of the people. Public opinion must first be convinced that hunted animals suffered more pain than they would if killed by other methods: 'To maintain . . . that hunting should be stopped because it is bad for man to kill for sport is to invade the sphere of individual conscience.'

When he moved the second reading, Mr Cocks ended an eloquent speech with: 'Attila or St Francis – that is the choice I ask the House to make.' Reluctantly, his colleagues then assumed the mantle of Attila. Mr Maurice Webb upheld the liberty of the subject, and argued that stories of cruelty had been grossly exaggerated, that the hazards faced by hunted hares and rabbits were not substantially greater than in Nature. Mr Tom (later Lord) Williams, Minister of Agriculture, said he had come round to the view that the Bill would lead to more cruelty than it would prevent. If it went through 'we should risk the loss of willing co-operation in a great national effort' (growing more food). There was even a chance that, if hunting stopped, shepherds and others might withdraw from outlying areas.

From the other side of the House came argument, mockery and patient instruction. 'Apparently,' said Sir Jocelyn Lucas, 'the criterion is that if one goes out with hounds or dogs to see them work one is committing a crime, but if one says that it is in the cause of food production and one hates doing it, then one may get away with it.' Mr R. E. Manningham-Buller (later Lord Dilhorne) pointed out that a century earlier the red deer of Exmoor nearly died out because they were not hunted; 'if the Bill is carried we shall see in a few years' time only a few crippled, suffering beasts crawling about Exmoor' (in *The Times* a resident of North Devon had complained, 'Fifty years ago there was no stag-hunting here and there were no deer. Now we have both.'). Earl Winterton said the opponents of hunting were 'Bloomsbury boys' who loathed the sport because it required courage, endurance and physical fitness ('their patron saint is Oscar Wilde'). He told how, fifteen or twenty years earlier, a young woman who had broken a leg while hunting received twenty letters expressing delight in her misfortune; 'one woman wrote to say that she would pray every night that this young lady would die as she had condemned the stag to die.'

Mr Anthony Greenwood sadly reproached his Government for urging people to do, not what was right, but what was politically expedient. The Bill was defeated by 214 votes to 101, and in the shires there was much jubilation. For once, town had been trounced by country.

The other Bill, which sought to prohibit fox-hunting, was withdrawn. As a sop, the Government appointed a committee to enquire into the treatment of wild animals in Britain. Its chairman was Mr John Scott-Henderson, KC, and other members included Mr W. J. Brown and Miss Frances Pitt, student of animal psychology and for more than twenty years a master of foxhounds. The unanimous report of this body, published in 1951, did not afford much encouragement to the more vocal humanitarians. Explaining its conception of cruelty, the Committee said: 'If, in pursuing or destroying a particular animal in the course of a sporting activity, the degree of suffering reasonably necessary is not more than would be involved in the use of other methods likely to achieve control or provide food with the infliction of the least amount of suffering, that particular sporting activity should not be regarded as cruel.' Ethics were not included in the Committee's terms of reference, which meant that its members were not concerned with the effect of hunting on those who took part in it. But they allowed themselves to say: 'If the ethical view . . . is taken to its logical conclusion it means that even if a field sport causes no more real suffering than any alternative method of control it should be forbidden, because it is carried on for sport, while alternative methods involving greater suffering are permitted. Presumably some people holding these views would like to prohibit fishing by line and hook because of the suffering which may be involved but would condone commercial net fishing. Fortunately for us, fish are not within our terms of reference . . .'

The cult of sportsmanship did not escape uncriticised. Future generations, the Committee thought, might well look on sportsmanship as 'an outmoded virtue, tainted by its origin.' The conduct of field sports appeared illogical, 'for if the pursuit itself involves suffering, the prolonging of that pursuit or the escape of the animal to be hunted again may very well have the effect of increasing the amount of suffering.' In shooting, pain was aggravated by those whose sportsmanship was not matched by their marksmanship: 'We think that a great deal of shooting is done by people who lack the necessary skill and experience.' Unless great care was taken, this could be 'an extremely cruel method of control.' Unfortunately, there seemed to be no way of enforcing tests for game shots.

For many popular misconceptions about animals the Committee blamed the 'Brumas attitude'.* This sentimental view was 'encouraged by articles and picture strips in the popular press and in children's papers, and by stories in books in which animals believe, speak and think like human beings.' Moreover, people tended to suppose that wild animals behaved like their own domestic pets, a notion exploited by some animal welfare organisations. The sentimental, as the Committee noted, reserved their sympathies for beautiful animals like deer, rabbits and foxes, caring little or nothing for the fate of the rat, an intelligent and highly sensitive creature which was destroyed by methods of great cruelty.

The two leading abolitionist bodies – the National Society for the Abolition of Cruel Sports and the League Against Cruel Sports – came in for careful scrutiny. Each had about 6,000 members, compared with the British Field Sports Society's 36,230, and it was reasonable to suppose that an

* Brumas was a much-photographed polar bear born in the London Zoo in 1949.

appreciable number belonged to both. These organisations claimed to speak on behalf of thirteen million people in various political, religious or social groups which had passed resolutions against field sports. 'An insignificant number of this very large number of people have been sufficiently interested . . . to help us in our inquiry,' said the Committee. 'The supporters of the general animal welfare organisations are divided in their views and we have no means of knowing how many are opposed to field sports.'

Having criticised those who imagined that animals shared the feelings of human beings, the Committee cautiously speculated on the emotions of a hunted animal:

'We are not . . . satisfied that wild animals suffer from apprehension or the after-effects of fear to the same extent as human beings. Wild animals must live very largely in the present and although a hunted fox, for example, may be aware that it is being hunted, and that if the hounds catch it something to be avoided will happen, we think it would be going beyond the evidence to say that a fox realises that it may be killed. We have been told by several witnesses of hunted foxes stopping to kill a chicken, but the scientific explanation of this is still uncertain.'

The Committee was firmly convinced that fox-hunting should be allowed to continue. Its abolition would lead only to an increase in the use of more cruel methods, and would be resented by most country people. Deliberate preservation of foxes was rarely practised, though there was 'a good deal of toleration' of foxes by hunt supporters who liked to have a fox found on their land. The Masters of Foxhounds Association had banned the 'objectionable practice' of using bag foxes or foxes which had been in any way handled.* It had also drawn up firm rules about digging out, a practice of perennial controversy. After the quarry had gone to ground, the Association said, three courses were open: to leave it there; to 'bolt' it and give it a fair chance to escape; or, if poultry preservation was the paramount need, to dig it out and kill it before giving it to the hounds. The Committee thought the second course

* The Association of Masters of Harriers and Beagles have a similar rule in respect of hares.

was needlessly cruel and ought to be prohibited (a recommendation which, in the view of the British Field Sports
Society, ran counter to the rule that every quarry should have
a fair chance of escape). Throwing a live fox to the hounds
'hardly ever' happened, the Committee was told; if it did,
severe action would be taken against the master responsible.
Some huntsmen carried humane killers, but this weapon was
not always safe to use; a sharp blow with a spade or a weighted
whip handle was preferable. On cubbing, the Committee said
the main object was to train young hounds, but experienced
hounds were always in the majority, so that there was no
additional cruelty. The cubs were fully grown animals, not
young and fluffy.

Deer-hunting, the Committee thought, was a useful and
necessary method of control, and should continue. It was very
unusual for the hounds actually to kill the quarry. Sometimes
they drowned a hind after it had taken to water by getting
on top of it (an M.P. told Parliament that such a thing was
impossible – the hounds were too busy swimming to do anything else). The usual way of dispatching a deer brought to
bay, the Committee noted, was the traditional one of cutting
the main artery of its throat, which usually caused a quick
death with little suffering. Huntsmen also carried a humane
killer and a twenty-bore folding gun, but it was not always
possible, or safe, to use these, and the method of dispatch was
left to the master's discretion. On the hunting of carted deer
the Committee made no recommendation. The sport did not
seem to serve any useful function other than to provide
exercise, but there was not enough evidence of suffering to
warrant legislation to ban it.

No criticism was offered of skilled stalking as practised in
Scotland. The Committee held, however, that to use rifles on
Exmoor, where winter visibility was bad, was dangerous.
During World War Two the Devon and Somerset Staghounds
had organised deer drives in conjunction with the war agricultural committees, but these shotgun operations had been
very difficult to control.

The sport which, in the Committee's view, involved a
greater degree of suffering than the others was otter-hunting,

which it thought should be thoroughly investigated. Witnesses had said that the 'stickle' – a line of people with sticks across the river – was no longer allowed (though it might have resulted in quicker kills); nor was it legitimate to lower the level of mill ponds or to pull out the otter by the tail to kill it. When an otter was evicted from tree roots, or some similar hide, the Committee thought it ought to be killed instead of being allowed to swim and then hunted again.

Coursing – branded from time to time in the press under headlines like 'Britain's Wickedest Sport' – came in for little criticism. Suspicious of the propaganda against this pastime, members of the Committee watched the Waterloo Cup at Altcar and revised their views. They saw no hares torn to pieces or made the subject of a tug-of-war. They were satisfied that the hounds usually killed the hare quickly by biting it across the back; if they did not kill it, an attendant did, sometimes by breaking its back with his foot (which was liable to be described as 'dancing on the hare'). The trainer was supposed to ensure that the hare was dead but did not always take as much care over this as he might do. On the whole, the Committee thought there could be 'no comparison between the lingering death of a hare that is shot at and wounded and the quick death of a hare that is coursed and caught.' It considered that the hare had a 50 per cent chance, though the National Coursing Club claimed that kills ranged from 20 to 30 per cent.

Badger-digging, classed as a field sport by animal welfare organisations but not by the British Field Sports Society, was an activity to which, the Committee noted, few people were willing to devote time and energy. When reached the badger was shot or hit on the head with a spade; if the object was to remove it to another area, it was tailed and boxed.

In its recommendations the Committee urged that all wild animals should be brought under the law's protection, with the stipulation that the hunting of deer, foxes, hares and otters should be legal if pursued under the rules of that sport. 'Any field sport which has a reasonable measure of support and is a traditional activity of the countryside, and which has some utilitarian value, should not be interfered with, except for some very good reason,' it concluded; adding that the use of unnecessary cruelty would be a good reason.

In the post-war years it became clear, save to the prejudiced, that most of the cruelty to deer was caused, not by hunters, but by the following: the fast-growing numbers of 'trigger-happy' sportsmen using weapons of the wrong calibre; youths, elated by possession of their first shotgun, who peppered anything in sight (some used bows and arrows, in imitation of American archer-huntsmen); infuriated smallholders and farmers defending their crops with shotguns or snares; and poaching gangs who dazzled their victims – stags, hinds and calves alike – with car headlights, mowed down what they could with what armoury they had and left the wounded to limp away.

The poaching problem became acute in Scotland. In 1957 and 1958 police stopped one hundred cars containing dead deer but could take no action against the offenders. To check this abuse, the Government introduced the Deer (Scotland) Bill in 1959, which was at once assailed as an attempt to protect and improve at public expense the interests of sporting landlords and their tenants. Cruelty, said the critics, lay in overstocking the deer forests, failing to provide winter feed and letting the animals stray from their unfenced areas to pillage other people's property. Keeping down deer was a task, they said, for professional game wardens. Mr Emrys Hughes doubted whether more cruelty was caused by poaching gangs than by society 'gangs', the members of which were chosen not for their marksmanship but for their money. The Bill, which was designed to stop not only car gangs, but to lay down close seasons and restrict the deer population, was passed.

In 1960 Earl Winterton and other peers tried to persuade the Government to protect English deer, estimated at 40,000 strong, which were the victims, not only of lone marksmen, but of organised drives with shotguns. Lord Massereene and Ferrard thought the only way to keep down deer in woodland areas was to shoot them at dawn as they went into the open to graze. In Europe this was done from forest platforms. Earl Bathurst thought little of deer drives, as occasionally organised by the Forestry Commission; 'I do not think they are very pleasant or very savoury spectacles at which to be present.'

Meanwhile, picketing and placarding went on in deer-hunting regions, notably in the West Country where the League Against Cruel Sports had established two deer sanctuaries on Exmoor, in the heart of the country hunted by the Devon and Somerset Staghounds. It was the League's view, perhaps an over-sanguine one, that 'but for the embarrassment which the Queen's patronage of hunting causes to the heads of the established British Church, the whole of this beastly form of amusement and the foul cruelties inseparable from it, would have been condemned by the Church of England, as it already has been by other denominational churches in Britain.'*

In 1962, when Prince Charles, at the age of thirteen, shot his first stag at Balmoral, the chairman of the League, Mr Edward Hemingway, invited the Duke of Edinburgh to say whether this act constituted a status symbol or a badge of brutality; a comment which, according to Mr David James, MP, in the *Daily Telegraph* of November 7, came strangely 'from the chairman of a league dedicated to obtaining the control of deer by firearms in the West Country.' Press comment on the Prince's feat was mixed. That deer, even Balmoral deer, had to be selectively culled, if starvation and crop raiding were to be avoided, was conceded; the point at controversy was simply whether culling should be performed by amateurs, for sport. A *Daily Telegraph* diarist noted that the Prince had still to emulate the feat recently achieved by the son and daughter of the Countess de la Valdene, tenant of Beaufort Castle; 'both of these young people killed a salmon, a stag and a grouse in one day . . . they had each bet £5 on this feat at 10 to 1.'†

Eventually, in 1963, a Deer Bill for England and Wales was introduced by Mr Jasper More, with the support of the British Field Sports Society, the Forestry Commission, the Nature Conservancy, the Devon and Somerset Staghounds and the New Forest Buckhounds. It was revealed, in one debate or another, that 60 per cent of all deer killed in the Forestry Commission woodlands in 1962 had gunshot wounds in them;

---

* *Daily Telegraph*, March 26, 1957.
† September 25, 1962.

that a British manufacturer had put on the market a cheap bow to meet the requirements of the amateur hunter*; and that a cross-bow was being sold for stalking (as it took three minutes to reload, it was essential that the first shot should be effective). Mr Anthony Greenwood agreed that the use of hounds might be necessary to track wounded game; 'but I feel it is more likely to be an economic and efficient way of controlling deer if the hounds are followed only by a small number of qualified foresters or pest officers rather than a large number of people for their personal enjoyment.' Special headlines were earned by Mr Nicholas Ridley, who said: 'There is something rather unpleasant about the way deer are often ensnared and shot when they are making love.' The Bill, which received the royal assent, established a close season for the four main species, prohibited snares, shooting from vehicles, night shooting and the use of weapons with inadequate stopping-power.

During the Bill's passage an unsuccessful attempt was made to outlaw the hunting of carted deer. Lord Crook called it a most un-English sport, but in fact it was peculiarly English. By now only one hunt – the Norwich Staghounds – still kept up the tradition, pursuing castrated (and hence hornless) stags with fangless hounds. The Mid-Kent had been forced to give up through the electrification of a railway line which ran through their country (deer had always shown a preference for following railway lines). The Norwich deer, some sixty in number, were kept like cows in a paddock at Winfarthing and were familiar with the sight of their pursuers. Each was chased twice a year. 'The hounds and the deer really appear to come to an understanding about this business,' said Lord Massereene and Ferrard. 'The deer does not run until he is utterly exhausted but will go and stand in a pond or in a field and the hounds never touch him; they know the game too well.' The deer might not enjoy the chase, but he enjoyed 'having a nice feed at the end of it.' Lord Massereene said he did not personally agree with carted deer-hunting; he thought it served no useful purpose and that anyone who wanted to gallop could

---

* 'Do not be surprised if the arrow passes entirely through the deer.' – Thomas A. Forbes: *New Guide to Better Archery* (1962, USA).

have as much fun on a drag hunt; but he successfully persuaded the Lords not to prohibit it, on the grounds that the Bill was not concerned with hunting. A few months later the Master of the Norwich Staghounds, which afforded perhaps more exercise to the press than to the deer of Winfarthing, announced that they would hunt deer no more. The reason given was lack of support; though *Baily's Hunting Directory* said, to the end, 'The pack is always welcome wherever it goes and is very popular with the farmers, a large number of whom support it.' Thus ended the fight which the Humanitarian League thought it had won sixty years earlier; but there is, of course, no legal reason why the sport should not be revived.

Baily's Hunting Directory is as anxious to improve the image of the huntsman as is the British Field Sports Society. Boors, according to the 1962–63 edition, can do great disservice to the cause; 'this is because the mounted man is not only raised on a pedestal for all to see, but physically looks down on the unmounted, a situation charged with psychological hazards.' Moreover, huntsmen tend to take the sport too seriously. 'Tense and earnest faces do in truth look incongruous and slightly ridiculous behind a gay and vivacious pack of hounds. The casual spectator is more likely to be amused than antagonised.' And the British Field Sports Society has implored its members, when writing reports of hunts for the press, to refrain from stressing details of the kill, or saying that the fox was dead-beat or that the hounds 'deserved a taste of blood.' It is sufficient, in the Society's view, to say that the quarry was 'accounted for'.

In the *New Statesman* the idea has been propounded more than once that if hunting were banned its followers would break out in worse ways. 'One does not have to be very sophisticated anthropologically,' wrote Mr Tony Gibson on March 23, 1957, 'to realise the significance which the hounding down of an antlered beast has for certain of the more primitive sub-groups of our rural communities. Some slight knowledge of their social habits provides the answer. Had we not better leave this regrettable custom untouched lest more harmful acts take its place to relieve the social and inter-familial tensions of our shires?' Mr Paul Johnson, writing on 'Hunting and Humbug' on July 12, 1963, had no doubt what the social habits of fox-hunters were: 'The hunting fraternity are notoriously lascivious and, in the season, the night air of Melton Mowbray is loud with the sighs of adulterers.'* Assuming there is a pinch of truth in this, is such behaviour fostered by hunting, or would it be far worse without hunting? There would seem to be scope here for the anthropologist.

* F. D. Smith and Barbara Wilcox, authors of *Sold For Two Farthings* (1950), a thoughtful book setting out the views of country-folk on cruelty, contend that field sports 'keep the countryman sweet and uninhibited.'

22

MORE RIGHTS FOR BIRDS

FOR much of the present century, the laws which were supposed to protect birds, especially wild birds, were a loose mesh of anomalies, pierced by scores of well-worn loopholes.

Two major abuses, already described in these pages, survived all attempts at legislation until 1921. Trap pigeon-shooting had come back into the headlines with the post-war resuscitation of Monte Carlo, where English visitors increasingly resented the 'slaughter in the sun.' *The Times* campaigned strongly against what it called a 'subsidised survival of medieval callousness.' Pressed to intervene, the Prince of Monaco, a scientist of repute, said he hated the sport but did not wish to act the autocrat and revoke a licence granted to the Casino directors thirty years earlier. Lord Rendlesham, president of the Gun Club and Britain's representative at Monte Carlo, insisted that pigeon-shooting was more sporting than game bird shooting and denied an allegation by H. W. Massingham that handicapped birds were freed from darkened traps. The birds' tails were lightly clipped, he said, to speed their exit and all the traps were grilled and faced south, receiving the full benefit of the Riviera sun. Unexpectedly the Casino directors announced that they would introduce clay pigeon-shooting, but it was soon apparent that the live shoots were merely being moved to nearby Cap Fleuri, in France. By Christmas barbarity had been restored in Monte Carlo.*

Meanwhile the press discovered that pigeon shoots were still being held in Britain. At a meeting in the ground of

* In 1963, after much sporting opposition, a mechanical pigeon was introduced.

Chatham Football Club a prize of £50 was offered to the sportsman who killed most birds. Indignation was by now considerable and Parliament without fuss passed an Act to prohibit the shooting of captive birds. This measure was piloted by Lord Lambourne, then chairman of the RSPCA, and Sir Burton Chadwick.

A much rougher passage awaited the Bill designed to ban the importation of plumage, for the friends of the feather trade in Parliament were ingenious in obstruction; but a Plumage Group of which H. W. Massingham was a member maintained strong pressure. When one of several plumage Bills failed eight times to find a quorum in Committee – after the Commons had overwhelmingly approved the principle at least ten times – the press began to accuse Members of devious practices. The successful Bill, prohibiting the import of a wide range of feathers, was steered by Trevelyan Thomson.

Some specialised Acts had followed the unsatisfactory wild bird protection measures of Victorian times. In 1904 the use of the pole trap was prohibited, though gamekeepers in 'ignorance' continued to use it for long afterwards. Four years later Sir Frederick (later Lord) Banbury, a renowned scourge of 'grandmotherly' legislation but a sharp foe of cruelty, persuaded Parliament to ban the sport, practised in Cornwall, of catching sea-birds on hooks. This was done by lowering lines down the cliff-face, or by setting out a short string, or 'teagle', with ten or twenty baited hooks on a clearing in the snow. Some birds were impaled, others tore themselves free with bent wires in their mouths or stomachs. This practice, for no logical reason, aroused more indignation than catching fish on hooks.

Was it, or was it not, cruel to keep wild birds in cages? The ghost of William Blake derived little satisfaction from the findings of a Departmental Committee on bird protection, which sat in 1921. 'Properly safeguarded, we see no reason why the practice should be accompanied by cruelty and many wild birds do in fact live in captivity in perfect health for long periods,' said the Committee. 'The keeping of cage birds provides many town dwellers with an innocent solace and amusement and we see no reason for its general abolition.'

From now on, the caged bird became a tiny pawn in the class struggle. Why (ran the argument) should the rich, with their gardens and aviaries, seek to deprive the poor townsman of the well-tended and well-loved linnet which was his only link with Nature?

The journal *Cage Birds* at this period had many advertisements offering British birds 'on approval'. 'Skylarks. Woodlarks. I have the finest collection of tame songsters in England,' said a dealer in Bishops Stortford. A Preston advertiser, 'winner of 5,000 prizes', boasted, 'I have supplied more British birds than any man alive.' Another announcement read: 'Larks. Larks. Don't forget the old reliable firm for quality; genuine cocks 8s doz.' An offer of 'Bird Catchers' Call Birds' was accompanied by the explanation: 'One of my best catchers given up owing to ill-health.' The birds in question were house-moulted cock linnets and cost 12s and 14s each. Clap nets, stuffed decoys, handy guides to the Bird Acts and manuals describing how to catch birds with lime were also on offer. One announcement said:

WORLD'S BEST BIRDLIME. Guaranteed to hold a pigeon; your money returned if not satisfied. I have hundreds of testimonials . . . It will hold in any weather and is always ready. Sample tins 6d and 1s. Large lever-lid tins 2s, 3s, 4s; all post-free; black or green; no waiting. F— A—, birdlime manufacturer, Hull.

In 1925 the use of birdlime became illegal under an Act which also prohibited the use of braced and blind decoys. It further laid down that a cage must be large enough to allow a bird 'freely to stretch its wings,' scarcely an extravagant requirement. But the measure which caused the biggest flutter in the Cage Bird Fancy was the Protection of Wild Birds Bill handled by Viscount Buckmaster of Cheddington and John Buchan in 1933. It was sponsored by the Royal Society for the Protection of Birds and backed by the RSPCA. The object of this measure, as its critics quickly recognised, was to wipe out the trade in British song-birds. Primarily it was aimed at the catchers, who were regarded as more cruel than the cagers; it did not affect canaries, budgerigars and other foreign birds. For some time the *Field* had been vigorously exposing conditions in the caged bird trade. Organisers of shows offered substantial prizes to those who could produce the best captive wild birds, including such species as night-ingales, thrushes, kingfishers, tree-creepers, swallows and water-ouzels. The chief focus of criticism was Club Row, in London, where bird-sellers had operated for many generations. Lord Buckmaster read to the Commons this extract from the *Field*: 'The woman in charge of the birds took linnet after linnet from a tiny cage. She held it by its tail and legs, dipped its beak into a little glass of dirty water, poked it head first in a cardboard box, closed the box and pocketed a shilling.'

The argument that caged birds escaped the rigours of Nature did not go unvoiced. A lark trilling at Heaven's gate was just as likely to be killed by a hawk up there as anywhere else, pointed out Major J. W. Hills, in the Commons. Sir Arnold Wilson, reminding the House that there were 780 caged bird societies in Britain, asked: 'Is it reasonable for us in haste to put a complete end to the sale of birds or the catching of birds when one sparrowhawk will probably kill 3,000 birds in a year and when frost and snow will kill hundreds and thousands in a day or two?' David (later Lord) Kirkwood preferred to oppose the measure because it came from the House of Lords and was an interference with working-class rights. When the Bill was considered by a Lords' Select Committee the manager of the Crystal Palace Bird Show said that, at the last display, robins and larks had been omitted; there was sentimental opposition by the public and it was therefore bad showmanship to include them. A spokesman of London Zoo said he thought shows helped people to care for their birds and demonstrated the perfection to which they could be brought.

The Government had doubted whether public opinion was ready for Lord Buckmaster's Bill but eventually decided to support it, and it went through. No traffic in British birds was now permissible unless they were born in captivity and close-ringed. In theory rings could be fitted only to fledgelings; but every law inspires its challenger, and catchers developed the knack of forcing rings on the legs of adult wild birds. Whether it is more cruel to hatch wild birds into captivity, depriving them of any chance of free flight, or to imprison wild birds which have already enjoyed freedom, is a subject which has not gone undebated; obviously there can be no authoritative answer. The Cage Bird Fancy, already irritated by the picketing which went on outside its shows, saw no virtue whatever in the Act, which it thought could only benefit foreign bird traders. *Cage Birds* of November 17, 1933 called on its readers to go in for breeding British birds and to make sure that they had adequate stocks before the Act came into force. 'Show our opponents that their efforts to eliminate British birds from our shows are going to be completely and utterly frustrated,' it said. ' "More British Birds Than Ever At Our Exhibitions" – let that be the Fancy's new slogan.'

During the 1930s some controversy was stirred up by the practice of buying caged birds and releasing them, not always to their advantage. In 1937 Miss Margaret Bradish and the RSPCA started an institution which, a hundred years earlier, would have been regarded as the ultimate in philanthropic eccentricity: a flying school for birds. It was part of the Home of Rest for Animals maintained at Ember Farm, near Thames Ditton. Birds seized in raids on dealers were put in an aviary and allowed to rediscover their wings, and confidence, before being freed; foreign birds which could not have survived in the open were kept as permanent boarders. This establishment, modelled on one at Neuchâtel, Switzerland, was officially opened by Miss Pauline Gower, the airwoman daughter of Sir Robert Gower, chairman of the RSPCA. She flew over it in salute.

One odd development of this decade was that Mussolini, the Italian Dictator, suddenly became a bird-lovers' hero. Axel Munthe in his *Story of San Michele* (1929) had turned publicity on the ruthless netting of birds on Capri. For centuries the island had been the seat of a bishopric entirely financed from the sales of netted migrants, lured by blind decoys. Munthe, protesting, gained an audience of the 'highest lady in the land'; she asked him to stay for lunch, where the first words on the menu were *pâté d'alouettes farcies*. He went to see the Pope and found him watching the netting of birds in the Vatican garden. Finally Munthe tried to buy the mountain where most of the netting was carried out. In 1933, unexpectedly, Mussolini declared Capri a bird sanctuary, an order which created considerable excitement in Italy and great pleasure elsewhere. 'In that moment,' said the *Queen*, 'his name was uttered affectionately by thousands who had never thought of it before. He became to us a living force, liberating to our isle a myriad sweet-voiced messengers who but for him had struggled in trappers' nets and ended their winged destiny on toast in French restaurants.'* Both Mussolini and Munthe were awarded the RSPCA's silver medal.

Not until after World War Two was the muddle of wild bird legislation reduced to reasonable order. The task of introducing the Protection of Wild Birds Bill in 1953 was undertaken by Lady Tweedsmuir, daughter-in-law of John Buchan who had moved the 1933 Bill. Her measure wiped out twenty-six previous Acts and 250 Regulations. It was the fruit of five years discussion by two advisory committees, one appointed by the Home Office, the other by the Scottish Office, with almost every interest consulted. The confusion that existed is shown by the fact that in the county of Flint one species of bird had its eggs protected, in Carmarthen 101, in the West Riding 161, in Cornwall 99 and in Bute none. The House was told that an avocet had settled in Suffolk, thus showing great intelligence, since if it had settled in Cambridgeshire it could have been shot for its skin. A species which had never visited Britain before could be destroyed with impunity because it was not listed on any county's schedule. Not the least objection to the system was that an impossible knowledge of ornithology was demanded of the village policeman.

Broadly, the idea of Lady Tweedsmuir's Bill was to protect all birds, their nests and eggs all the year round, with three major exceptions: food and game birds; black-listed birds, like carrion crows and jays; and common wild birds on an agreed list. Lady Tweedsmuir was not the only Member anxious that bird-nesting by boys should not be made a criminal offence (though in respect of certain birds it already was). 'Children do not as a rule come upon the rare species,' said Lady Tweedsmuir, 'and they take a great delight in bird-nesting.

* Quoted by Quentin Crewe: *The Frontiers of Privilege.*

I do not think the House would like to ban what is not only a most exciting pleasure but one which gives a lasting interest in wild life.' She thought that parents and teachers had already done much to encourage children to respect the eggs; hooligan destruction of eggs ought to be countered by other means.

Lady Tweedsmuir's Bill also proscribed the more murderous forms of punt gun, the use of artificial lights, poisoned bait, 'floating containers holding explosives,' rocket-propelled nets and other crude aids to slaughter. But it does not stop pest officers burning the nightingales out of a stretch of countryside in order to kill off a few rabbits. Nor does it prevent the use of crop dressings which litter the land with bird corpses. The Tweedsmuir Bill is not the final word on bird protection; but not all latter-day legislation can be listed here.

It is far easier to pass bird legislation than to enforce it. The RSPCA and the Royal Society for the Protection of Birds (which now has twenty bird sanctuaries) have prosecuted many trappers and egg-dealers, and fines as high as £210 have been imposed. The latter Society has also taken to court 'bird-lovers' who collect rare eggs to gloat over in private. But 'trigger-happy' marksmen remain a considerable problem. As these lines are written the press is full of reports that townsmen armed with guns overrun shores, farms and woodlands at week-ends, shooting at anything in sight; the same complaint that roused widespread anger a hundred years earlier. Today the guns are enormously improved, even if the standard of marksmanship is not.

For sea birds, the twentieth century brought an enduring scourge beyond the reach of any one nation's legislature: pollution from waste oil. A 1922 Act designed to limit this nuisance in coastal waters was evaded by taking vessels beyond the three-mile limit to flush out tanks; the oil then drifted ashore as hitherto. A series of international conferences resulted in the Convention of 1954 (effective in 1959); subsequent amendments have still to be ratified by many countries. In 1964 leading British oil companies gave a valuable lead by undertaking to stop the cleaning of tankers at sea

Cleansing of bedraggled and immobilised birds has been

one of the more publicised chores of the protection societies. It is not enough to purify the bird's plumage; the creature has to be detained long enough for its feathers to recover their water-repellent state. At Mousehole, in Cornwall, the RSPCA took over and operated a rehabilitation centre for oiled sea birds, founded by two sisters, the Misses Yglesias.*

* A. W. Moss: *Valiant Crusade.*

23

ARE WE PROGRESSING?

IN the last twenty years many old cruelties have been outlawed, but these were overshadowed in many minds by
such dubious new practices as ill-controlled poison-spraying,
deliberate disease-spreading and the conversion of animals into
factory units. To some, it appeared that while humanity
tidied up a few forgotten drawers, science was wrecking the
house. In 1949 the nicking and docking of horses was at last
prohibited, but how much cruelty did the hackney horse suffer
compared with the millions of birds needlessly poisoned? In
1951 an Act was passed to control conditions in pet shops,
but already huge colonies of hens were living out their lives
in perpetual twilight.

One post-war reform at least was a major one: the abolition
of the gin trap. The amount of cruelty caused by this device,
down the centuries, does not bear contemplation. It was
employed primarily not to control rabbits but to catch them
for market, though this aspect was sedulously obscured. Many
a prize had been offered for a more humane method of taking
wild animals, but no device caught as many as the gin trap;
one of its attractions was that it held the animal alive and the
flesh did not deteriorate. In 1935 a Gin Traps (Prohibition)
Bill narrowly failed. Viscount Tredegar informed the Lords
that 'the intention of this Bill is to abolish cruelty and not to
suit human convenience,' and reminded his hearers that the
gin trap for human beings was abolished in 1827. According
to an estimate by the University of London Animal Welfare
Society, which was behind the Bill, 1,800,000 birds (from tits
upwards), 124,000 cats and 35 million rabbits were caught

annually in gin traps, as well as numerous other creatures from foxhounds to cows (often seized by the lip). The British Field Sports Society said it was anxious to restrict the setting of gins in the open, but thought the measure unworkable; and it was not eager to have inspectors poking about on private land. Lord Merthyr spoke of 'the intense feeling of indignation' felt by sporting people towards this Society – 'They are tired of foxes with three legs, and I have also heard of a bag of seven pheasants with eight legs between them.'

In 1949 the Scott-Henderson Committee described the gin trap as 'a diabolical instrument which causes an incalculable amount of suffering' and urged its prohibition. Between three and three-and-a-half million traps were then in use. In 1951 a Spring Traps Bill was lost, but the 1954 Pests Act made the gin trap illegal from August 1, 1958. Other, more humane, devices were then available.

Much hard work on this campaign was put in by the Universities Federation for Animal Welfare, which had argued throughout that the best way to abolish the gin trap was to abolish the trapping industry by a thorough campaign of rabbit clearance, using gas and other methods. The Federation now directs attention to the fact that many furs on the market are the result of gin-trapping in other lands. A woman wearing a wild-mink coat parades the agony of a hundred animals. The pain to a trapped animal has been likened to that of a man with his hand trapped in a car door, left to starve, freeze or twist his hand off. Leg-hold traps now in use in the American continent first grasp the animal by the leg then clamp it higher up to prevent it 'wringing off' – gnawing or twisting off the imprisoned paw. Other traps hoist the animal into the air to preserve it from predators.*

Ironically, by the time Parliament had decided to abolish the gin trap much of Britain's rabbit population had been wiped out by plague. The ravages of myxomatosis caused deep revulsion among those who witnessed its effects. Ordinarily the control of pests by spreading disease or disability among them was practised on creatures too small for their sufferings to be visible, or too repulsive to qualify for pity.

* F. Jean Vinter: *Facts About Furs* (UFAW, 1957).

A Fougasse poster for the Universities Federation
for Animal Welfare

Infecting rabbits was not a new idea; in 1887 Pasteur, in hope of winning a £25,000 reward offered in New South Wales for a means of wiping out rabbits, conceived the idea of spreading chicken cholera among them, but his experiments were stopped because of the danger to poultry.* Between the world wars scientists carried out tests with the myxomatosis virus in South America, Australia and Britain. They were anxious on two points: that there should be no risk of the disease infecting creatures other than rabbits; and that it should lose none of its virulence once it was propagated. As it happened, the plague proved extremely difficult to start. In Australia and Europe alike dozens of attempts failed. But in the early 1950s the disease was successfully spread in Australia, rabbits died by the million and, in the first year, agricultural profits rose by £50 million. On an estate near Paris, in 1952, Professor Armand Delille inoculated two wild rabbits and released them, in an effort to kill off the rest of his rabbits – and the disease swept France. His action was later compared to the use of an H-bomb to bring down a covey of partridges.† British farmers and landowners watched with mixed feelings. They had little sentiment for rabbits and the Government was always calling for more energetic action against this pest. In 1951 the Scott-Henderson Committee had said: 'We . . . recommend that the Agricultural Departments should seriously consider obtaining Parliamentary sanction for a policy of extermination.' Then, late in 1953, rabbits at Edenbridge, Kent, were found to be infected, by what agency is unknown. The temptation to spread the disease was strong, but public opinion was against such a policy; instead, efforts were made to contain the outbreak. As the Minister of Agriculture, Mr Heathcoat Amory, later explained: 'It seemed clear that on humanitarian and other grounds there was a case against allowing the disease to become established if we could prevent it, at any rate until we knew more about its implications.'‡

* Harry V. Thompson and Alastair N. Worden: *The Rabbit* (1956).
† The Professor was sued in the civil court at Dreux by an 'association for defence against epidemics', representing breeders, hotel-keepers, sportsmen, gunsmiths, cartridge-makers, hatters and others. They lost their claim for a symbolic award of one franc damages.
‡ House of Commons, October 22, 1954.

A Myxomatosis Advisory Committee studied the disease, conceded that attempts at restraint were useless, but urged that no deliberate efforts be made to spread it; a view with which the Government agreed.

Before the plague started, rabbits had been costing Britain £50 million a year. To many a farmer who faced an annual loss of up to half the value of his crops from this cause, the policy of containment seemed absurd. *The Times* on June 18, 1954 printed a letter from a farmer near Andover calling for 'a determined attempt to infect the whole rabbit population with myxomatosis.' In some areas pairs of infected carcasses changed hands for sums up to £10 and were then 'planted' in as yet uncontaminated fields. But most farmers found they had little stomach for this form of pesticide once they had seen such sights as (to quote one witness) 'a wretched creature, sightless, nearly hairless, and half its entrails exposed, battering itself against the wall of the house.'

In the worst-affected regions, the plague assumed macabre proportions. Lanes in Essex became almost unusable because of the stench of putrid bodies in the surrounding fields and ditches. Cats and dogs brought dying rabbits, hideously swollen, into houses. School-children, confronted everywhere with blinded, bleeding, misshapen rabbits, came home in tears. Housewives shut all their windows against swarms of blow-flies. A man who went into a wood to kill off a diseased rabbit said, 'I had to leave it. The wood was full of dead and dying rabbits. I had to come out. The smell was so awful . . . and the flies . . .'* On the Sussex Downs hundreds of rabbit corpses became a disposal problem for Eastbourne Corporation.

The RSPCA began to organise 'mercy squads' to shoot the diseased victims and these were joined by farm workers in their spare time. In the first year they destroyed more than a quarter of a million rabbits, at no small cost in cartridges. The 'mercy squads' were in no sense preventive and the disease rolled on. Food rabbits vanished from the shops and, as a crowning irony, scientists began to take precautions to save their laboratory rabbits.

Moral censure came from many quarters. Leading church-

* Dr Horace King, House of Commons, November 4, 1954.

men called the deliberate spreading of myxomatosis an act of impiety and sacrilege. Here and there a farmer denied that diseased rabbits suffered; they were stupefied and died peacefully. All that scientists could say (and on the whole they said little) was that food production was paramount and that some degree of cruelty must, in the circumstances, be accepted.

Meanwhile Australia, after four years' experience, had discovered that myxomatosis was not, to use a genocidal phrase, the 'final solution'. The Commonwealth Scientific and Industrial Research Organisation, meeting at Melbourne, recommended that for maximum results the disease should be followed by extensive mopping-up operations, using other methods. A year later it was reported that the Australian rabbit population had been reduced by 90 per cent.

In Britain, Parliament was petitioned to make the deliberate propagation of myxomatosis illegal. The subject was raised, with force and passion, in 1954 when the Minister of Agriculture moved his Pests Bill. Mr Amory did not think it necessary to make disease-spreading an offence, as the disease would spread anyway; but the feeling of the House was against him. Dr Horace King, Member for Southampton, argued that, even though it might be impossible to catch offenders, the establishment of a penalty would at least show that the act was regarded as morally wrong. 'Let us have a Geneva Convention in our rabbit war,' he said. When Mr Amory gave in, other Members who had been proposing to speak in support of Dr King tore up their speeches. Later Dr King referred to a reported declaration by Cornish farmers that their task was to spread myxomatosis in the few days that remained between the third reading and the royal assent. He hoped these farmers would feel ashamed of themselves. Mr Amory said he did not believe that farmers in general had yielded to the temptation to spread the disease.

It would be rash to conclude, from the myxomatosis episode, that the Australians are less squeamish than the British. If rabbits had been a comparable menace in Britain, it is unlikely that any British Government would have long withstood pressure to tackle the problem 'scientifically'.

The humanitarian now faces the considerable dilemma

posed by new methods of pesticide, the situation summed up in J. W. Taylor's *Punch* drawing which showed two men surveying a dead dog in a farmyard: 'This is the dog that bit the cat that killed the rat that ate the malt that came from the grain that Jack sprayed.' Scientists maintain, and probably with good reason, that the world's population increase makes necessary the use of powerful insecticides; scores upon scores of these were produced in the post-war years and the ultimate effects of many are still unknown. In the 1950s some of the more immediate effects were apparent enough, as game birds died from organo-phosphorus poisons. The spring of 1960 brought a massacre of birds from chlorinated hydrocarbon seed dressings. Now the repeated discovery of sterile eggs in the nests of predatory birds has set man worrying about the long-term effect of crop sprays on his own body. In parts of America woodcocks and pheasants have been rendered unfit for consumption by their high content of heptachlor and DDT. In 1963, not before time, a voluntary committee was set up by the British agricultural chemical industry, with the co-operation of the Nature Conservancy (which was already working on the problem) and wild life preservation societies, to survey the effects of chemicals on wild life.

The suburban gardener, encouraged to adopt scientific methods, and fortified by the Ministry of Agriculture's pamphlet *Chemicals for the Gardener*, also engages in chemical warfare against trivial pests, upsetting such balance of Nature as survives in his plot and killing off his and his neighbour's birds. The Royal Society for the Protection of Birds has pressed the Government to withdraw that pamphlet, on the grounds that 'wide distribution . . . and unquestioning acceptance of its advice can only lead to a further decrease of our garden birds.'*

A more emotional controversy surrounds the big development in 'industrial' farming of livestock; that is, the indoor rearing of food animals and birds in wholly unnatural conditions. These methods are said to be essential if an expanding population is to enjoy its supposed birthright of cheap food and if the taste of chicken and veal is to be shared by those

* *Daily Telegraph*, October 12, 1963.

hitherto unable to indulge it. By now the conditions which prevail in broiler-houses, veal-houses, pig 'sweat-boxes' and hen batteries are uncomfortably familiar, thanks to the popular press – notably the *People* – and, more recently, the publication of Ruth Harrison's book *Animal Machines* (1964). Unmothered, fed artificially, warmed artificially, 'protected' from sunlight, moonlight and even from motor car headlights, stuffed with antibiotics and sedatives, the units in these factories have no contact with the Nature of which they are a part; their only function is to put on flesh. Those who farm them are mathematicians: 'The Performance Efficiency Ratio is obtained by multiplying the liveweight by 100 and then dividing the result by the Food Conversion Ratio. The Food Conversion Ratio is the result of dividing the food consumption by the liveweight.'* The stockman on an indoor farm feeds his fowls by pulling switches. Every trick of lighting – from bright 'stimulighting' to 'twilighting' and red-lighting – has been tried out in an effort to encourage body-building or egg-laying without encouraging exercise or 'vice'. To prevent feather-pecking and cannibalism, birds are often de-beaked. There have been attempts to interest British operators in the American practice of fitting hens with cheap, rose-coloured contact lenses, which are supposed to calm them; one extra egg offsets the cost. In the euphemistically-named packing stations hens are slung upside down on a conveyor belt and their throats are cut manually – sometimes after electric stunning, but often not. The difficulty appears to be to devise a stunner efficient and economical enough to deal with 4,500 birds an hour; any slowing-up device slows up the rate of profit. Mrs Harrison quotes the Humane Slaughter Association as saying that two out of five birds pass from the bleeding tunnel into the steam room alive; others say that the flapping of the birds is caused only by muscular spasms. Calves reared for quality veal spend their brief lives – perhaps fourteen weeks – restrained by the head in such a way that they can lie down, but not exercise. Their feet are deformed by the slats on which they live, but death comes before deformity is far advanced. Sometimes they are 'bled' before death, by giving them diets to cause anaemia.

* Ray Feltwell: *Broiler Farming* (1960).

'Sweat-box' pigs are kept packed together in near-darkness in a high temperature which stifles bacteria. Their vice is tail-biting.

Just before Mrs Harrison's book was published the Ministry of Agriculture took the unusual course of calling a press conference to defend the practices under criticism. Its main contentions were that animals would not thrive if they were suffering and that the infliction of 'boredom' was not cruelty. The *Observer** quoted Sir Harold Sanders, chief scientific adviser to the Ministry, as saying that 'no case had been established for making it an offence merely to deprive animals of light, freedom to exercise or pasture,' which, in his view, did not cause suffering. The word 'merely' stuck in a good many gullets; and there were sceptics who wanted to know how Sir Harold could be sure that these deprivations did not constitute suffering. In intensive farming there is rarely cruelty of the kind punishable under the 1911 Act or any of the bird protection Acts. Defenders of the new methods point out that the inmates are preserved from the chills, damps, quarrels, bullying and other indignities of the old-fashioned farm and instead pass their lives in an ultra-hygienic club. Hygiene is not yet absolute, for disease can spread through the club rapidly. Whether the flesh produced in this way is tasteless or even pernicious is not an issue here. The basic question is: has man a right to treat animals as vegetables? Some of the earlier excesses of industrial farming have been toned down, others may yet be limited by law, as in Denmark; but as these lines are written Parliament has shown little concern over this issue, other than to set up a technical committee of enquiry. The *Guardian,* suspicious of the easy reassurances from interested parties, ventured a comment which would have been commended by St Thomas Aquinas: 'The fact is that an increasing contempt for lower forms of life may be leading us, especially in an agnostic age, to a contempt for man himself. How big a step is it from the broiler-house to Auschwitz?'† And the *Guardian*'s cartoonist Papas dramatised this thought with a picture of a conveyor

* March 8, 1964.
† March 9, 1964.

belt in which the naked suspended corpses of fowls gradually turned into the naked suspended corpses of humans.

What would have been the verdict of John Lawrence or Jeremy Bentham after touring an automated farm? Would they have regarded the system as an infraction of the animals' rights for which they campaigned? And what would Richard Martin have thought of some less publicised methods of tinkering with Nature's machinery? In Martin's day chickens were caponised surgically, if surgically is not too flattering a word. On balance he might conclude that, if caponising must be done, the hormone gun now used is an improvement. He might or might not be impressed by the ingenuity of our technicians who have made it possible for one bull to have 100,000 calves without serving a single cow. They have also enabled a single pedigree cow to have a score of calves a year without giving birth to any of them; the feat is performed by injecting the fertilised 'mother' with a pituitary hormone to increase the supply of eggs from her ovaries and transplanting them to inferior cows which in due course calve naturally. Thus, the mother is a mere link in the chain of procreation. She knows no sire and licks no children.* Applied to the human race, this system would be regarded as obscene and blasphemous; is it any the less blasphemous when applied to animals? Technically, again, no cruelty is involved. Breeders say it is a sensible method of speeding the propagation of a superior strain. What (they might argue) is the difference between taking away eggs from a cow and taking away eggs from a hen?

Descartes said that animals were machines. The twentieth century technocrat knows that the Cartesian view is nonsense, but he sees no harm in using animals as machines, and carrying out all sorts of ingenious modifications on them. Of the many ethical problems posed in these pages, this one ought to attract more hard thinking than it does at present.

* Dr J. Gordon Cook: *The Fight for Food* (1955).

INDEX